Your Pregnancy™ QUESTIONS & ANSWERS

THIRD EDITION

Dr. Glade B. Curtis, OB/GYN
Judith Schuler, M.S.

A Member of the Perseus Books Group

Text design by Jeff Williams
Set in 11-point Berling Roman by Perseus Publishing Services
Illustrations by Les Young

Cataloging-in-Publication data for this book is available from the Library of Congress.

First Da Capo Press edition 2004
ISBN 0–7382–1003–X

Published by Da Capo Press
A Member of the Perseus Books Group
http://www.dacapopress.com

Note: The information in this book is true and complete to the best of our knowledge. This book is intended only as an informative guide for those wishing to know more about pregnancy. In no way is this book intended to replace, countermand or conflict with the advice given to you by your own physician. The ultimate decision concerning your care should be made between you and your doctor. We strongly recommend that you follow his or her advice. The information in this book is general and is offered with no guarantees on the part of the authors or Da Capo Press. The authors and publisher disclaim all liability in connection with the use of this book. The names and identifying details of people associated with events described in this book have been changed. Any similarity to actual persons is coincidental.

4 5 6 7 8 9—08 07 06 05

ACKNOWLEDGMENTS

Glade B. Curtis, M.D.—I have the honor of sharing the joy, the excitement and even the heartbreak associated with the miracle of childbirth on a daily (and nightly) basis. I thank my patients and their families for allowing me to share in their experiences. I have answered many questions hundreds, if not thousands, of times, yet to the person asking the questions, the answer is critical.

My thanks to my wife, Debbie, and our family, who have supported me in the pursuit of a profession that requires me to give a lot of time and energy to my patients. Their unfailing support, which is an inspiration to me, has continued during this and other projects. My thanks also to my parents for their endless love and support.

Judi Schuler's insight, persistence and commitment to excellence and accuracy continue to inspire and to challenge me. I appreciate her drive and ability to "pull things together" and keep me focused. I also appreciate the input and assistance from Cynthia Deines, Nancy L. Thompson, Janet L. Hawley, David Fischer and Dr. Ted Noon.

Judith Schuler, M.S.—Thanks to my son, Ian, and my parents, Bob and Kay Gordon, for their love and continued belief in me. Thanks to Bob Rucinski for his support and help. I can always count on you to help me find a solution, no matter what the problem is!

Authors' Note to Readers

We are always happy to hear from the readers of our books. You are welcome to address letters to us via our publisher, DaCapo Press, or you may send them to us by email. If you use email, we will probably be able to reply more quickly. Our email address is **yourpregnancy@juno.com.**

When you send us an email, please do not ask us medical questions about your particular situation. We are unable to reply to these letters, except to suggest you discuss your question with your own physician. We are happy to answer general questions about areas we address in our books. We are also happy to clear up any confusion regarding information we present. If you have comments or suggestions for areas to address in future books, we are always glad to receive these suggestions.

If you send us an email, please do not include any attachments. We will not open these because of the problem with viruses. In addition, we ask that you do not add us to any lists for stories, chain letters, prayers, political or other causes, charitable donations or any other lists you can think of.

We will attempt to answer your emails as quickly as possible, but please understand that with all the books we have published, we are kept busy updating them and doing research for new books. In addition, Dr. Curtis sees patients nearly every day. We'll get back to you as soon as we can!

CONTENTS

PART ONE

Before Pregnancy

1

Preparing for Pregnancy

Before a woman becomes pregnant, it's important for her to prepare for the many changes her body will experience. Sometimes, a pregnancy is a surprise, so a woman cannot prepare for it. However, when it is possible, think about and make plans for how you will take care of yourself during this wondrous time. Preparing for a pregnancy allows you to make changes *before* you get pregnant so your baby gets a healthy start in life. To that end, many physicians and other healthcare workers now consider pregnancy a 12-month term.

The actual length of a pregnancy (growth from a fertilized egg into a normal-size baby) is only 9 months. But we now know that the few months before you get pregnant can be as important as the 9 months the fetus develops inside of you.

With good preparation on your part, you can give your baby the best start toward a healthy life. The months that you plan for your pregnancy give you time to prepare your body and make any necessary lifestyle changes. You can eat nutritiously, cut out alcohol and tobacco use, begin an exercise program, get your weight under control and talk to your doctor about any other medical concerns you have.

What lab tests should I have done before I get pregnant?

Your doctor may order a range of tests for you, including the following:

- Pap smear
- Rh-factor test

- blood typing
- rubella titers
- mammogram, if you are 35 or older

If you know you have other specific or chronic medical problems, such as diabetes, have them checked. If you have been exposed to hepatitis or AIDS, you should be tested for these.

My last two pregnancies ended in miscarriages. Should I talk with my doctor before I get pregnant or can I wait until my first visit when I am pregnant?

The history of previous pregnancies can be important in the success of your next pregnancy. It's true that in many situations there's nothing you can do to avoid problems. The safest thing to do is talk with your doctor before you try to conceive. Tell your doctor what has happened in the past. Find out if there is anything you can do now or if there are risks you may have to deal with.

YOUR BODY DURING PREGNANCY

How will my body change during pregnancy?

Your body goes through incredible changes during pregnancy! Your breasts enlarge, and the number of milk ducts to produce breast milk actually increases. Your organs are crowded by your enlarging uterus, which may cause more frequent urination, heartburn or indigestion. Your legs, feet and hands may swell. Your hair and skin often undergo changes. Compare the illustration on page 6 with that on page 175 to see what changes a woman's body may undergo during pregnancy.

What role does the menstrual cycle play in my getting pregnant?

During a menstrual cycle, your body prepares for the possibility of pregnancy. An egg is released from one of your ovaries, and changes take place in the lining of your uterus to provide an environment for the development of a fertilized egg. If fertilization does not take place, the enriched lining is discarded through the menstrual flow.

PREPREGNANCY CHECKLIST

Attention to these details *before* you get pregnant makes your pregnancy safer and more enjoyable.

- Exercise regularly.
- Find out if you can decrease or discontinue medications you take regularly. Ask your physician if they are safe to take during pregnancy.
- Get your weight under control. Pregnancy is not the time to lose weight.
- If you need X-rays, vaccinations or medical tests, get them done *before* trying to get pregnant.
- Control or eliminate tobacco, alcohol or drug use.
- Decide who will deliver your baby.
- Check on your insurance coverage for pregnancy.

Should I see my doctor before I get pregnant or wait until I am pregnant?

If possible, see your doctor before you get pregnant. A visit before pregnancy answers questions you may have about medications you take. You can have a Pap smear and any other tests your doctor decides are necessary. With your doctor, you can evaluate your current weight and set a target weight gain for a pregnancy. You will know you're in good health before getting pregnant; if you're not, you can make plans to get into the best shape possible **before** *you get pregnant.*

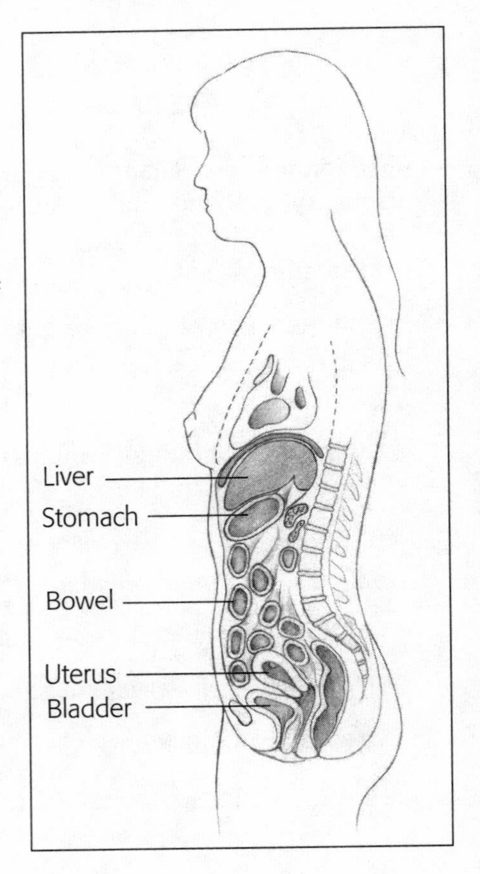

This illustration of a woman's body shows a nonpregnant uterus and various organs. Compare it with the illustration of a pregnant woman's body on page 175. Pregnancy causes many changes!

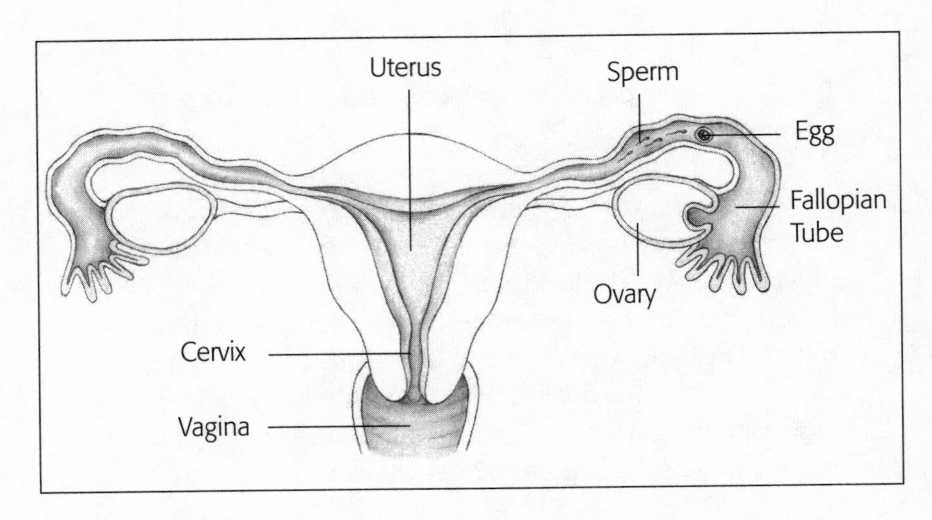

Pregnancy begins when the sperm fertilizes the egg.

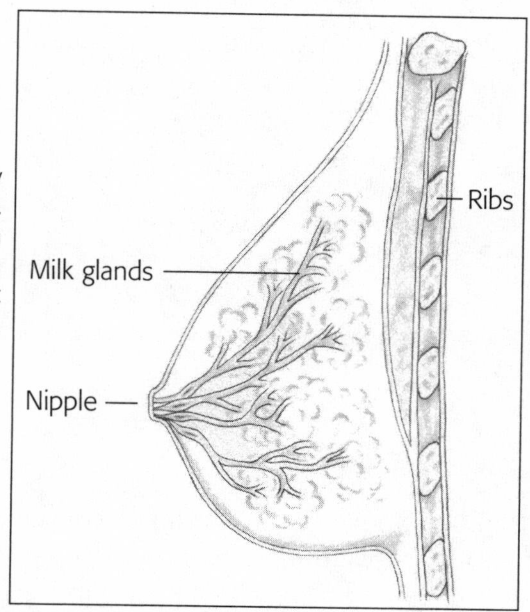

Your breasts go through many changes during pregnancy. Compare this illustration of a breast in a nonpregnant woman with the illustration of a pregnant woman's breast on page 195.

How does fertilization of the egg occur?

Fertilization is believed to occur in the middle part of the tube called the *ampulla (Fallopian tube)*, not inside the uterus. Sperm travel through the uterine cavity and out into the tube to meet the egg that comes from the ovary. (See the illustration on page 6.)

What happens after fertilization?

The fertilized egg begins to divide and to grow. Within 3 to 7 days, it travels down the Fallopian tube into the uterus and attaches to the wall of the uterus. The developing baby is called an *embryo.* (After 8 weeks it is called a *fetus.*)

By about day 12, the amniotic sac begins to form around the developing embryo. The sac contains fluid in which the baby can easily move around. Amniotic fluid also cushions the fetus against injury and regulates temperature.

YOUR CURRENT CONTRACEPTION METHODS

How long should my IUD be out before I try to conceive?

The best and easiest time to remove an intrauterine device (IUD) is during your period. Wait for a couple of normal cycles after your

If I want to get pregnant soon, when should I stop my birth-control pills?

Most doctors recommend staying off the pill for two or three normal menstrual cycles before trying to get pregnant. Use some other form of contraception, such as a barrier method (condom), until you want to get pregnant.

IUD is removed before trying to conceive. Use barrier contraception during the waiting time.

I use Norplant for birth control. Is it OK to get pregnant right after it is taken out?

After the Norplant implant is removed, wait at least two or three menstrual cycles before trying to get pregnant.

If I use Depo-provera for birth control, how long do I have to wait after my last shot to try to get pregnant?

The injection works for 3 months. A new monthly injection may also be available in your area. After stopping either injection, you should have at least two normal periods before you attempt a pregnancy.

YOUR PREPREGNANCY HEALTH

Can I have a successful pregnancy even though I have chronic health problems?

Yes, in many cases. Women with health problems can have successful pregnancies and healthy babies. It is very important for you to discuss your particular situation with your doctor before becoming pregnant. Follow his or her instructions carefully.

I have diabetes, and I really want to have a baby. Is it possible?

Progress has been made in handling diabetes during pregnancy; however, diabetes can still have serious effects during pregnancy. Risks to you and your baby can be decreased with good control of your blood sugar. Discuss your concerns with your doctor *before* you try to conceive.

How long must the diabetes be under control before I get pregnant?

The longer the better, but most doctors recommend 2 or 3 months before pregnancy begins. This helps lower the risk of miscarriage. It may also prevent problems with fetal development.

Will pregnancy affect my insulin requirements?

Pregnancy can increase your body's need for insulin.

When do most pregnancy problems occur for diabetic women?

Most problems occur during the 1st trimester—the first 13 weeks of pregnancy. However, problems can occur throughout pregnancy, so it's important to have your diabetes under good control before you conceive. A woman's insulin requirement often increases in the last 13 weeks of pregnancy.

Will pregnancy affect my asthma?

There is no way to predict ahead of time if pregnancy will affect your asthma. About 50% of women see no change in their asthma during pregnancy. About 25% have improved symptoms, while 25% have increased problems.

Is my asthma medication safe to take during pregnancy?

Most medications prescribed for asthma are safe to use during pregnancy. Discuss your medication use with your doctor.

Is there anything else I can do to avoid asthma problems?

Avoid substances that trigger your asthma attacks, such as particular foods or anything you are allergic to.

I have high blood pressure, and I want to get pregnant. How will my blood pressure affect pregnancy?

High blood pressure can cause problems for the mother and baby. These include kidney damage, stroke or headaches in the mother-to-be and decreased blood flow to the fetus. The decreased blood flow can cause intrauterine-growth restriction (inadequate growth of the fetus).

Can I continue taking my blood-pressure medication during pregnancy?

Some medications are safe to take during pregnancy; others are not. Do *not* stop or decrease any medication on your own! Discuss your situation with your doctor.

I've had heart problems for quite a while, but I want to have a baby. Is this dangerous?

Some heart problems may be serious during pregnancy and require special care. Other heart problems may affect your health so adversely that your physician will advise against pregnancy. Discuss this serious question with your heart specialist and your obstetrician *before* you get pregnant.

I have lupus, and my kidneys were affected by my first flareup. Is this a serious consideration before I get pregnant?

Any situation that results in loss of kidney function can be serious during pregnancy. Be sure your physician knows about this situation before you get pregnant. You will need to make a plan to follow during your pregnancy.

My mother always warned me not to try to have a baby because I have epilepsy. Should I avoid pregnancy?

We can't answer this question without knowing your full medical history. Some seizure medications are safe to take during pregnancy, and women with epilepsy have had successful pregnancies.

What kind of seizure medication is safest to take during pregnancy?

Phenobarbital has long been regarded as safe to use during pregnancy, but this is now being questioned. Discuss its use or the use of other medications with your physician, but do not discontinue or decrease your medication on your own!

I've been anemic in the past. Should I start taking iron now?

Your doctor can check you for anemia. Pregnancy puts great demands on your body's iron supplies. Many women start taking vitamins or iron before getting pregnant. Because you have had a problem in the past, it's better to discuss this with your doctor before pregnancy.

I use hydroxyurea for sickle cell anemia. Can I continue to use it while I try to get pregnant?

This medication has proved to be the first effective treatment of sickle cell anemia. It helps reduce the excruciating pain of some sickle cell attacks, but its use carries some risk and it cannot be given to all sickle cell sufferers. We do not know the long-term effects of the drug, so women contemplating pregnancy should not use it.

I take medication for a thyroid problem. Do I need to change the dosage or stop taking it if I want to get pregnant?

Don't make any changes without first consulting your doctor. Medication for thyroid problems is very important during pregnancy.

Will an occasional bladder infection before pregnancy cause problems during pregnancy?

It shouldn't, so don't be alarmed if you have a bladder or urinary-tract infection before or during pregnancy.

My friend had surgery for breast cancer a few months ago, and now she's talking about getting pregnant. Is that dangerous?

This is an individual problem and depends on the seriousness of her cancer and the type of treatment your friend received. It is very important for your friend to talk to her doctor if she is thinking about getting pregnant and she is being treated for cancer. It is much easier and safer for the woman to make decisions about treatments or medications before becoming pregnant than after.

I've been having a lot of back problems and my orthopedic surgeon wants to do some X-rays, a CT-scan and an MRI. Should I have them before I get pregnant?

Yes, these tests should be completed while you are still using contraception, before you consider conceiving. A good time to schedule these tests is right after the end of your period so you know you're not pregnant.

I just got a vaccination for rubella. Is it OK to stop my birth control and try to get pregnant?

No. Some vaccinations are safe during pregnancy, and some are not. Most physicians believe it's wise to continue contraception for at least 3 months after receiving any type of vaccination.

I often have to take medications for various problems. Can you give me some good advice about medication use before pregnancy?

Be cautious with your use of medications while you prepare for pregnancy and while you are trying to conceive. Follow the guidelines in the box below for safe use.

SAFE MEDICATION USE

- Ask your doctor if the medications you take are safe to use during pregnancy.
- Take all prescription medications as prescribed.
- Don't use old medications for current problems.
- Be careful with over-the-counter medications. Many contain caffeine, alcohol and other additives.
- Never use anyone else's medication for your medical problem.
- Notify your doctor immediately if you use medication and believe you might be pregnant.

I often take vitamins and herbs. Can I continue to take them while I prepare for pregnancy?

It's not a good idea to self-medicate while preparing for pregnancy or during your pregnancy. In excessive amounts, certain vitamins, such as vitamin A, can increase the risk of birth defects. A multivitamin is the only supplementation most women need while they are trying to conceive.

GENETIC COUNSELING

My sister had a baby last year that was born with Down syndrome. I'm considering pregnancy. Should I have genetic counseling?

This is something to discuss with your doctor. The answer is based on many factors, including your age, your past health, your partner's health and your family medical history.

What can genetic counseling tell me?

A counselor can discuss possibilities or probabilities regarding a planned pregnancy and your baby. In a situation like the one you describe with your sister, ask your doctor's advice.

Should everyone consider genetic counseling?

It isn't necessary for most women. If you have a family history of problems, you may want to seek counseling. Other situations in which you might consider genetic counseling include those listed below:

- You will be 35 or older when you deliver.
- Either you or your partner has a birth defect.
- You have had a baby with a birth defect.
- You have had three or more miscarriages in a row.
- You and your partner are related.

PREGNANCY FOR OLDER COUPLES

I'm 40 years old this month and want to have another baby. How will this pregnancy be different from my earlier one?

There are several advantages to being older. You are more mature and probably have more patience. Your financial situation may be better than when you were younger. On the other hand, problems you have with chronic illnesses, such as high blood pressure or diabetes, can worsen and affect both you and your baby. There are also increased risks for the baby. For a thorough discussion of pregnancy in the older woman, read our book *Your Pregnancy after 35*.

Does this mean I shouldn't get pregnant now that I'm older?

No, but a pregnancy may be a little more difficult for you. This is an individual situation that you and your partner should discuss with your doctor.

I am 39 and hope to be pregnant soon. Will I need any special tests during pregnancy?

With increasing maternal age, tests to consider include the following:

- ultrasound
- amniocentesis
- chorionic villus sampling
- alpha-fetoprotein testing
- diabetes testing
- mammogram (if you haven't had one)

What are some of the possible problems I might have if I am older than 35 and get pregnant?

Risks are varied and include the following:

- a slightly increased risk of a baby with Down syndrome
- a higher risk of Cesarean section
- problems with diabetes or high blood pressure
- a harder, longer labor

If you have other chronic medical problems, such as thyroid disease, or take medications regularly, discuss your concerns with your doctor before getting pregnant.

My husband is older, and we've heard that his age can affect my pregnancy and our baby. Is this true?

Some researchers believe this may be true. It has been shown that chromosomal abnormalities occur more often in babies born to women over 35 and men over 40. Men over age 55 are twice as likely as younger men to father a child with Down syndrome.

NUTRITION BEFORE PREGNANCY

I want to be pregnant soon. I love hamburgers, French fries and other junk food. Will this be a problem when I get pregnant?

A recent study showed that women who eat high amounts of saturated fat—the kind found in cheese and red meat—in the year before they got pregnant had a higher risk of suffering severe morning sickness during pregnancy.

The best plan is to start eating nutritiously *before* you get pregnant. By the time many women know they're pregnant, they are 7 or 8 weeks into the pregnancy—or more! The early weeks of pregnancy are important in the development of your baby.

Can't I just start eating better when I find out I'm pregnant?

It is best for you and your developing baby if you develop good eating habits before you get pregnant. It's important to your health and to the development of your baby for you to eat nutritiously for the entire 12 months of pregnancy.

I plan to start watching my weight once I'm pregnant. Is there a problem with this plan?

Pregnancy is *not* the time to start a new diet or to try to lose weight. Dieting can cause temporary deficiencies in vitamins and minerals that are important to a developing baby. Ask your doctor about a good eating plan before getting pregnant, and make necessary changes before pregnancy.

EXERCISING BEFORE PREGNANCY

I don't really like to work out. Is exercise that important?

Exercise is good for you, whether or not you are pregnant. Develop a good exercise program before getting pregnant to help you feel better, control weight and increase stamina. Exercise can also help make labor and delivery easier.

How can I find and maintain a good exercise program?

Find exercise you enjoy and can do in any type of weather. Information on various types of exercise programs is available from your local hospital, your doctor and health clubs. The American College of Obstetricians and Gynecologists (ACOG) has tapes available on exercise during and after pregnancy. Ask your doctor for information on ordering them.

SUBSTANCE USE

My friend just found out that she is 8 weeks' pregnant. She uses cocaine once or twice a week but says she'll stop now that she's pregnant. How does this affect the baby?

Drug use can be harmful during pregnancy. A woman should get these problems under control before stopping birth control or try-

EXERCISE GUIDELINES

Some general guidelines for safe exercise before and during pregnancy include the following.

- Before starting a new program, consult your doctor about past medical problems and past pregnancy complications.
- Start exercising *before* you get pregnant.
- Exercise on a regular basis.
- Start gradually, and increase as you build strength.
- Wear comfortable clothing.
- Avoid contact sports or risky exercise, such as water skiing or horseback riding.
- Allow plenty of time for warming up and cooling down.
- Check your pulse every 10 to 15 minutes during exercise. Keep your pulse under 140 beats a minute.
- Once you're pregnant, be careful when changing positions.
- After the 4th month of pregnancy, don't lie flat on your back when exercising. This decreases blood flow to your baby.
- Stop exercising and consult your doctor if you experience bleeding, loss of fluid from the vagina, shortness of breath, dizziness, abdominal pain or other serious problems.

ing to conceive. A doctor can help a woman find assistance. (Doctors who deal specifically with these problems are called *addictionologists, addictionists* or *addiction specialists.*) It is extremely important to stop using cocaine before conceiving. Research has shown that damage to the baby can occur as early as 3 days after conception! Cocaine use increases risk of miscarriage and intrauterine-growth restriction. For the mother-to-be, problems are many, including malnutrition.

I've tried to stop smoking, but I don't know if I can. Can cigarette smoking harm a growing baby?

Smoking can affect pregnancy and fetal development. Low birthweight and a slower growth rate are problems in babies born to mothers who smoke. For your health and the health of your baby, try to stop smoking before you consider pregnancy.

I read somewhere that caffeine can make a woman infertile. Is that true?

Studies have shown that drinking 8 cups of coffee a day (1,600mg of caffeine) is associated with a decrease in a woman's ability to get pregnant. Some researchers have found an association between excessive caffeine consumption and miscarriage.

My friend told me she stopped drinking alcohol before she got pregnant, but I don't drink very much. I don't have to stop, do I?

In the past, we believed a little alcohol was OK during pregnancy, but times have changed. Most doctors believe it's best not to drink any alcohol during pregnancy. Every time you take a drink, your baby does too! Stop using alcohol from the time you are preparing to conceive until after your baby is born.

There really aren't many side effects from marijuana; I always feel relaxed when I smoke it. Is it bad for the baby?

Marijuana contains tars, resins and other substances that can be dangerous during pregnancy. It crosses the placenta and enters the baby's system. We know it can cause attention deficit, impaired decision making and memory problems in childhood years if a fetus is exposed. Stop before you get pregnant.

WORKING BEFORE PREGNANCY

At work I am exposed to an X-ray machine and chemicals every day. Will this be a problem when I am pregnant?

Get answers to these questions *before* you get pregnant. Many workplace exposures, such as X-rays and chemicals, could be harmful. If you wait to ask these questions until after you find out you're pregnant, you may have already exposed your developing fetus to various dangers during some of the most important weeks of development.

My job requires me to stand for a 10-hour shift; I'm used to it. Will this be a problem when I am pregnant?

Studies have shown that women who stand for a long time each day have smaller babies. If you have had premature deliveries or an incompetent cervix in the past, or if your job requires that you stand a lot, discuss the situation with your doctor.

I pay for healthcare coverage out of my check at work. Will this cover me when I get pregnant in a few months?

Not all insurance plans include maternity coverage. Some have a waiting period to pay for surgery or having a baby. Some may not cover your doctor or the hospital you want to go to. Having a baby costs a lot of money; find out ahead of time what your coverage is. Planning ahead may save you money and the trouble of changing doctors or hospitals.

SEXUALLY TRANSMITTED DISEASES

In the last 2 years, I've had a sexually transmitted disease four times. Can this cause problems when I want to get pregnant in a few months?

Sexually transmitted diseases (STDs) can damage your uterus or Fallopian tubes, making it more difficult to get pregnant. If you get an STD while you're pregnant, it could affect your pregnancy.

STDs include gonorrhea, chlamydia, genital herpes, genital warts (condyloma), syphilis and HIV (the virus that causes AIDS). Use a condom before trying to get pregnant if you have a problem with infections or are exposed to infections frequently, even if you use other forms of birth control. If you get an infection, take care of it before you try to get pregnant.

How can I protect myself from STDs?

Having your partner use condoms is a good way to protect yourself against STDs, especially if you have more than one sexual partner.

PART TWO

Your Pregnancy

2

Your Health and Medical Concerns

Your health can affect your pregnancy in many ways. If you are in good health before pregnancy, try to maintain it while you're pregnant by eating healthfully, getting enough rest, drinking lots of fluids, taking good care of yourself and keeping all your prenatal appointments.

Even if you begin pregnancy in good health, you may experience some common discomforts as your pregnancy progresses. You may experience nausea (with or without vomiting), frequent urination, fatigue, breast changes and breast tenderness. Don't worry—these are common in pregnancy, and luckily they aren't usually serious.

You have an incredible effect on the health of your growing baby. As we state in the previous chapter, planning for pregnancy is important. Even more important is how you treat yourself (and the developing fetus) *during* your pregnancy. Good nutrition, proper exercise, sufficient rest and taking care of yourself all have an impact on your pregnancy.

We cover many aspects of your health care in this chapter, such as what prenatal care is and what kind of care you should expect during pregnancy; choosing whom you want to take care of you; how to deal with morning sickness; how your health affects your baby; some discomforts you may experience; special pregnancy concerns and what to do about pre-existing medical conditions. It's a fairly long chapter, so you may want to read only those parts that concern you at this time. You can read about other areas as they become important to you. To be sure you get the best medical treatment you can during pregnancy, contact your doctor as soon as you believe you might be pregnant.

PRENATAL CARE

What is "prenatal care" and why do I need it?

Prenatal means before birth; prenatal care is the care you receive during pregnancy. You need this special care to help you discover any problems before they become serious. Healthcare professionals who are specially trained to deal with pregnancy can answer your questions and respond to your concerns during this important time.

How does the care I receive affect my pregnancy?

You want to feel confident that the care you receive is the best you can find, so you'll be able to relax and enjoy your pregnancy. It really is a special time in your life and an enjoyable one. You want to do everything you can to make it the best possible time for your growing baby.

What can I expect on my first prenatal visit?

Your first visit may be one of your longest. You will be asked a lot of questions, and you will undergo a physical exam. Lab tests may be ordered now or at your next visit.

What kinds of questions will I be asked?

You will be asked for a complete medical history, including information about your periods, recent birth-control methods and previ-

BENEFITS OF PREGNANCY

- The natural steroids produced during pregnancy may reduce symptoms of allergies and asthma.
- Women who suffer from rheumatoid arthritis, systemic lupus erythematosus, inflammatory bowel disease or other autoimmune disorders may do better when they are pregnant. Natural steroids produced by the placenta can reduce inflammation, common in these diseases.
- Pregnancy may protect you from breast or ovarian cancer. The younger you are when you start having babies, and the more pregnancies you have, the greater the protection.
- Migraine headaches often disappear during the 2nd and 3rd trimesters of pregnancy.
- Menstrual cramps are a thing of the past during pregnancy. An added benefit—they may not return after baby is born!
- Endometriosis (when endometrial tissue attaches to parts of the ovaries and other sites outside the uterus) causes pelvic pain, heavy bleeding, infertility and other problems during menstruation for some women. Pregnancy stops the growth of endometrial tissue when ovulation stops and therefore may help relieve moderate endometriosis.

ous pregnancies. Tell your doctor about any miscarriages or abortions. Be sure to include information about hospital stays or surgeries you have had.

What other information will my doctor want to know?

Your doctor needs to know about any medications you take or are allergic to. Your family's medical history may be important, such as the occurrence of diabetes or other illnesses. Be sure to tell your doctor about any chronic medical problems you have. If you have medical records, bring them with you.

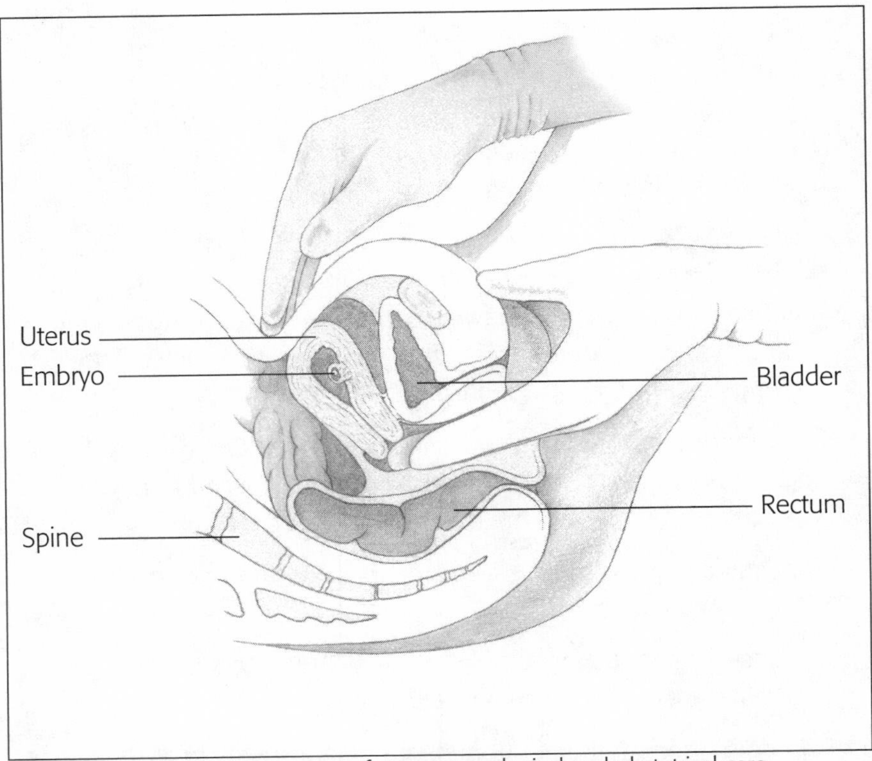

A pelvic exam is a necessary part of your gynecological and obstetrical care.

I hate having a pelvic exam. Will I need one?

Yes, you probably will. A pelvic exam helps your doctor determine if your uterus is the appropriate size for how far along you are in pregnancy, which can be helpful in determining your due date. You will also have a Pap smear if you haven't had one in the last year.

How often will I have to go to the doctor?

In most cases, you will go every 4 weeks for the first 7 months, then every 2 weeks until the last month, then once a week. If problems arise, more frequent visits may be necessary.

What kind of lab tests will I need?

Several tests will probably be ordered during the first or second visit. These may include any of the following:

- a complete blood count (CBC)
- urinalysis and urine culture
- Pap smear
- cervical cultures, as indicated
- blood-sugar test (for diabetes; may be done later in pregnancy)
- rubella titers (for immunity against rubella)
- blood typing
- Rh-factor
- test for syphilis
- test for hepatitis antibodies
- alpha-fetoprotein test
- triple screen
- quad screen

CHOOSING YOUR DOCTOR

I have a friend who says I need to go to a special kind of doctor for prenatal care and delivery of my baby. Is this true?

You have many choices when it comes to choosing your doctor for pregnancy. You can choose an obstetrician, a family practitioner or a certified nurse-midwife to oversee your prenatal care.

What is an obstetrician?

An obstetrician is a medical doctor or an osteopathic physician who specializes in the care of pregnant women, including delivering babies. He or she has completed further training in obstetrics and gynecology after medical school.

What is a family practitioner?

A family practitioner, sometimes called a *general practitioner,* often provides care for the entire family. Many family practitioners are experienced in delivering babies. In some cases, an obstetrician may not be available in a community because it is small or remote. In these cases, a family practitioner often delivers babies. If problems arise, your family practitioner may refer you to an obstetrician for prenatal care.

What is a certified nurse-midwife?

A certified nurse-midwife is a trained professional who cares for women who have low-risk, uncomplicated pregnancies and delivers their babies. These professionals are registered nurses who have additional professional training and certification in nurse-midwifery. They are supervised by a physician and call him or her if complications occur.

What is a perinatologist?

A perinatologist is an obstetrician who specializes in high-risk pregnancies. Only about 10% of all pregnant women need to see one. If you have serious problems during pregnancy, you may be referred to a perinatologist. You may need to see one if you experienced problems with past pregnancies.

If I see a perinatologist, will my doctor still deliver the baby?

It may be possible for you to deliver with your doctor, or you may have to deliver your baby at a hospital other than the one you chose. Usually this is because of specialized facilities or the availability of specialized tests for you or your baby.

How can I find the best caregiver for me?

If you have an obstetrician you like, you may not have to look any further. If you don't have one, call your local medical society and ask for a referral. Ask for recommendations from friends who have recently had babies. Ask the opinion of a labor-delivery nurse. Sometimes another doctor, such as a pediatrician or internist, can refer you to an obstetrician. Ask your local librarian for publications that list physicians in your area.

Who can answer my questions and help me with my fears while I'm pregnant?

It's important to establish communication with your doctor so you can ask him or her anything about your condition. Read articles and books, such as this one and our other books, *Your Pregnancy Week by*

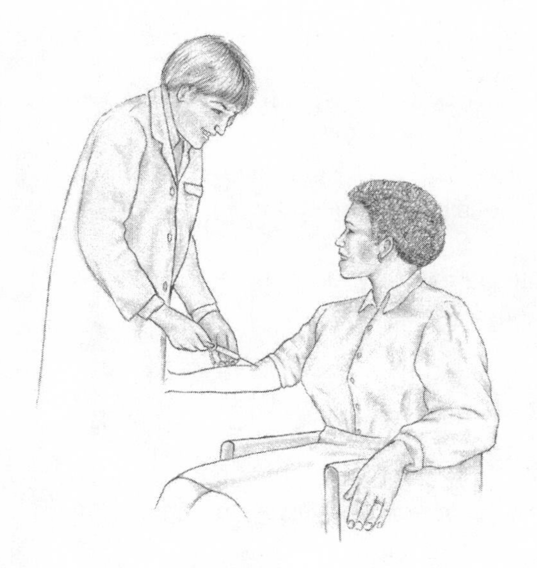

Blood tests are done to ensure that you and your baby are healthy.

Week, Your Pregnancy: Every Woman's Guide and *Your Pregnancy after 35*. They help you prepare questions to ask. *Never* substitute any information you receive from other sources in place of information you receive from your doctor about your personal pregnancy. He or she knows you, your history and what has occurred during this pregnancy. Always discuss your concerns with him or her!

I feel embarrassed asking some of the questions I have. They seem silly or stupid.

Don't be afraid to ask any question! Your doctor has probably already heard it, so don't be embarrassed. It's possible a situation is unwise or risky for you, so check even the smallest details. It's better to take time to get answers to all your questions than to wait until a problem develops.

DEALING WITH MORNING SICKNESS

I feel so nauseated in the morning that I can't eat anything. Does this last throughout pregnancy?

Nausea is typically the worst at the beginning of pregnancy; most often it is bad in the morning and improves during the day. Morning

WHAT CAN I DO ABOUT NAUSEA?

Many things may help you deal with nausea and vomiting related to morning sickness. Try the following suggestions and use what works for you.

- Spread meals throughout the day so you eat several nutritious snacks instead of a few large meals.
- Eat a snack before you get up, such as crackers or rice cakes. Or ask your partner to make you some dry toast.
- Avoid heavy, fatty foods.
- Keep up your fluid intake, which may be easier to handle than solids and will help avoid dehydration.
- Alternate wet foods with dry foods. Eat only dry foods at one meal, then liquids at the next.
- Try fresh ginger—it's a natural remedy for nausea. Grate it on vegetables and other foods.
- Suck on a fresh cut lemon when you feel nauseated.
- Avoid things that trigger your nausea, such as odors, movement or noise.
- Get plenty of rest.
- Avoid getting sweaty or overheated, which can contribute to your nausea.

sickness usually begins around week 6 and lasts until week 12 or 13, when it lessens and disappears.

Can't I take medication for morning sickness?

A pill to relieve the symptoms of morning sickness is on the market again in the United States. Sold under the trade name Bendectin, it was removed in the early 1980s because some claimed it caused

birth defects. Studies have not supported these claims, however, and have actually proved it is safe to use during pregnancy. The FDA re-examined the studies and research data and has determined the drug to be safe.

I have nausea and vomiting, but it's only at night. Is this the same thing as morning sickness?

Nausea and vomiting with pregnancy can occur at *any* time of the day or night. Sometimes it lasts all day long.

I'm nauseated every morning but don't throw up. My friend had to go to the hospital for I.V.s when she had morning sickness. Is this the same thing?

Probably. An early symptom of pregnancy for many women is nausea, with or without vomiting. A more serious condition, called *hyperemesis gravidarum*, results when a woman experiences a great deal of vomiting and the inability to eat foods or to drink fluids. If a woman has this problem, she may need to be treated in the hospital with I.V.s (intravenous fluid) and medicines for nausea.

Do I have to go into the hospital if I have hyperemesis gravidarum?

A new medical approach involves use of Reglan (metoclopramide), which suppresses your vomiting reflex. A catheter is inserted into your abdomen or thigh. This is attached to a tiny pump, which pumps a steady dose of Reglan, so you can lead a normal life. It has been used during the 1st trimester with no harmful effects on the fetus. Hypnotherapy is another effective treatment.

My sister had to go into the hospital when she had morning sickness. Why?

If a woman gets dehydrated or loses a substantial amount of weight with morning sickness, she may have to be put in the hospital where she can be fed intravenously. Usually after a couple of days in the hospital, the woman can resume eating solids. The main purpose in putting her in the hospital is to keep her fluid intake up and to give her the nourishment she needs.

A friend told me her dentist warned her to take care of her teeth if she had morning sickness. How were her teeth affected?

When you vomit, stomach acid that enters the mouth can cause a breakdown in tooth enamel. Brush your teeth after vomiting to remove any residue.

This may sound weird, but I've heard that a man can suffer from morning sickness when his wife is pregnant. Is this true?

Many fathers-to-be experience various physical problems during their wife's pregnancy. The condition is called *couvade,* from a Carib Indian tribe in which every expectant father engages in rituals that enable him to understand what his wife is experiencing. A father-to-be may experience nausea, headaches, back and muscle aches, insomnia, fatigue or depression.

HOW YOUR HEALTH AFFECTS YOUR GROWING BABY

How does my health affect my baby?

Your baby is totally dependent on you for all its needs. To make sure he or she gets the best possible start in life, it's important for you to eat right, get enough rest and stay as healthy as possible throughout your pregnancy.

I've heard that some infections and illnesses I have can affect the development of my baby. Is that true?

Yes. That's why it's important to remind your doctor you're pregnant when you call him or her about any medical problems. See the chart below, which lists some illnesses and the effects each illness can have on a developing fetus.

Fever

If I have a fever, especially a high one, can it hurt my baby?

It may. Your baby relies on you for its temperature control. A *prolonged* high fever, especially in the 1st trimester (first 13 weeks), may affect a developing fetus.

POSSIBLE PRENATAL EFFECTS OF MOTHER'S ILLNESS

Illness in Mother	Possible Effect on Fetus
Chicken pox	Heart problems
Cytomegalovirus	Microcephaly, brain damage, hearing loss
Group-B streptococcus	Pneumonia, meningitis, cerebral palsy, damage to lungs or kidneys
Hepatitis	Liver damage, death
Lupus	Miscarriage, premature delivery
Lyme disease	Preterm labor, fetal death, rash in newborn
Rubella (German measles)	Cataracts, deafness, heart lesions; can involve all organs
Shingles	Possible effects on all organs
Syphilis	Skin defects, fetal death
Toxoplasmosis	Possible effects on all organs

Is there anything I can do, which won't harm the baby, to bring down a high fever?

Drink lots of liquids, take acetaminophen (Tylenol) and dress appropriately to help you cool down. If your physician prescribes medication for a cold, bladder infection or other illness, take *all* of it as prescribed.

Hepatitis B

I read that hepatitis is becoming more serious for pregnant women. What do I need to be aware of?

Hepatitis is a viral infection of the liver and is one of the most serious infections that can occur during pregnancy. Your doctor will probably test you for hepatitis B at the beginning of your pregnancy.

How is hepatitis B transmitted?

Hepatitis B is spread from one person to another by the reuse of intravenous needles and by sexual contact. It is responsible for nearly 50% of the hepatitis cases in the United States. This type of hepatitis can be transmitted to a developing fetus.

What are the symptoms of hepatitis?

Hepatitis can cause flulike symptoms and nausea and pain in the area of the liver or upper-right abdomen. The person may appear yellow (jaundiced), and urine may be darker than normal.

How can hepatitis affect a developing baby?

A developing baby can get hepatitis from its mother. Hepatitis affects the liver. A fetus that gets hepatitis is at serious risk for liver damage or stillbirth.

What can be done about hepatitis?

If a baby is born to a mother who tests positive for hepatitis at the beginning of pregnancy, it may be necessary to give the baby immune globulin after it is born. It is now recommended that all newborns receive hepatitis vaccine shortly after birth. Ask your pediatrician if the vaccine is available in your area.

Group-B Streptococcus

I read that Group-B streptococcus infection in a mother-to-be can cause problems for her baby. What kind of problems?

Group-B streptococcus (GBS) rarely causes problems in adults but is the leading cause of life-threatening infection in newborns.

What are the symptoms of GBS?

There usually aren't any symptoms, but sometimes a woman will have vaginal discharge.

How could I get GBS?

GBS is often found in the mouth or lower-digestive, urinary or reproductive organs. In women, it is most often found in the vagina or rectum. You get an infection when your immunity or resistance is down. It is common to "carry" the bacteria in your system (about 30% of women are "carriers") and not be sick or have any symptoms.

How will I know if I have GBS?

As mentioned above, it's common to have GBS in your system and not be sick or have any symptoms. At this time, we don't have an ideal screening test for GBS; however, your doctor may recommend taking a swab of your vagina or rectum at around 28 to 36 weeks of pregnancy. This is cultured to test for the presence of GBS; the test identifies 90% of all women who will carry the bacteria at the time of birth. There are faster tests that can be used during labor to detect GBS, but they are not as accurate.

Risk increases with premature labor, premature rupture of membranes or a previous GBS infection.

Can GBS be treated?

Yes, GBS is treated with antibiotics.

Fifth Disease

One of my friends, who's a teacher, was worried about fifth disease while she was pregnant. What is it?

Fifth disease, also called *parvovirus B19*, is a mild, moderately contagious airborne infection that spreads easily through groups, such as classrooms or day-care centers. (It is *not* the same infection that affects dogs.) The rash of the disease looks like skin reddening caused by a slap. Reddening fades and recurs and can last from 2 to 34 days. There is no treatment, but it is important to distinguish it from rubella, especially if you are pregnant.

Should I be concerned about it?

It is something to know about. This virus is important during pregnancy because it interferes with the production of red blood cells. If you are exposed to fifth disease, contact your doctor, who will do a blood test that determines whether you have had the virus before. If you have not, he or she can monitor you to detect fetal problems. Some fetal problems can be dealt with before the baby is born.

Bacterial Vaginosis

What is bacterial vaginosis? I've heard it can cause problems for pregnant women.

Bacterial vaginosis (BV) is a vaginal infection that affects pregnant and nonpregnant women. Some researchers estimate that up to 20% of all pregnant women have BV. It increases a pregnant woman's risk of having a low birthweight baby or of going into premature labor. It occurs when bacteria that can cause you problems multiply due to suppression or killing of good bacteria. Most women are *not* routinely screened for BV.

What are the symptoms of bacterial vaginosis?

It is possible to have BV without any symptoms, but symptoms you may notice include the following:

- mild vaginal irritation
- a fishy odor
- increased creamy discharge from the vagina

How can I be tested for BV?

Your doctor can do a vaginal swab if he or she suspects BV.

What is the treatment for bacterial vaginosis?

Creams and oral antibiotics are used to treat BV. Treatment may increase a woman's chances of carrying her baby to full term.

Lyme Disease

Lyme disease is prevalent in our area. Is it dangerous for my baby if I get Lyme disease during pregnancy?

Lyme disease is an infection carried and transmitted to humans by ticks. Lyme disease does cross the placenta. Complications from this infection include preterm labor, fetal death or a rashlike illness in the newborn.

What are the symptoms of Lyme disease?

There are several stages of the disease. In most people, a skin lesion with a distinctive look, called a *bull's eye,* appears at the site of the bite. Flulike symptoms appear, and after 4 to 6 weeks there may be signs of heart problems or neurological problems. Arthritis may be a problem later.

If I do get Lyme disease, how it is treated?

Treatment includes antibiotic therapy. Many medications used to treat Lyme disease are safe to use during pregnancy.

How can I avoid exposure to Lyme disease?

Stay out of areas that are known to have ticks, such as heavily wooded areas. If you can't avoid them, wear long-sleeved shirts, long pants, socks and boots or closed shoes. Check your hair for ticks; they often attach themselves to the hair or the scalp.

Lupus

What is lupus?

Lupus (systemic lupus erythematosus or SLE) is a disease of unknown cause that affects women more often than men (about 9 to 1). A woman with lupus has a large number of antibodies in her bloodstream that are directed toward her own tissues. This can affect various parts of the body, including the joints, skin, kidneys, muscles, lungs, brain and central nervous system.

Why is lupus a concern in pregnancy?

Lupus occurs most often in young or middle-aged women who may become pregnant. The risk of miscarriage, premature delivery and complications around the time of delivery may increase in women with lupus.

What are the symptoms of lupus?

The most common symptom is joint pain. Other symptoms include a rash, skin sores, fever, kidney problems and hypertension.

How is lupus treated?

Steroids is the drug of choice to treat lupus. The most commonly prescribed steroid is prednisone. Many studies on the safety of prednisone during pregnancy have found it to be safe.

Toxic Streptococcus A

I've heard a lot lately about toxic streptococcus A, the flesh-eating bacteria. What is it?

Toxic streptococcus A is a bacterial infection that usually starts in a cut on the skin, not as a sore throat. It spreads very quickly and can soon involve the entire body.

How does it get into my system?

Bacteria can enter through a very small scratch, scrape or cut in the skin. The skin then turns red and becomes swollen, painful and infected very quickly.

What are the symptoms of toxic streptococcus A?

Symptoms include the following:

- fever above 102F (39C)
- an inflamed cut or scratch
- flulike symptoms
- unusually cold extremities (feet, hands, legs and arms)

Is there anything I can do to prevent toxic strep A?

Yes. Any time you cut or scratch yourself, clean the affected area with soap and water, alcohol or hydrogen peroxide. All are safe to use during pregnancy. After careful washing, apply antibiotic cream or ointment (available over the counter) to the area. Use a light bandage, if necessary. Keep the area clean, and reapply antibiotic ointment as needed. These same measures can and should be used with every member of your family.

Diarrhea

I've been having some diarrhea lately. Should I be concerned?

Diarrhea during pregnancy can cause you concern. If the diarrhea doesn't go away in 24 hours, or if it keeps returning, contact your doctor. He or she may prescribe medication for the problem. Do not take any medication for diarrhea without discussing it with your doctor first.

Is there anything I can do for myself if I have diarrhea?

One of the best things you can do is increase your fluid intake. Drink a lot of water, juice and other clear fluids, such as broth. (Avoid apple juice because it can act as a laxative.) You may feel better eating a bland diet, without solid foods, until your diarrhea stops.

Is it dangerous for my baby if I don't eat solids?

No, it isn't harmful for a few days if you keep up your fluid intake. Solid foods may actually cause you more gastrointestinal distress. Avoid milk products while you have diarrhea; they can make it worse.

Toxoplasmosis

My vet told me to be careful about caring for my cat. What does caring for my cat have to do with my pregnancy?

If you have a cat, you may be exposed to *toxoplasma gondii,* a protozoa that causes toxoplasmosis. The disease is spread by eating raw, infected meat or by contact with infected cat feces. You can pick up protozoa from an infected cat's litterbox, from counters, other surfaces the cat walks on or from the cat itself when you pet it.

What problems can toxoplasmosis cause me or my baby?

Infection during pregnancy can lead to miscarriage or an infected infant at birth. Usually an infection in the mother causes no symptoms.

How can I protect myself from toxoplasmosis?

Avoid exposure to cat feces; get someone else to change the kitty litter. Keep cats off counters and other areas where you could pick up the protozoa. Wash your hands thoroughly after contact with your cat or contact with raw meat. Keep counters clean, and cook meat thoroughly. Hygienic measures prevent transmission of the protozoa.

Cytomegalovirus

What is cytomegalovirus?

Cytomegalovirus (CMV) is a member of the herpes-virus family. It is transmitted in humans by contact with saliva or urine. Day-care centers are a common source of the infection. CMV can also be passed by sexual contact.

How can cytomegalovirus affect me?

Most CMV infections do not cause any symptoms. When symptoms do occur, they include a fever, sore throat and joint pain.

Can cytomegalovirus affect my growing baby?

Yes, it can cause various problems in an infant, including low birthweight, eye problems, jaundice and anemia.

Rubella

I've heard about a pregnant woman getting rubella. What is it exactly?

Rubella, also called *German measles,* is a viral infection that causes few problems in the nonpregnant woman. It is more serious during pregnancy, especially in the 1st trimester.

What are the symptoms of rubella?

The most common symptom of rubella is a skin rash. You may also experience flulike symptoms.

How can rubella affect my growing baby?

Rubella infection during pregnancy can increase the rate of miscarriage and cause problems in the baby, especially deafness and heart defects.

Chicken Pox

I've been exposed to chicken pox. Can they hurt me or my baby?

If you have had chicken pox before, it shouldn't be a problem now. If you haven't had chicken pox, exposure during the 1st trimester can result in birth defects, such as heart problems. Exposure close to delivery (within 1 week) can result in chicken pox in the baby.

How can chicken pox affect me?

Adults don't tolerate chicken pox as well as children do. Contraction of the disease can result in painful lesions, high fever and severe flulike symptoms.

I'm not sure if I've had chicken pox before. What can I do?

Avoid exposure to the disease, if possible.

Shingles

I just read about shingles. What is it exactly?

Shingles (sometimes called *varicella-zoster*) is in the herpes virus and chicken pox family. It may remain latent for years, only to be reactivated.

What are the symptoms of shingles?

Pain is the main symptom; a rash or lesions may accompany this.

How can shingles affect me?

If you get shingles while you're pregnant, it can cause severe pain and even breathing problems. Fortunately, it is rare.

How can shingles affect my growing baby?

It may cause birth defects if you are exposed early in pregnancy. If you are exposed within 2 weeks of delivery, the baby may catch the disease.

ENVIRONMENTAL POISONS AND POLLUTANTS

I've heard environmental poisons can be dangerous to a pregnant woman. What are they?

Environmental poisons and pollutants that can harm a developing fetus include lead, mercury, PCBs and pesticides.

How can lead harm a developing baby?

Lead is readily transported across the placenta to the baby. Exposure to lead can cause an increase in the chance of miscarriage. Poisoning can occur as early as the 12th week of pregnancy.

How could I be exposed to lead?

Lead exposure may come from many sources, including water pipes, solders, storage batteries, some construction materials, paints,

INCIDENCE OF BIRTH DEFECTS

Parents-to-be want to know how often birth defects occur. Luckily, they don't happen that often. The chart below shows how often specific defects occur in North America.

Cleft lip/cleft palate	1 in 730 births
Clubfoot	1 in 1,000 births
Congenital heart defects	1 in 125 births
Dislocated hips	1 in 400 births
Down syndrome	1 in 900 births (incidence is correlated to mother's age)
Neural-tube defects	1 in 1,600 births
Pyloric stenosis	1 in 250 births
Sickle cell anemia	1 in 400 births of African-American babies

dyes and wood preservatives. You may also be exposed in your workplace; find out if you are at risk.

How can mercury harm a developing baby?

Reports of mercury exposure have been linked to cerebral palsy and microcephaly.

How could I be exposed to mercury?

Exposure usually occurs from eating contaminated fish.

How can PCBs harm a developing baby?

PCBs (polychlorinated biphenyls) are not single compounds but mixtures of several compounds. Most fish, birds and humans have small, measurable amounts of PCBs in their tissues. PCBs have been blamed for miscarriage and intrauterine-growth restriction.

How could I be exposed to PCBs?

We are exposed to PCBs through some of the foods we eat, such as fish.

How can pesticides harm a developing baby?

Pesticides have been held responsible for an increase in miscarriage and intrauterine-growth restriction.

How could I be exposed to pesticides?

Pesticides include a large number of agents used to control unwanted plants and animals. Human exposure is common because of the extensive use of pesticides. Those of most concern include DDT, chlordane, heptachlor and lindane.

How can I protect myself against these agents?

The safest course is to avoid exposure, through the foods you eat or the air you breathe. Thoroughly wash all fruits and vegetables before eating. It may not be possible to eliminate all contact. If you know you will be around certain chemicals, wash your hands thoroughly after exposure.

COMMON DISCOMFORTS OF PREGNANCY

Heartburn and Indigestion

I've had a lot of problems with heartburn during my pregnancy. What causes it?

Discomfort from heartburn is one of the most common complaints during pregnancy. It may begin early in pregnancy, although it generally becomes more severe as pregnancy progresses. Heartburn is caused by reflux (regurgitation) of stomach contents into the esophagus.

I don't usually have heartburn when I'm not pregnant. Why does it occur so much during pregnancy?

It occurs more frequently during pregnancy because of two factors:

1. decreased gastrointestinal function
2. compression of the stomach by the uterus as it grows larger and moves up into the abdomen

Is there anything I can do about heartburn?

Antacids may provide considerable relief. Follow your doctor's instructions or the directions relating to pregnancy on the package. Don't overdo it and take too much in an effort to find relief. You can use some antacids without much concern, such as Amphojel, Gelusil, milk of magnesia and Maalox. Avoid sodium bicarbonate because it might cause you to retain water. In addition to antacids, the following tips may provide some relief.

- Eat smaller, more frequent meals.
- Avoid eating before bedtime.
- When lying down, elevate your head and shoulders.

Can the foods I eat affect my heartburn?

Some foods *do* affect heartburn. Try to find foods (and amounts) that don't give you heartburn. Eliminate foods that cause you problems. Add foods you tolerate well that benefit you and your growing baby.

What's the difference between heartburn and indigestion?

Heartburn is a burning discomfort felt behind the lower part of the sternum (breastbone). *Indigestion* refers to the inability to digest food or difficulty digesting food.

If I have indigestion, is there anything I can do about it?

Eat foods that agree with you. Avoid spicy foods. Eat small meals frequently. If you need them, take antacids after meals, but don't overmedicate yourself.

Hemorrhoids

I've never had hemorrhoids before, and now I do. Why?

Hemorrhoids are caused by increased blood flow in the pelvis and the increased weight and size of the uterus, which blocks blood flow.

HEMORRHOID RELIEF

- Eat adequate amounts of fiber.
- Drink lots of fluid.
- Sitz baths help.
- Suppository medications, available without a prescription, can provide relief. You may need stool softeners.
- Apply ice packs or cotton balls soaked in witch hazel to the affected area.
- Discuss it with your doctor if hemorrhoids become a major problem for you.

What exactly are hemorrhoids?

They are dilated blood vessels around the anus or inside the anus. They can itch, bleed and hurt.

Headaches

I have headaches but don't want to take medication if I don't have to during pregnancy. What can I do about them?

You may experience more tension headaches during pregnancy because of sleep disturbances, nausea and vomiting, and stress (emotional and physical). You may get fewer tension headaches during the 2nd and 3rd trimesters as your body (and mind) adjust to your pregnancy.

It's a good idea to try to deal with your problem without medication. There are several things you can try that are medicine free (see the box below).

If my headaches won't go away using these techniques, is there any medicine I can take?

Acetaminophen (Tylenol) is recommended for headaches. You can take the regular or extra-strength version. If this doesn't help, call your doctor.

HEADACHE RELIEF WITHOUT MEDICATION

- Try various relaxation methods, such as listening to relaxation tapes, learning deep-breathing exercises or practicing meditation or yoga.
- Close your eyes and rest in a quiet place.
- Apply an ice pack to the back of your head for a tension headache, or lie in a darkened room with a cold compress on your forehead for a migraine.
- Eat regularly. Avoid foods or substances that might trigger a headache, such as aged cheese, cured meat, chocolate or substances that contain caffeine.
- Avoid bright lights, cigarette or cigar smoke, stress or disruptions in sleeping or eating patterns.
- Get enough sleep.

I suffer from migraine headaches. What can I do about them during pregnancy?

Try the techniques described above. If they don't help, discuss the problem with your doctor. Do not take any medications for a migraine headache without discussing it with your physician first.

Allergies

Will my allergies cause problems during pregnancy?

Your allergies may change during pregnancy. Sometimes they get worse; sometimes they improve.

What can I do for my allergies while I'm pregnant?

Drink plenty of fluid, especially during hot weather. If you're sensitive to certain foods, be careful about what you eat. Avoid anything you might be sensitive to, such as animals or cigarette smoke.

LEG CRAMP RELIEF

Leg cramps are not uncommon during pregnancy. The following advice may help you deal with leg cramps you experience at any time of day.

- Wear support hose during the day.
- Take warm baths.
- Have your partner massage your legs.
- Wear comfortable clothing that is not restrictive.
- Take acetaminophen (Tylenol) for pain.
- Rest on your side.
- Use a heating pad for up to 15 minutes when you experience pain.
- Avoid standing for long periods of time.

Can I take my regular allergy medications while I'm pregnant?

Ask your doctor or pharmacist *before* taking any medication, whether it's a prescription or over-the-counter (OTC) medication. Don't assume it's OK. It's safer and easier to ask ahead of time rather than take a chance with a medication.

Nasal Problems

My nose has been stuffed up ever since I got pregnant. Is this normal?

Some women complain of nasal stuffiness or nosebleeds during pregnancy. We believe these occur because circulation changes caused by hormonal changes cause mucous membranes of the nose and nasal passages to swell and to bleed more easily.

What can I do about my stuffed up nose?

Do not use decongestants or nasal sprays to relieve stuffiness without first asking your doctor. Many are combinations of several medications that you should not use during pregnancy. Try a humidifier to relieve stuffiness. Increase your fluid intake, and use a gentle lubricant, such as petroleum jelly. Discuss it at a prenatal visit if these remedies don't provide relief.

SPECIAL CONCERNS OF PREGNANCY

Rh-Factor

My mother told me to discuss my Rh-factor with my doctor. Why?

You may be Rh-negative, which requires some additional attention during pregnancy and after your baby is born.

What does it mean to be Rh-negative?

Your blood type, such as O, A, B, AB, contains a factor that determines if it is positive or negative. In the past, Rh-negative women who carried an Rh-positive child faced complicated pregnancies that could result in a very sick baby. Today, most of these problems can be prevented. If you are Rh-negative, you and your doctor need to know it.

Why is being Rh-negative a problem?

If you have had a previous pregnancy, you have had a blood transfusion or you received blood products of some kind, you could become Rh-sensitized (isoimmunized). This could affect your baby if he or she is Rh-negative.

What does it mean to be isoimmunized?

If you are *isoimmunized*, you have antibodies that circulate inside your system. They won't harm you, but they can attack the blood of an Rh-positive fetus. Antibodies from you can cross the placenta and attack your baby's blood. This can make your baby anemic while it is still inside the uterus and can be very serious.

How does a woman become sensitized?

An Rh-negative woman becomes sensitized when Rh-positive blood gets into her bloodstream. This can happen with a blood transfusion, amniocentesis, the previous birth of an Rh-positive baby, a miscarriage or an ectopic pregnancy.

What can I do about this problem?

Most problems can be prevented with the use of Rho-GAM, which is Rh-immune globulin. If you are Rh-negative and pregnant, you will receive an injection of RhoGAM at 28 weeks' pregnancy to prevent sensitization before delivery. Rho-GAM is a blood product; if you have any personal, religious or ethical reasons for not using blood products, discuss it with your doctor.

Do I receive any more injections?

Within 72 hours after delivery, you will be given a second injection of RhoGAM, if your baby is Rh-positive.

Not all babies are Rh-positive, are they?

No. Some women who are Rh-negative carry a child who is also Rh-negative. In this case, no RhoGAM injection is given after delivery.

Are there other situations in which RhoGAM is used?

Yes. If you have an ectopic pregnancy and are Rh-negative, you should receive RhoGAM. This also applies to miscarriages and abortions. If you are Rh-negative and have amniocentesis, you will also receive RhoGAM.

Anemia

My doctor says I have anemia now that I'm pregnant. What is it?

Anemia is a common medical problem in many pregnant women. The number of red blood cells in your blood is low; the quantity of these cells is inadequate to provide the oxygen your body needs.

Why does anemia occur so often in pregnancy?

Your blood volume increases up to 50% during pregnancy. Blood is made up of fluid and cells. The fluid usually increases faster than the cells. This may result in a drop in your hematocrit (the volume, amount or percent of red cells in the blood). This drop can result in anemia.

Why is it important to treat anemia during pregnancy?

If you suffer from anemia, you won't feel well during pregnancy and you'll tire more easily. You may also experience dizziness. If you're anemic when you go into labor, you're at higher risk of needing a blood transfusion when your baby is born. Pregnancy anemia can cause an increased risk of preterm delivery, growth restriction in the baby and low birthweight. Your doctor will determine if you are anemic and prescribe a course of treatment for you.

What is the most common type of anemia during pregnancy?

The most common type is *iron-deficiency anemia.* While you're pregnant, your baby uses some of your iron stores. With iron-deficiency anemia, your body does not make enough red blood cells to keep up with the increased demand.

What causes iron-deficiency anemia?

Several factors can cause this condition:

- bleeding during pregnancy
- multiple fetuses
- recent surgery on your stomach or small bowel
- frequent antacid use
- poor dietary habits

Is iron-deficiency anemia easy to control?

Yes, it usually is. Most prenatal vitamins contain iron; if you can't take a prenatal vitamin, you may be given iron supplementation. Eating certain foods, such as liver or spinach, also helps increase your iron intake.

What is thalassemia?

Thalassemia is a type of anemia that occurs most often in people of Mediterranean descent. The body doesn't produce enough globulin, which makes up red blood cells, and anemia results. If you have a family history of thalassemia, tell your doctor.

What is sickle cell anemia?

Sickle cell anemia occurs when a person's bone marrow makes abnormal red blood cells. It occurs most often in people of African or Mediterranean descent.

How do I know if I have sickle cell anemia?

Your doctor can perform a blood test to see if you have this disease.

Doesn't sickle cell anemia also cause pain?

Yes, a sickle crisis can cause pain in the abdomen or limbs. This can happen at any time, not just during pregnancy.

Are there any other problems with sickle cell anemia?

In addition to pain, a mother-to-be can suffer more frequent infections. Risks to the fetus include miscarriage and stillbirth.

What about using hydroxyurea to treat sickle cell disease? Can a pregnant woman take it?

Hydroxyurea is the first effective treatment of sickle cell anemia. It reduces some of the excruciating pain, but its use carries some risk. Because we do not know the long-term effects, pregnant women should not use it.

Incompetent Cervix

A woman I met at my doctor's office told me she had an incompetent cervix with her last pregnancy. What is that?

An incompetent cervix is a condition in which a woman has painless premature stretching (dilatation) of the cervix. It is usually unnoticed by the woman. Membranes may rupture without any warning, and it usually results in premature delivery of the baby.

How will I know if this is happening to me?

The problem is not usually diagnosed until after one or more deliveries of a premature infant without any pain before delivery. If it's your first pregnancy, there is no way for you to know if you have an incompetent cervix.

What causes an incompetent cervix?

Some researchers believe it occurs because of previous trauma to the cervix, such as a D&C (dilatation and curettage) for an abortion or a miscarriage. It may also occur if surgery has been performed on the cervix.

If this problem occurs, is there any treatment for it?

Treatment is usually surgical. Sewing the cervix shut can reinforce a weak cervix. When the woman goes into labor, the suture is opened and the baby can be born normally.

Changes in Blood Pressure

At my last appointment my doctor said my blood pressure was up. Should I be concerned?

It's normal for your blood pressure to change a little during pregnancy. It often decreases a little during the 2nd trimester of pregnancy and increases toward the end of pregnancy.

What can I do about high blood pressure if it becomes a problem?

Resting in bed on your side can help. If your blood pressure remains elevated, medication may be necessary to lower it.

My sister had pregnancy-induced hypertension. What is it?

Pregnancy-induced hypertension is high blood pressure that occurs only during pregnancy. It will disappear after the baby is born. It develops in about 3% of women under age 40, and in 10% of women over 40.

What can be done about pregnancy-induced hypertension?

It is treated with bed rest, drinking lots of fluid and avoiding salt and foods containing large amounts of sodium. Medications to lower blood pressure may be prescribed. Hypertension can also be a symptom of pre-eclampsia. (For further information, see the discussion of pre-eclampsia on page 273.)

I feel dizzy a lot. Should I worry?

Feeling dizzy while you're pregnant is a fairly common symptom. Anemia can cause dizziness any time during pregnancy and can be checked with a blood count. Another cause of dizziness is hypotension (low blood pressure). Hypotension in pregnancy usually occurs during the 2nd trimester.

What causes hypotension in pregnancy?

There are two causes.

1. The enlarging uterus puts pressure on large blood vessels, such as your aorta and vena cava. This is called *supine hypotension* and may occur when you lie down. Don't lie on your back, especially after 16 weeks.
2. The second cause is rising rapidly from a sitting, kneeling or squatting position, called *postural hypotension*. When you rise rapidly, gravity causes blood to leave your brain, which may result in a drop in blood pressure. Avoid the problem by rising slowly from a sitting or lying position.

Bladder and Urinary-Tract Infections

What is the difference between a urinary-tract infection (UTI) and a bladder infection?

UTI refers to an infection anywhere in the urinary tract, including the bladder, the urethra, the ureters and the kidneys. A *bladder infection* refers to an infection in the bladder only. The terms are often used interchangeably.

Why do I get more bladder infections now that I'm pregnant?

This happens because of changes in your urinary tract. The uterus sits directly on top of the bladder and on the tubes leading from the kidneys to the bladder, called *ureters*. As the uterus grows, its increased weight can block the drainage of urine from the bladder, causing a bladder infection. Between 5 and 10% of all pregnant women experience bladder infections.

SYMPTOMS OF A BLADDER INFECTION

Call your doctor if you experience the following symptoms:

- frequent urination
- burning urination
- feeling as though you need to urinate and nothing will come out
- blood in your urine (with severe infection)

How does my doctor check for bladder infections?

Usually your doctor will do a urinalysis and a urine culture at your first visit. He or she may also check your urine for infections on subsequent visits.

I've heard about a more serious urinary-tract infection called *pyelonephritis.* What is it?

Pyelonephritis is an infection of the urinary tract that also involves the kidneys. It occurs in 1 to 2% of all pregnant women.

What are the symptoms of pyelonephritis?

In addition to the symptoms of a bladder infection, symptoms of pyelonephritis include high fever, chills and back pain.

How is pyelonephritis treated?

It may require hospitalization and treatment with intravenous antibiotics.

Kidney Stones

How often do kidney stones occur during pregnancy?

Kidney stones, also called *urinary calculi,* occur about once in every 1,500 pregnancies.

What are the symptoms of a kidney stone?

Symptoms usually include severe pain in the back and blood in the urine.

How is a kidney stone diagnosed?

In pregnancy, ultrasound is usually used to diagnose a kidney stone.

How is a kidney stone treated?

In pregnancy, it can usually be treated with pain medication and by drinking lots of fluid or receiving I.V.s.

PRE-EXISTING MEDICAL CONDITIONS

Before pregnancy, I often visited a chiropractor for back pain. Can I go to a chiropractor if I have back pain during pregnancy?

Low back pain is common during pregnancy—nearly half of all pregnant women suffer from it. If you have problems that you believe might be helped by chiropractic manipulation, discuss it with your doctor before you do anything! Whatever you do, avoid X-rays of your pelvis and lower back area.

Blood Sugar Problems

Can problems with my blood sugar cause dizziness?

Yes. Either high blood sugar (hyperglycemia) or low blood sugar (hypoglycemia) can make you feel dizzy or faint. Many doctors routinely test pregnant women for problems with blood sugar.

If I have a problem with blood sugar, what can I do?

Eat a balanced diet, don't skip meals and don't go a long time without eating. If it is more serious, you may need to see a dietitian. If blood tests show diabetes, you may be referred to an internist.

My friend said she had gestational diabetes while she was pregnant. What is it?

Sometimes called *pregnancy-induced diabetes,* gestational diabetes happens in about 10% of all pregnancies. With this problem, your blood sugar is too high. This can cause problems for you associated with too much weight gain. Problems for the baby include birth defects and a large baby. (See page 262 for more information on gestational diabetes.)

Diabetes

I have diabetes. How can it affect my pregnancy?

Diabetes was once a serious medical problem during pregnancy. It continues to be an important complication of pregnancy, but today many diabetic women can have safe pregnancies with proper medical care and a good diet if they follow their doctor's instructions. Using a glucometer to measure blood sugar is essential for diabetes control during pregnancy.

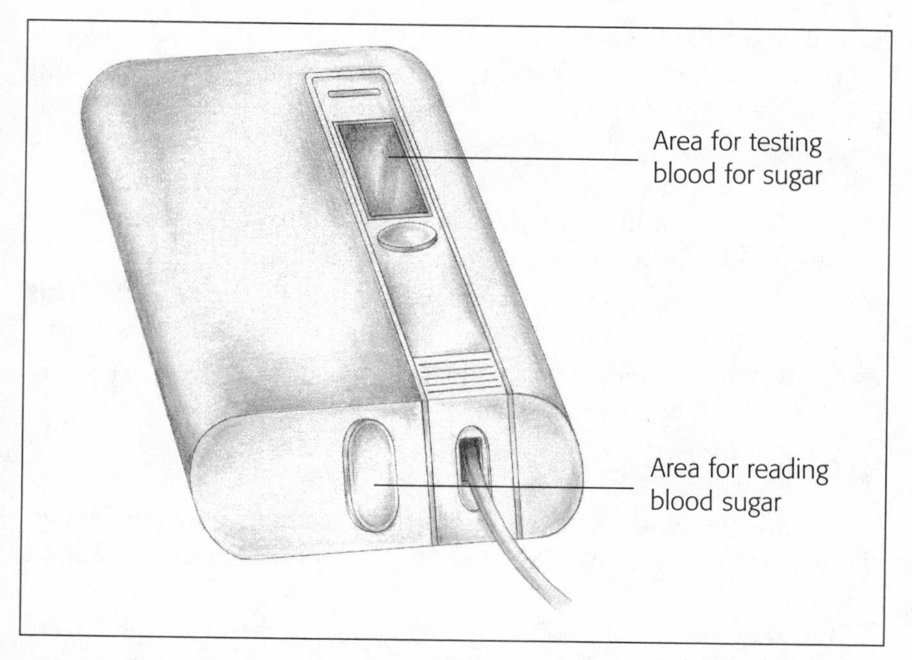

A glucometer measures the amount of sugar in a diabetic woman's blood. Blood-sugar control is important during pregnancy for a diabetic woman.

What are the symptoms of diabetes?

The symptoms of diabetes include the following:

- an increase in urination
- blurred vision
- weight loss
- dizziness
- increased hunger

Why is diabetes serious in pregnancy?

Diabetes can cause medical problems that could be serious for you and your baby. If your diabetes is not treated, you expose your baby to a high concentration of sugar, a condition called *hyperglycemia,* which is not healthy for the baby.

Uncontrolled diabetes puts you at significantly increased risk of miscarriage and problems at the time of birth. The most common fetal problems are heart, genitourinary and gastrointestinal problems. Diabetes can also cause large babies.

How is diabetes diagnosed?

Diabetes is diagnosed with blood tests: a fasting blood-sugar or a glucose-tolerance test. This test is usually done around 28 weeks of pregnancy.

If there is sugar in my urine, does it mean I have diabetes?

Not necessarily. It is common for nondiabetic pregnant women to have a small amount of sugar in their urine, called *glucosuria.* This occurs because of changes in your sugar levels and changes in the way your kidneys handle sugar during pregnancy.

Epilepsy

I have epilepsy, and I just found out I'm pregnant. I'm very excited about the pregnancy, but I'm concerned about the medicine I take. What should I do?

Tell your doctor immediately that you are pregnant and have epilepsy. Most medications to control seizures are safe during pregnancy. However, some medications are safer than others.

What medications are OK to use?

During pregnancy, phenobarbital is often used to control seizures, but its safety is now being questioned. Dilantin is *not* recommended because it can cause birth defects. Discuss this important issue with your doctor as soon as possible.

Asthma

I suffer from asthma. Can I have a safe pregnancy?

Most women with asthma can have a safe pregnancy. If you have severe asthma attacks before pregnancy, you may have them during pregnancy. Usually you can use the medications you used before pregnancy. Discuss medication use with your doctor.

Besides taking my medicine, is there anything else I can do for my asthma during pregnancy?

Many women feel better and have fewer problems with their asthma if they increase their fluid intake during pregnancy. Try it—you should increase your fluid intake during pregnancy anyway.

An asthma attack can be frightening, especially during pregnancy. If you suffer from asthma, tell your doctor. Some asthma medications are safe to use during pregnancy.

Cancer

A pregnant woman I know just found out she has cancer. Isn't this uncommon?

You're right; cancer during pregnancy is rare. Fortunately, many cancers in women occur after menopause, which lowers the likelihood of cancer in pregnancy. However, cancer does occasionally occur during pregnancy.

I hate to think about cancer during pregnancy. Should I be concerned about it?

It's not a pleasant subject to think about or to discuss, and most women don't need to be concerned about it. However, it's better to be aware that these problems occur than to know nothing about them.

What is the most common type of cancer discovered during pregnancy?

The most common cancer found is breast cancer. Gynecologic cancers, leukemia, lymphoma, melanoma and bone tumors also occur.

Is there any reason these cancers might appear during pregnancy?

Researchers believe there are a couple of reasons cancers could appear during pregnancy.

- Some cancers arise from tissues or organs that are influenced by the increase in hormone levels caused by pregnancy.
- Increased blood flow and changes in the lymphatic system may contribute to the spread of cancer to other parts of the body.

I've heard it's harder to find breast cancer during pregnancy. Why?

Changes in the breasts, including breast tenderness, increased size and even lumpiness, may make it harder to discover this type of cancer. Of all women who have breast cancer, about 2% are pregnant when it is diagnosed.

How is breast cancer treated during pregnancy?

Treatment varies: surgery, chemotherapy, radiation or a combination of treatments may be used.

If a woman has breast cancer, can she breastfeed?

A woman should not breastfeed if she has breast cancer.

Are treatments for cancer during pregnancy dangerous?

Cancer treatments can cause problems. A pregnant woman may experience side effects from the treatment.

I've been having chemotherapy for 6 months and just found out I'm 8 weeks' pregnant. What should I do?

Talk to your doctor immediately! What you do depends on the medications you are taking.

PREGNANCY AND THE OLDER WOMAN

I've heard in the news about older women having more babies. What is the average age for a woman to give birth in North America?

A recent study showed that 27 is the average age at which women give birth. More women give birth in their twenties than at any other age.

I'm almost 36 and about 7 weeks' pregnant. Is there anything I should worry about because of my age?

Today, more couples are waiting to start their families, so you're not alone. There are a few more risks for the older mother-to-be and her baby, but it's more likely than ever before that you and your baby will be OK. Risks include Down syndrome in the baby and, in the mother, high blood pressure, Cesarean delivery, multiple births, pre-eclampsia, placental abruption, bleeding and other complications. For more information, read our book *Your Pregnancy after 35*.

I'm 35 and pregnant with my third child. I'm a lot more tired than I remember being before. What's wrong with me?

It's simply harder to be pregnant when you're 35 than it is when you're 25. It doesn't necessarily mean anything is wrong; you just have more demands on your time and energy and more to do.

I'm over 35. What are my chances of having a baby with Down syndrome?

As you get older, the risk of delivering a baby with Down syndrome increases.

- at age 25, the risk is 1 in 1,300 births
- at 30, 1 in 965 births
- at 35, 1 in 365 births
- at 40, 1 in 109 births
- at 45, 1 in 32 births
- at 49, 1 in 12 births

But let's look at it in a more positive light. If you're 45, you have a 97% chance of *not* having a baby born with Down syndrome. If you're 49, you have a 92% chance of delivering a child *without* Down syndrome. (See also the discussion of Down Syndrome on pages 68–69.)

3

Tests on You and Your Growing Baby

You may be surprised by how many tests you will undergo during your pregnancy. The various tests help your doctor learn about the health of your developing pregnancy, including specific tests to gauge your health and tests that tell him or her certain things about your baby's health. At each prenatal appointment, your doctor will weigh you and take your blood pressure. These two simple tests can tell him or her a lot about your pregnancy.

Most of the tests you will take are routine tests that every pregnant woman has. Your doctor may order other tests to learn more about your health or your baby's health. Don't be afraid to ask why a test is being done, and be sure to check on results.

The first test you will probably have is a pregnancy test. You may take this at home or in your doctor's office. Home-pregnancy-test kits are very accurate today.

Once you know you're pregnant, your doctor will perform a lot of tests at your first or second visit. These tests tell your doctor how healthy you are at this time and whether he or she needs to caution you about certain things to avoid or to watch out for. Some tests are repeated during pregnancy, if necessary. Because all these tests are important, cooperate with your doctor about having them.

PREGNANCY TESTS

I am really eager to be pregnant. When will a pregnancy test be positive?

Pregnancy tests can be positive (show you're pregnant) even before you miss a menstrual period. Most tests are positive 7 to 10 days after you conceive; this includes blood, urine and home pregnancy tests. To save you money and emotional energy, wait until you miss your period before having a test.

When my sister-in-law thought she was pregnant, her doctor told her to do a home pregnancy test first. Why?

Home pregnancy tests are so accurate now that your doctor may rely on them as an initial screening for pregnancy, before you go into the office. Sometimes a woman misses a period because of stress, excessive physical exertion or dieting and is not pregnant. If your test is positive, make an appointment to see your physician.

I did a home pregnancy test last night, and it was positive. How soon should I see my doctor?

Most doctors will want to see you within a few weeks, unless you are having problems and need to go in right away. Good prenatal care is an important part of having a healthy baby. Don't wait for weeks or months to make an appointment; starting early is important for your health and the health of your baby.

OTHER COMMON TESTS

My friend had a pregnancy test called a *quantitative HCG test* because she was having problems; the result was a number. What kind of test is it?

A quantitative HCG (human chorionic gonadotropin) test is a blood test done in the 1st trimester if there is concern about miscarriage or ectopic pregnancy. The test measures the HCG, which is produced early in pregnancy and increases rapidly. Two or more tests done a few days apart are more useful than one test because it is the change in the amount of the hormone that is significant. An ultrasound is often done when a quantitative HCG test is ordered.

A friend told me I should ask a lot of questions before I have any tests. What questions should I ask?

Some tests are fairly routine, so you don't need to ask many questions. But you want information about procedures that are more involved. Your goal in asking these questions about *any* test or procedure is to ensure the benefits of the test outweigh any risks. Ask any of the following questions before any test.

- Why are you doing this test?
- How will the test be performed?
- What risks does this test pose to me or the baby?
- How experienced is the person doing the test?
- How experienced is the lab doing the test?
- How dependable are the results?
- When will I get the results?
- What happens after I get the results?
- What is the possibility of false-positive or false-negative results?
- What will happen if we don't do the test?
- How will the results affect my pregnancy?
- Is there any other way to get the same information?
- What is the cost of the test?
- Will my insurance cover the test?

My doctor said I'm going to have a lot of tests done when I go in next time. What kind of tests will I need?

Your doctor will probably order several tests at the first or second visit, including any of the following:

- complete blood count (CBC)
- urinalysis and urine culture

- syphilis test
- cervical cultures
- rubella titers
- blood type
- Rh-factor
- test for hepatitis-B antibodies
- alpha-fetoprotein test
- ultrasound
- Pap smear

See the chart on the opposite page for a description of some common tests done during pregnancy.

Why do I need to have all these tests?

The results of these tests provide vital information. For example, if testing shows you have never had rubella (German measles) or rubella vaccine, you need to avoid exposure and receive the vaccine before your next pregnancy. Rubella can be responsible for miscarriage or birth defects if a woman contracts the disease during pregnancy.

I'm 28 weeks' pregnant, and my doctor says I need more tests. Why?

Many doctors repeat tests or perform new tests at this time. For example, the 28th week of pregnancy is the best time to discover any blood-sugar problems. At this point in pregnancy, RhoGAM is given to an Rh-negative woman to protect her from becoming sensitized.

GENETIC COUNSELING AND TESTING

I'm pregnant for the first time and want everything to be all right. Do I need genetic counseling?

Probably not. Individuals who need genetic counseling are usually those who have had a malformed infant, those with a family history of inherited diseases, women who have had recurrent miscar-

COMMON TESTS

Test	How It's Done	What You and Your Doctor Can Learn
Alpha-fetoprotein	Blood sample drawn from mother	May indicate neural-tube defects (spina bifida) or risk of Down syndrome
Amniocentesis	Sample of amniotic fluid drawn by needle from uterus	Early in pregnancy, indicates chromosomal problems (Down syndrome), neural-tube defects, genetic disorders (cystic fibrosis), sex of fetus; late in pregnancy, indicates whether baby's lungs are developed
Biophysical profile	Variety of tests, including ultrasound, monitoring and observation	Used to show fetal well-being and to look for fetal stress
Chorionic villus sampling	Sample of placental tissue drawn from placenta through abdomen or vagina	Used to determine many diseases, such as Down syndrome, some biochemical diseases, such as Tay-Sachs disease, and other fetal conditions, such as cystic fibrosis
Stress/nonstress test	Fetal activity is monitored by mother-to-be and fetal monitor	Used to show fetal well-being and to look for fetal stress
Ultrasound	Soundwaves produce picture of uterus, placenta and fetus on a screen	Age of fetus, fetal position, heart rate, movement, number of fetuses, some birth defects, fetal sex (sometimes)

riages (usually three or more) and women who will be 35 or older at the time of birth.

What happens when a couple goes for genetic counseling?

You and your partner participate in this counseling together. The counselor asks detailed questions about your medical history, other pregnancies, medication usage and the family medical history of you and your partner. If it is necessary to do chromosome tests, blood samples are taken from both of you. You are advised about the potential for problems in a pregnancy.

NEW GENETIC TESTS

Prenatal genetic tests are being used in some areas to detect the following diseases.

- **Familial Mediterranean fever** is found in people of Armenian, Arabic, Turkish or Sephardic Jewish background. Prenatal testing helps identify carriers of the recessive gene so diagnosis can be made quickly in a newborn, avoiding a potentially fatal medical problem.
- **Canavan's disease** is common in people of Ashkenazi Jewish descent. Canavan's disease can be screened in combination with Tay-Sachs screening to determine if a fetus is affected.
- **Congenital deafness** caused by the connexin–26 gene. If a couple has a family history of inherited deafness, this test may identify the problem before birth, so that measures can be taken immediately to manage the problem.

DOWN SYNDROME

What is Down syndrome?

Down syndrome is a condition caused by a defect in the baby's chromosomes. A baby is mentally retarded and may have a somewhat dwarfed appearance, with a sloping forehead, short, broad hands, a flat nose and low-set ears. He or she may also have heart problems, gastrointestinal defects or leukemia.

How can Down syndrome be diagnosed?

Down syndrome can be diagnosed during pregnancy by amniocentesis; alpha-fetoprotein, triple screen, quad screen and other blood tests; chorionic villus sampling and ultrasound (in some cases). A blood test that measures HCG and pregnancy-associated protein A may be helpful in detecting Down syndrome. If abnormal amounts are in the mother's blood, amniocentesis or chorionic villus sampling may be recommended for further evaluation.

A new urine test, not yet available commercially, holds promise as a prenatal predictor of Down syndrome. Urine is examined for hyperglycosylated HCG (HHCG). Combined with ultrasound measurements, the results are valuable in detecting the problem.

Another new test, called *nuchal translucency screening,* combines detailed ultrasound, a blood test and the mother-to-be's age to gauge a woman's risk of having a baby with Down syndrome. This test is not widely available, but there are no known risk factors. Results depend on the accuracy of the ultrasound test.

ULTRASOUND

All my friends have had ultrasounds during pregnancy. Will I have one?

Many doctors routinely perform ultrasounds, but not all do them with every woman. Some perform them only when there is a problem or a definite reason for doing one (see the box on page 72).

I'm confused about ultrasound and sonograms. What's the difference?

Ultrasound, sonogram and *sonography* refer to the same test. Ultrasound is a valuable medical tool, especially in pregnancy.

What exactly is an ultrasound?

Ultrasound is a test that gives a 2- or 3-dimensional picture of the developing embryo or fetus. It involves the use of high-frequency sound waves made by applying an alternating current to a transducer. This transducer is placed on the abdomen or in the vagina. Sound waves projected from the transducer travel through the abdomen or

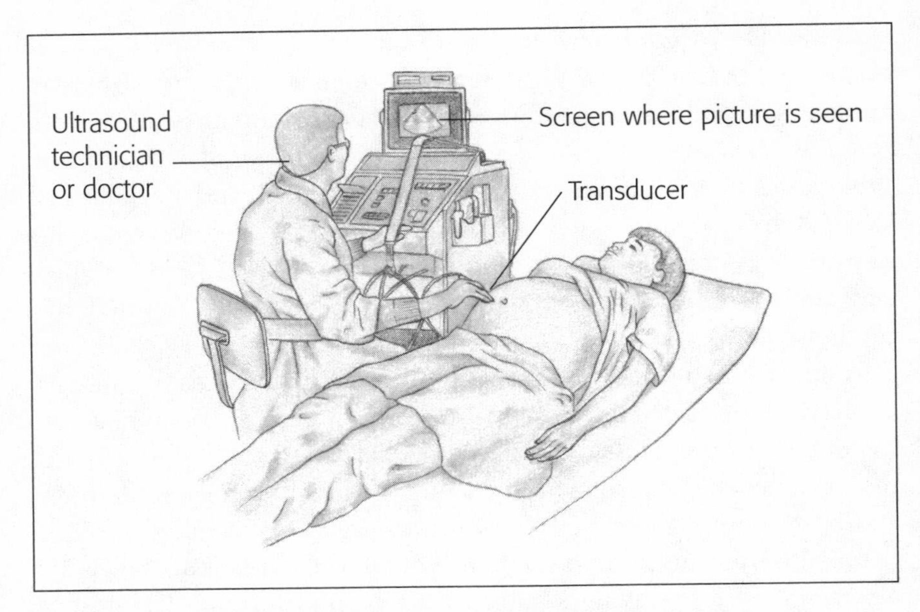

Ultrasound examination is a useful tool your doctor may order for you.

vagina, bounce off tissues and bounce back to the transducer. Reflected sound waves are translated into a picture

What is a 3-dimensional ultrasound?

This ultrasound test is available in some areas. It provides clear, detailed pictures of the fetus in the womb. They're so clear, the

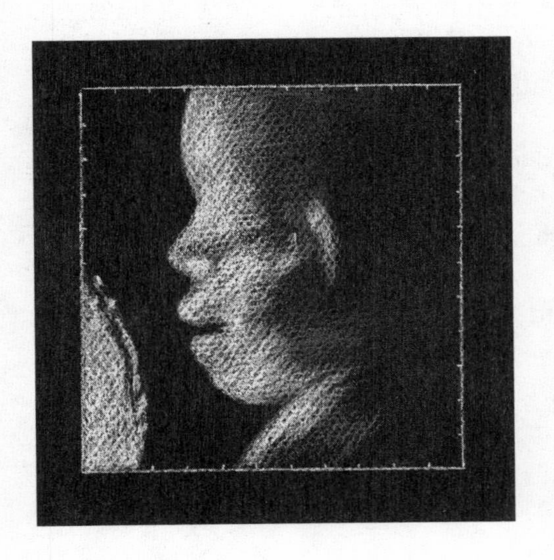

This ultrasound picture shows a baby's profile inside the uterus.

image almost looks like a photograph. For the pregnant woman, the test is almost the same as a regular ultrasound. The difference is that computer software translates the picture into a 3-D image. At this time, this advanced ultrasound is used when there is suspicion of abnormalities and the doctor wants to take a closer look

Is ultrasound safe?

Yes. The possibility of ultrasound having adverse effects has been studied many times without evidence that the test causes any problems.

How early in pregnancy can I have an ultrasound?

That depends on your doctor. If you're having problems, you may have an ultrasound early in your pregnancy.

Can an ultrasound help determine when I'm due?

Yes. Your doctor can take measurements of the baby with an ultrasound, then compare these measurements with charts that have averages to help approximate your due date.

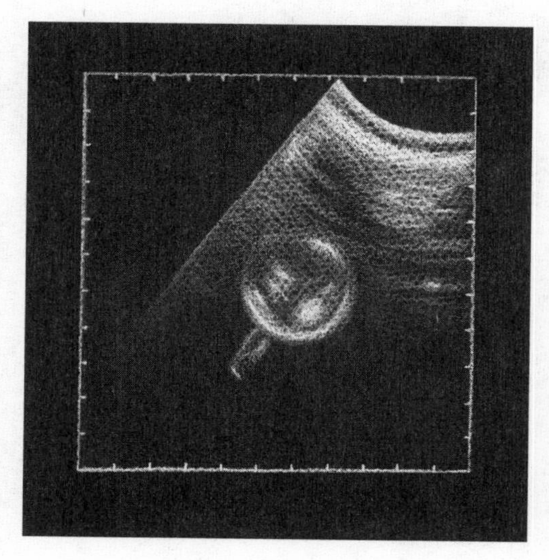

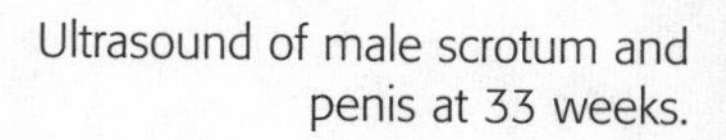

Ultrasound of male scrotum and penis at 33 weeks.

REASONS FOR ULTRASOUND

You may have an ultrasound for any number of reasons:

- to help confirm or determine the due date by measuring the fetal head, abdomen or thighbone
- to determine whether there is more than one baby
- if you've had problems during pregnancy, such as bleeding
- if you've had previous problem pregnancies
- to identify an early pregnancy
- to examine the size and growth of the embryo or fetus
- to identify some fetuses with Down syndrome
- to identify some fetal abnormalities, such as hydrocephalus
- to measure the amount of amniotic fluid
- to identify the location, size and maturity of the placenta
- to identify abnormalities of the placenta
- to detect an IUD (intrauterine device)
- to differentiate among a miscarriage, an ectopic pregnancy and a normal pregnancy
- to find a safe location to perform an amniocentesis

Most doctors like to do at least one ultrasound during a pregnancy, but not all agree on this. Your insurance coverage also plays a role in whether and how often you have an ultrasound. If your pregnancy is high risk, you may have several ultrasounds.

I've heard that sometimes the ultrasound instrument is put in the vagina. Is that dangerous? Could it make me bleed or miscarry?

This type of ultrasound is called *vaginal ultrasound*. It can be very helpful in evaluating problems early in pregnancy, such as possible miscarriage or an ectopic pregnancy. The instrument (probe or

Will I be able to find out if I am having a boy or girl when I have my ultrasound?

This is the most common question expectant parents ask. If you are 18 weeks' or more when you have an ultrasound, you may be able to determine the sex of your baby, but don't count on it. It isn't always possible to tell the sex if the baby has its legs crossed or is in a breech presentation.

Even if your doctor makes a prediction, keep in mind that ultrasound is a test, and tests can sometimes be wrong. Don't start buying for one sex or the other based on an ultrasound. If you do buy anything, save the receipts!

transducer) is put just inside the opening of the vagina, so it does not touch the cervix and will not cause bleeding or miscarriage. This type of ultrasound sometimes gives better information earlier in pregnancy than an abdominal ultrasound.

I'm supposed to have an ultrasound next week, and they told me to drink 32 ounces of water before I come and not to empty my bladder. Why?

Your bladder is in front of your uterus. When your bladder is full, your uterus rises out of the pelvis and becomes easier to see. When your bladder is empty, your uterus is farther down in your pelvis, and it's harder to see it. The full bladder acts as a window from the outside of your abdomen into your uterus. With a vaginal ultrasound, your bladder doesn't have to be full.

Where are most ultrasounds done?

Some doctors have ultrasound training and an ultrasound machine in their office. Some prefer to have you go to the hospital to have the ultrasound done and read by a radiologist. In certain high-risk situations, your doctor may send you to an ultrasound specialist to perform your ultrasound. Ask where your ultrasound will be done.

My friend has a videotape of her ultrasound. Can I get one of mine?

Ask about it when you schedule your ultrasound. Not all ultrasound machines are capable of making a video recording. Ask ahead of time if you need to bring a blank videotape.

Can I get pictures from my ultrasound?

Most ultrasounds include black-and-white photos. Baby pictures before you have the baby!

How much does an ultrasound cost?

It varies depending on where the test is done and where you live. An average cost is about $150, but it can range from $100 to $300. With many insurance plans, ultrasound is an extra and not part of the normal fee for prenatal care. Ask about cost and coverage before having an ultrasound. Some insurance plans require preapproval before an ultrasound is done.

I'm having an ultrasound next week. Can my partner come with me?

Yes. This is something your partner will probably enjoy, so arrange to have the ultrasound when he can come. You may want to have others, such as your mother or older children, come when possible. Ask about this when you schedule your ultrasound.

AMNIOCENTESIS

I heard some women talking about amniocentesis. Is this test for everyone?

No, not all pregnant women need amniocentesis. It is usually performed on women in the following circumstances:

- women who will deliver after their 35th birthday
- women who have had a previous baby with a birth defect
- women who have a family history of birth defects

- women who have a birth defect
- women whose partners have a birth defect

When is the test done?

Amniocentesis is usually performed for prenatal evaluation between 16 and 20 weeks of pregnancy. Some doctors use amniocentesis at 11 or 12 weeks of pregnancy. However, risks are higher when it is done at this time; the test is still considered experimental when done this early.

How is amniocentesis performed?

Ultrasound is used to locate a pocket of fluid where the fetus and placenta are out of the way. Skin over the abdomen is cleaned and numbed with a local anesthetic. A long needle is then passed through the abdomen into the uterus, and fluid is withdrawn from the amniotic cavity with a syringe.

How much fluid is withdrawn?

About 1 ounce (30ml) of amniotic fluid is needed to perform tests.

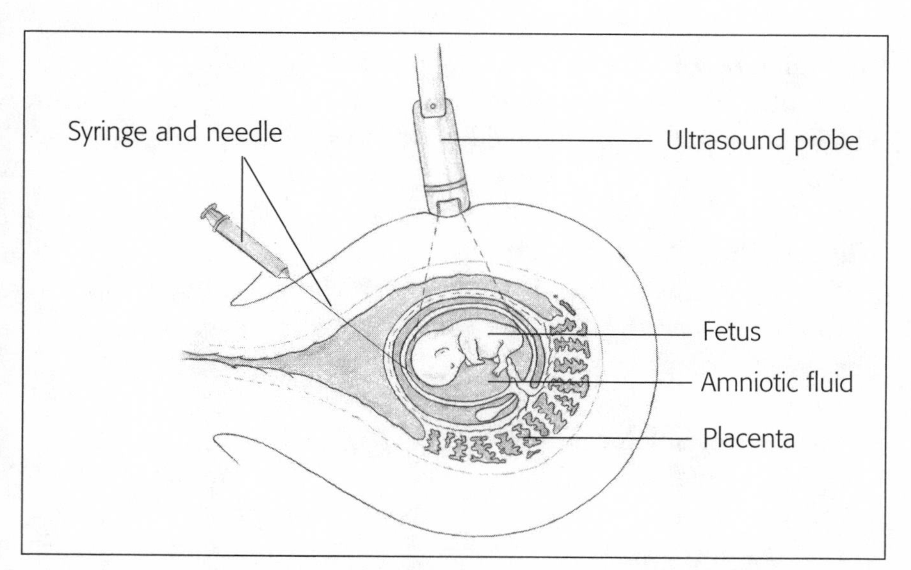

Amniocentesis is usually performed between the 16th and 20th weeks of pregnancy.

What do they do with the amniotic fluid?

Fetal cells that float in the amniotic fluid can be grown in cultures. These cells are used to identify fetal abnormalities or to reassure you that your baby is healthy.

How many abnormalities can amniocentesis identify?

We know of more than 400 abnormalities a child can be born with. Amniocentesis can identify about 10% of them, or about 40 problems.

What kind of abnormalities can be found with amniocentesis?

The problems a physician can identify include the following:

- chromosomal problems, particularly Down syndrome
- skeletal diseases, such as osteogenesis imperfecta (fragility of the baby's bones)
- fetal infections, such as herpes or rubella
- central-nervous-system disease, such as anencephaly
- blood diseases, such as erythroblastosis fetalis
- chemical problems or deficiencies, such as cystinuria or maple-syrup–urine disease

Can't amniocentesis also determine the baby's sex?

Yes, but the test is not used for this purpose, except in cases in which the sex of the baby could predict a problem, such as hemophilia.

What are the risks of this test?

Risks are relatively low: Fetal loss from complications is estimated to be between 0.5 and 3%. Discuss it with your doctor before you have the test.

Who performs amniocentesis?

Only someone who has experience should perform the test, such as a physician at a medical center. Your doctor will be able to give you more information.

If I wouldn't end my pregnancy regardless of the baby's condition, why have amniocentesis?

If your doctor suggests it, you should seriously consider having the test. If a problem is detected, you and your family can prepare for it. You can gather information about the problem. The test may also indicate the need for additional tests to determine if the fetus might have other problems. If any are found, you and your physician can take steps to ensure a smooth delivery and have any necessary procedures done as soon after the birth as possible. It is still a personal decision. Discuss it carefully with your doctor and your partner.

THE ALPHA-FETOPROTEIN TEST

A friend told me about a blood test she had that can detect problems with the baby. What is it?

You probably mean the maternal alpha-fetoprotein (AFP) test. It is a blood test done on you to determine abnormalities in your baby. Measurement of the amount of alpha-fetoprotein in your blood can help your doctor predict problems, such as Down syndrome and spina bifida.

Is the AFP test done on all pregnant women?

At this time, it is not performed on all pregnant women. However, it is required in some states, such as California and New York. If the test is not offered to you, discuss it with your doctor.

When is the test done?

It is usually performed between 16 and 20 weeks of pregnancy. Test results must be correlated with the mother-to-be's age and weight, and the gestational age of the fetus. If AFP detects some problem, additional, more definitive testing is usually ordered.

What kind of abnormalities can AFP detect?

The test is designed to detect babies with the following conditions:

- neural-tube defects
- severe kidney disease
- severe liver disease
- esophageal or intestinal blockage
- Down syndrome
- urinary obstruction
- osteogenesis imperfecta (fragility of the baby's bones)

I've heard that if I have an alpha-fetoprotein test, chances are rather high that it will be abnormal, even if there are no problems. Is this true?

Yes. The test is not specific enough. For example, if 1,000 women are tested, 40 tests will come back abnormal. Of those 40 tests, only 1 or 2 actually have a problem. So if you have AFP and your test result is abnormal, don't panic. Another AFP test will be done to correlate results, and an ultrasound will be performed. Be sure you understand what false-positive and false-negative test results mean. Ask your doctor to explain what each result can mean to you.

CHORIONIC VILLUS SAMPLING

I've heard about a test called chorionic villus sampling. What is it?

Chorionic villus sampling (CVS) is done to detect genetic abnormalities. Sampling is done early in pregnancy, usually between the 9th and 11th weeks.

How is the test done?

Ultrasound is used to locate the fetus and the placenta. A small piece of tissue is removed from the placental area with an instrument placed through the cervix or with a needle inserted through the abdomen (see the illustration on the opposite page).

Are there risks in having CVS done?

There is a small risk of miscarriage with this procedure. Only someone with experience should perform this test.

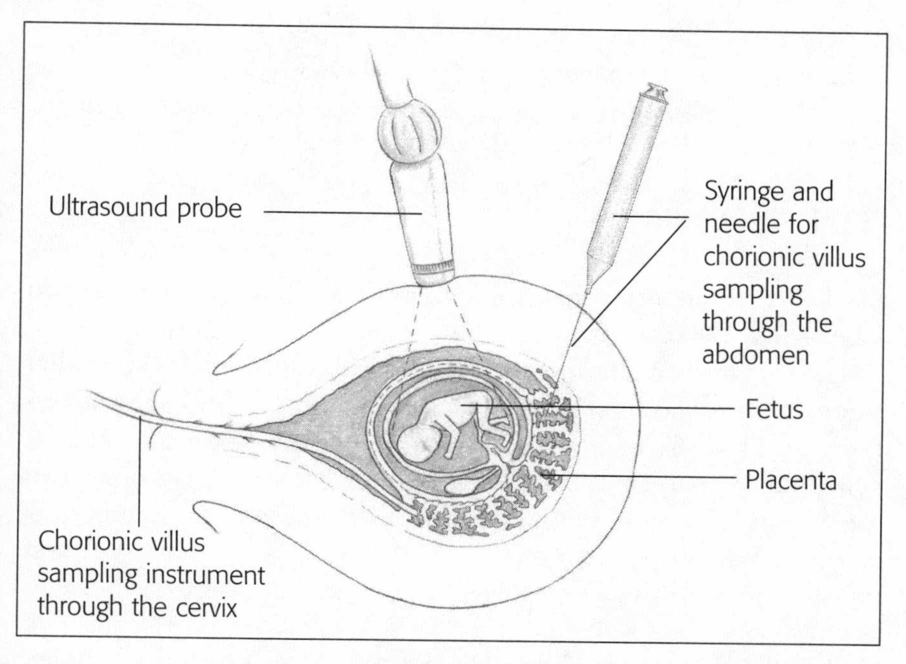

Chorionic villus sampling can be done earlier in pregnancy than other tests and is a valuable diagnostic tool.

Why is this test ordered?

The advantage of CVS is an earlier diagnosis than amniocentesis, if a problem exists. The test can determine various fetal problems, such as Down syndrome, Tay-Sachs disease and cystic fibrosis. Some women choose to have this test because they want results earlier so they can make decisions about the pregnancy.

Is CVS better than amniocentesis?

CVS can be done much earlier in pregnancy, and results are available in about a week. If the woman decides to terminate the pregnancy after learning results of the test, the procedure can be performed earlier in pregnancy and may carry fewer risks. On the other hand, the risk of disturbing a normal pregnancy is slightly higher with CVS than with amniocentesis.

Should I have this test done?

Each woman's pregnancy is different. Discuss this test with your doctor, who will help you determine if your particular case requires it.

FETAL FIBRONECTIN

I've heard about a test that can help predict if a woman will go into labor early. What is it?

The test you are referring to is the fetal fibronectin (fFN) test. fFN is a protein found in the amniotic sac and fetal membranes during the first 22 weeks of pregnancy. If a physician believes a woman is going into premature labor, he or she can test the woman's cervical-vaginal secretions; if fFN is present after 22 weeks, it indicates increased risk for preterm delivery. If it is absent, the risk is low and the woman probably won't deliver in the next 2 weeks.

How is the fFN test performed?

It is performed like a Pap smear. Your doctor takes a swab of cervical-vaginal secretions from the top of the vagina, behind the cervix. Results are available from the lab within 24 hours.

FETOSCOPY

What's the test that uses some kind of scope to look at the baby?

You are probably referring to fetoscopy. It is performed on the fetus and placenta while both are still inside your uterus. It provides a view of the baby and placenta.

What is fetoscopy used for?

The doctor can see the baby through the fetoscope and detect some abnormalities and problems. This very specialized test is not performed often.

How is the procedure done?

A small incision is made in the mother's abdomen, and a scope similar to the one used in laparoscopy is placed through the abdomen into the uterus. The doctor uses the fetoscope to examine the fetus and placenta.

Should I have fetoscopy?

If your doctor suggests fetoscopy to you, discuss the reason with him or her. This test is not done often but is used when it is necessary to look directly at the fetus or placenta.

Are there risks to fetoscopy?

Risk of miscarriage is 3 to 4% with this procedure. Only someone experienced with the technique should perform this test.

OTHER TESTS FOR THE MOTHER-TO-BE

Doppler

My friend told me about a special stethoscope that my doctor will use to let me hear my baby's heartbeat. What is it?

You're probably referring to a *doppler.* It is not actually a stethoscope. It magnifies the sound of the baby's heartbeat so you can hear it.

When will I be able to hear the baby's heartbeat?

Around the 12-week visit. If your doctor doesn't offer it to you, ask about it.

Tests that Use Radiation

I'm concerned about having tests that use radiation during my pregnancy. Can they hurt my baby?

Avoid exposure to X-rays during pregnancy, unless it is an emergency. There is no known safe amount of radiation for a developing fetus. Dangers to the baby include an increased risk of birth defects and an increased risk of cancer later in life.

I have to go to the dentist next week. Should I let them X-ray my teeth?

If possible, avoid dental X-rays while you're pregnant. If you must have a dental X-ray, be sure your abdomen and pelvis are completely shielded by a lead apron.

What should I do if I break my leg and need an X-ray while I'm pregnant?

There are medical reasons for X-rays, but the need for the X-ray must be weighed against the risk to your pregnancy. If you have injured your foot or hand, it is fairly easy to shield the uterus with a lead apron while the area is X-rayed. However, if your injury is in your back or any place near the pelvic area, the risks increase. Discuss it with your doctor before having any X-rays.

Are there any other reasons to do an X-ray during pregnancy?

Some problems, other than broken bones, may require X-rays. Pneumonia and appendicitis are two possibilities. Again, discuss the situation with your doctor.

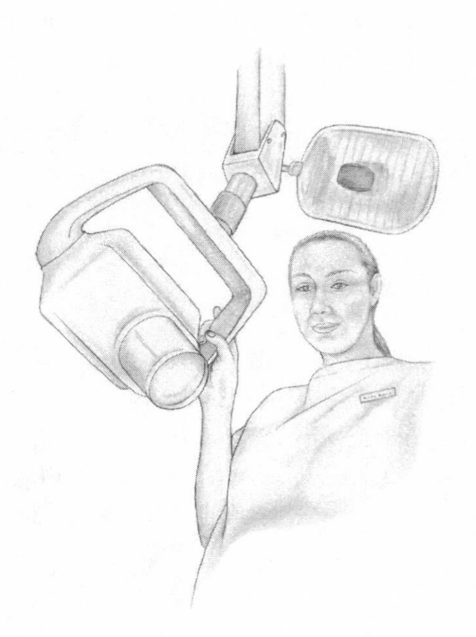

Be careful with X-rays, whether a test requires them or your job exposes you to them. They could be harmful to your developing baby.

What about CT scans—are they the same as X-rays?

Computerized tomographic scans, also called *CT scans* and *CAT scans,* are a form of specialized X-ray. The technique involves the use of X-ray with computer analysis. Many researchers believe the amount of radiation received from a CT scan is much lower than a regular X-ray. However, it is probably wise to avoid even this amount of exposure, if possible.

When is the fetus most susceptible to the harmful effects of radiation from X-rays?

Risk to a fetus appears to be the greatest between 8 and 15 weeks of pregnancy (between the fetal age of 6 and 13 weeks). Some believe the only safe amount of radiation exposure for a fetus is *no exposure.*

I've heard about a test called MRI. Is it the same as an X-ray?

No. Magnetic resonance imaging, also called *MRI,* is a diagnostic tool widely used today. At this time, no harmful effects in pregnancy have been reported from its use, but pregnant women are advised to avoid an MRI during the 1st trimester of pregnancy for the safety of the fetus.

A new ultra-fast MRI may provide additional information on fetal abnormalities. This may be done when results of an ultrasound are abnormal or don't provide enough information. The test is useful in identifying conjoined twins, a diaphragmatic hernia, oligohydramnios and various large tumors. It is not available everywhere, and it is expensive ($1,000 to $1,400). This test is *not* necessary for every pregnant woman.

Pap Smears

I'm going for my first visit, and they told me that the doctor will want to do a Pap smear. What is a Pap smear?

A Pap smear removes some cells from your cervix and tests for abnormal cells in the cervical area.

Why does the doctor do a Pap smear at this time?

If you had a normal Pap smear in the last few months, you won't need it. If it has been a year or more since you had the test, you should have a Pap smear. The goal of a Pap smear is to find problems early so they are easier to deal with.

I saw my obstetrician a week ago, and the office just called to tell me my Pap smear wasn't normal. Will I need a biopsy?

It depends on how serious the problem might be. Usually a biopsy is not done while you're pregnant. Your doctor will probably wait until after your pregnancy for further testing. Instead of removing tissue for a biopsy, he or she may do a colposcopy (a very careful look at the cervix). An abnormal Pap smear during pregnancy is an individual situation and must be handled carefully.

I had a Pap smear after my baby was born and it was normal, but the Pap smear I had before that was abnormal. Is this a mistake?

Not necessarily. Women who deliver vaginally may see a change in abnormal Pap smears. One study showed that 60% of a group of women who were diagnosed with high-grade squamous intra-epithelial lesions in the cervix before giving birth had normal Pap smears after their baby was born. Researchers believe that dilatation of the cervix during labor may slough off the precancerous cells, or the baby may scrape them off as it moves down the birth canal.

Pelvic Exams

I'm close to delivery, and my doctor said I will have a pelvic exam the next time I come to the office. Why now, when I haven't had one for so long?

A pelvic exam is needed late in pregnancy because it tells us a lot of things:

- presentation of the baby: whether the baby is head first or in a breech position
- dilatation of the cervix: how much the cervix has opened
- effacement: how much the cervix has thinned

- shape and size of your birth canal or pelvic bones
- station: how low the baby is in your birth canal

After my pelvic exam, my obstetrician said I was "2 and 50%." Why did he tell me this?

This information is important for two reasons. First, it tells you your cervix is open 2cm and thinned out 50%, or halfway. (This is not an indication of when your baby will be born.) Second, this information is helpful if you go to the hospital thinking you're in labor. At the hospital, you'll be checked again. Knowing what you were at your last pelvic exam can help determine if you are in labor.

I had a pelvic exam today and I was not dilated and my cervix had not thinned out. Does that mean I have a lot longer to go?

No. The pelvic exam tells you where you were at that time. Labor may begin at any time.

When my obstetrician does a pelvic exam, does that tell him when I will go into labor?

No. At this point in your pregnancy, labor might start at any time, no matter what condition your cervix is in.

Home Uterine Monitoring

What is home uterine monitoring?

Home uterine monitoring is a way to monitor a pregnant woman's uterine contractions in her home. Doctors use this type of testing or monitoring when there could be a problem with premature labor.

How does home uterine monitoring work?

A recording of uterine contractions is transmitted from the woman's home, via telephone, to a center where contractions can be evaluated. Your doctor may be able to view the recordings on his or her own home or office computer.

HOME UTERINE MONITORING

The following conditions may require home uterine monitoring:

- previous preterm delivery
- infections in the mother-to-be
- premature rupture of membranes
- pregnancy-induced hypertension
- multiple fetuses

What does home monitoring cost?

Costs vary but run about $100 a day.

TESTS FOR YOUR DEVELOPING BABY

Nonstress Test

My doctor wants me to have a nonstress test. What is that?

A *nonstress test* is a procedure done in the doctor's office, in the labor room or in the delivery room. While you are lying down, a fetal monitor is attached to your abdomen. Every time you feel the baby move, you push a button to make a mark on the monitor paper. At the same time, the fetal monitor records the baby's heartbeat on the same paper.

What will a nonstress test show?

The information gained from a nonstress test gives reassurance that your baby is doing OK.

If my nonstress test isn't OK, what happens next?

Additional tests will be done, including a biophysical profile or a contraction stress test.

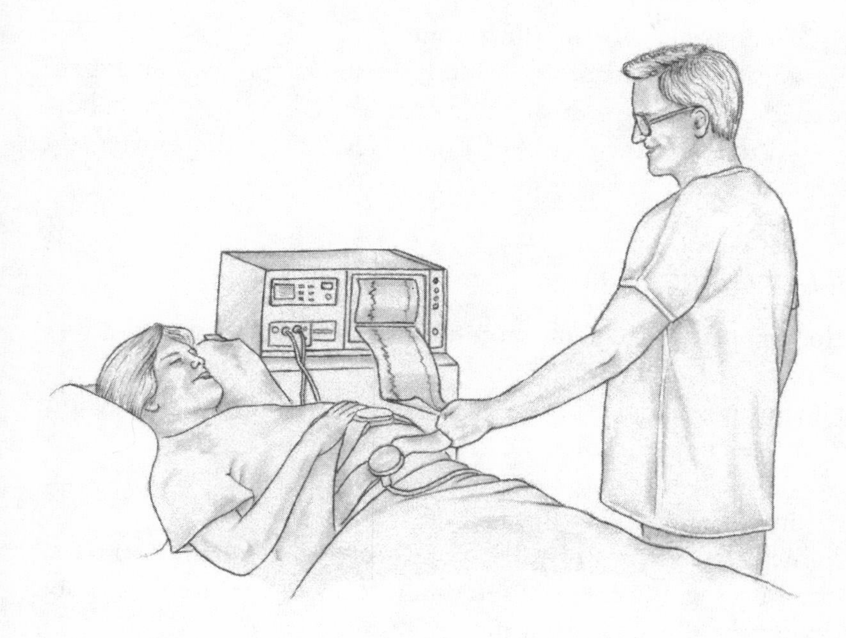

A nonstress test and a contraction stress test are done to evaluate the fetus.

Contraction Stress Test

What is a contraction stress test?

A contraction stress test (CST), also called a *stress test*, is another test used to evaluate the well-being of the baby.

How is a contraction stress test done?

A monitor is placed on the woman's abdomen to record the fetal heart rate. Sometimes nipple stimulation is used to make the woman's uterus contract, or an I.V. is started to give oxytocin in small amounts to make the uterus contract. Results indicate how well a baby will tolerate contractions and labor.

What can a contraction stress test indicate?

If the baby doesn't respond well to the contractions, it can be a sign of fetal distress.

When is a contraction stress test done?

If a woman has had problem pregnancies in the past or experiences medical problems during this pregnancy, her doctor may have her tested the last few weeks of pregnancy. This is done when the nonstress test is not reassuring.

Fetal Monitoring

My doctor mentioned fetal monitoring during labor and delivery. What is it?

In many hospitals, a baby's heartbeat is monitored throughout labor to detect any problems early so they can be resolved.

What kind of monitoring do they do?

There are two types of fetal monitoring during labor—external fetal monitoring and internal fetal monitoring. (See the illustration below and the illustration on the opposite page.)

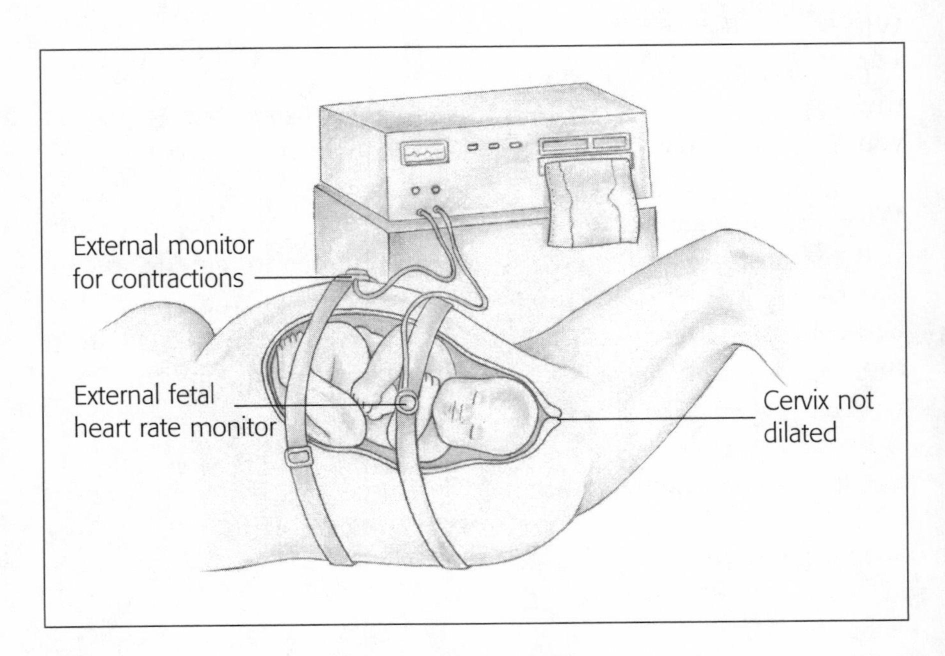

External fetal monitoring, with membranes intact (bag of waters has not broken).

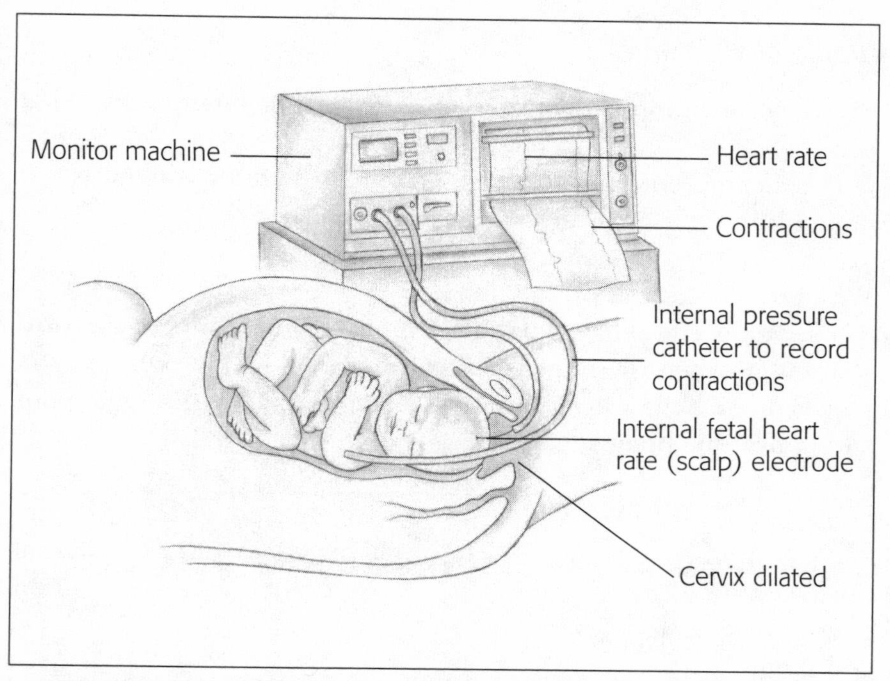

Internal fetal monitoring during labor; membranes (bag of waters) have ruptured.

What is external fetal monitoring?

A belt with a receiver is strapped to your abdomen, and it records the baby's heartbeat. This type of monitoring can be done before your membranes rupture.

What is internal fetal monitoring?

It is a more precise method of monitoring the baby. An electrode is placed on the fetal scalp to give a more exact reading of the fetal heart rate than external monitoring can. Your membranes must be ruptured for internal monitoring.

Is there any way to monitor my baby's oxygen during labor?

Yes! We can now monitor baby's oxygen *inside* the womb, before birth. A new technology uses light to measure the oxygen level in fetal blood, accurately indicating whether baby's oxygen levels are in a safe range. A probe is placed inside the womb and on baby's skin. This relatively noninvasive approach, called *OxiFirst fetal oxygen monitoring,* is used during labor.

Biophysical Profile

My doctor mentioned doing a biophysical profile on my baby. What is it?

It is a comprehensive test that examines the fetus while it is still in your uterus. It helps determine the baby's health.

Why is a biophysical profile done?

The test is useful in evaluating an infant with intrauterine-growth restriction, when the mother-to-be is diabetic, with a pregnancy in which the baby doesn't move very much, in high-risk pregnancies and in overdue pregnancies.

BIOPHYSICAL PROFILE: WHAT DOES IT MEASURE?

- fetal breathing movements
- fetal body movements
- fetal tone (tightening or contractibility of muscles)
- reactive fetal heart rate (increase in heart rate when baby moves)
- amount of amniotic fluid

How is the test performed?

Ultrasound, external monitors and observation are used to make the different measurements.

How is the test scored?

Each area (see box above) is given a score of 0, 1 or 2. A total is obtained by adding all five scores together. The higher the score, the better the baby's condition. A low score may indicate problems.

If a baby has a low score, what can be done?

The situation will be evaluated—the baby may need to be delivered immediately. The test may be repeated at intervals. It may be necessary to repeat the test the following day. Your doctor will evaluate the scores, your health and the pregnancy before making any decisions.

Fetal Blood Sampling

I recently read about fetal blood sampling during labor. What is this test?

It is another way of evaluating how well a baby is tolerating the stress of labor.

How is fetal blood sampling during labor done?

Your membranes must be ruptured, and you cervix must be dilated at least 2cm. Your physician places an instrument inside you to make a small nick in the baby's scalp. The baby's blood is collected in a small tube, and the pH (acidity) is checked.

What can the doctor learn from fetal blood sampling?

The pH level can help determine whether the baby is having trouble during labor and is under stress. The test helps the physician decide whether labor can continue or if you need a C-section.

Fetal Lung Maturity

I've heard about some test they can do to see if a baby is ready to be born; it has something to do with the baby's lungs. Why is it done?

You are probably referring to a couple of tests that are done to evaluate the maturity of fetal lungs. When a baby is born prematurely, a common problem is immaturity of the lungs, which can lead to development of respiratory-distress syndrome in the baby. Lungs are not completely mature, and the baby cannot breathe on its own without assistance.

Why is it important for the baby's lungs to be mature?

The last fetal system that matures is the respiratory system. If your doctor knows the baby's lungs are mature, it aids him or her in making a decision about early delivery, if it must be considered.

What are the tests called that check fetal lung maturity?

The *L/S ratio* measures the ratio of lecithin to sphingomyelin. Results give the doctor an index of the maturity of the baby's lungs. The *phosphatidyl glycerol (PG)* test gives either a positive or negative result. If the result shows phosphatidyl glycerol is present, there is greater assurance that the baby will not develop respiratory-distress syndrome. Both tests are performed by amniocentesis (see page 74). Other tests are being developed.

If the baby's lungs have not developed enough, what can be done?

The first course of action is to avoid premature delivery, if possible. If this cannot be done, tests are done immediately after birth to determine if the baby has surfactant in its lungs. Surfactant is a chemical essential for respiration. If it is not present, the baby's doctor may introduce surfactant directly into the lungs of the newborn, preventing respiratory-distress syndrome. The baby will not have to be put on a respirator—it can breathe on its own!

4

Medications and Treatments for You

Before pregnancy, you may not think too much about taking aspirin or ibuprofen for a headache. Or you might take cough medicine or a cold preparation whenever you have a cough or cold. Nasal spray may help you breathe more easily during an allergy attack. However, now that you're pregnant, *you must be very careful about every medication you take!*

When we talk about medications, we're not referring only to prescriptions your doctor may write for you. We're also talking about over-the-counter preparations, vitamins, minerals and herbs. Any of these substances may affect a developing baby. What may seem like only a little to you could pass through the placenta to your developing fetus.

If possible, discuss different medications you must take for medical conditions *before* you get pregnant. If you were unable to do this, discuss all medications (prescription and over-the-counter) you take on a regular basis at your first prenatal visit. You may need to adjust your dosage, or you may have to stop taking a particular substance. However, *never* stop taking any medication that you take for a chronic problem without first consulting your doctor! Some medication cannot and should not be stopped during pregnancy. Talk to your doctor before making any decisions about medication use.

I've read that some of the medications I take can affect my growing baby. What are they and what are the effects?

Various substances you ingest affect your developing baby in many ways. See the chart on page 96, which lists some substances and their effects.

When should I discuss with my doctor the different medications I must take for my medical conditions?

Ideally, you will have had this discussion *before* you got pregnant. If you were unable to do this, discuss all medications (prescription and over-the-counter) you take on a regular basis at your first prenatal visit. You may need to adjust your dosage or stop taking a particular substance.

Can't I just stop taking the medicine before I visit the doctor? I'm not that sick.

Never stop taking any medication that you take for a chronic problem without first consulting your doctor! Some medication *cannot* and *should not* be stopped during pregnancy.

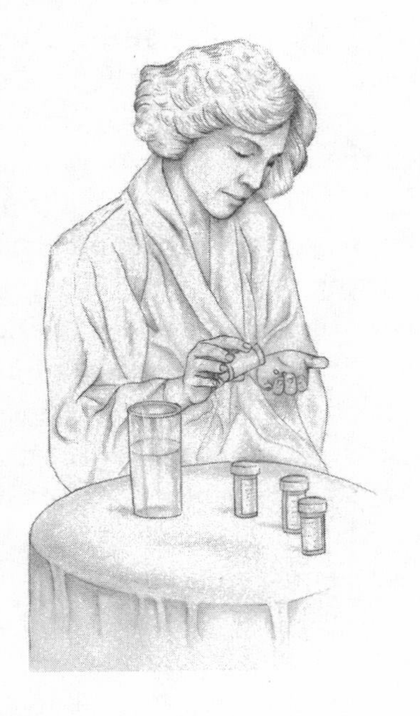

Medication usage is very important during pregnancy. Check with your doctor before you take (or stop taking) any medication.

There are so many different kinds of medicine. How can I remember which are safe to take?

You don't have to remember them all. Ask your doctor about those that pertain to your own special care. Much of the information in this chapter may not apply to you, but it's good information to have at hand. The important thing is to call your doctor about any medication before you take it. And remember to read labels!

PRESCRIPTION MEDICATIONS

Why should I discuss my prescription medications with my doctor?

This is a very important aspect of your prenatal care. Discuss all medications (prescription and over-the-counter) you take on a regular basis at your first prenatal visit. You may need to have your dosage adjusted, you may have to stop taking a particular substance or certain conditions may require additional medication.

I take thyroid medication. Is it necessary during pregnancy?

Yes, it's very important to continue taking your thyroid medication throughout your pregnancy. Be sure your doctor knows what you take.

Why is thyroid medication important in pregnancy?

Thyroid hormone is made in the thyroid gland. This hormone affects your entire body and is important in your metabolism. Thyroid hormone is also important in your ability to get pregnant.

Can medications for thyroid problems be taken safely during pregnancy?

Thyroxin (medication for low thyroid or hypothyroid) is acceptable to use. Propylthiouracil (high-thyroid or hyperthyroid medication) passes to the baby; you will probably be given the lowest amount possible during your pregnancy.

POSSIBLE EFFECTS OF SOME MEDICATIONS ON THE FETUS

Medication	Possible Effects
Androgens (male hormones)	Ambiguous genital development (depends on dose given and stage of pregnancy when given)
Anticoagulants (warfarin)	Bone and hand abnormalities, intrauterine-growth restriction, central-nervous-system abnormalities, eye abnormalities
Antithyroid drugs (propylthiouracil, iodide, methimazole)	Hypothyroidism, fetal goiter
Chemotherapeutic drugs (methotrexate, aminopterin)	Increased risk of miscarriage
Diethylstilbestrol (DES)	Abnormalities of female-reproductive organs, female and male infertility
Isotretinoin (Accutane)	Increased miscarriage rate, nervous-system defects, facial defects, cleft palate
Lithium	Congenital heart disease
Phenytoin (Dilantin)	Growth restriction, mental retardation, microcephaly
Streptomycin	Hearing loss, cranial-nerve damage
Tetracycline	Hypoplasia of tooth enamel, discoloration of permanent teeth
Thalidomide	Severe limb defects
Trimethadione	Cleft lip, cleft palate, growth restriction, miscarriage
Valproic acid	Neural-tube defects

(Chart modified from *ACOG Technical Bulletin #84, Teratology,* 2/85, American College of Obstetricians and Gynecologists.)

I have lupus, and I take medication every day. Can this affect my pregnancy?

The medication used to treat lupus is steroids; the primary steroid given is prednisone. Many studies have been done on the safety of prednisone during pregnancy, and it has been found to be safe.

Before pregnancy, I took Prozac for depression. Can I continue taking it?

Studies indicate Prozac is acceptable for use during pregnancy.

Skin Medication

I asked my doctor for a prescription for Accutane to treat my acne, but she told me she couldn't prescribe it because I'm pregnant. Why?

Accutane (retinoic acid isotretinoin) is a common treatment for acne. However, pregnant women must *not* take it! There is a higher frequency of miscarriage and fetal malformation if a woman takes Accutane during the 1st trimester of pregnancy.

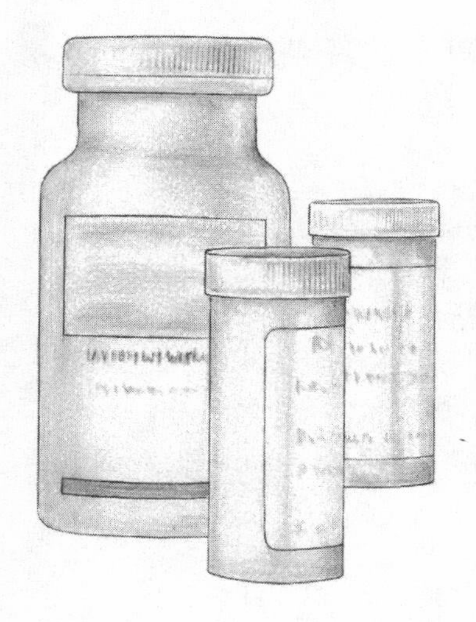

Consult your doctor about all medications you are now taking.

I use Retin-A for my skin. Should I discontinue using it now that I'm pregnant?

Yes. Any type of medication you use can get into your bloodstream, which could be passed to your baby. Avoid Retin-A during pregnancy because we don't know the extent of its effects on the fetus.

I often take tetracycline for a skin problem, but my brother warned me it can harm my baby. How?

Do not take tetracycline during pregnancy because it can cause discoloration of your baby's permanent teeth later in life. For that reason, tetracyclines should not be prescribed for any child under age 8.

I occasionally use a steroid cream for a skin condition I have. Can I use it during pregnancy?

It's best to discuss this with your doctor. There may be another preparation you can use that is safer during pregnancy.

NONPRESCRIPTION MEDICATIONS

Is it OK for a pregnant woman to take medicines that don't require a prescription?

Over-the-counter (OTC) medications should be taken with care during pregnancy. Many OTCs contain aspirin, caffeine or phenacetin—all should be avoided during pregnancy. Limit your use of cough syrups, which may contain as much as 25% alcohol. Be careful with medications containing ibuprofen, such as Advil, Motrin and Rufen. Avoid newer medicines, such as Aleve and Orudis, until we know more about them and their safety in pregnancy. Read package labels, and ask your doctor or pharmacist before taking anything.

SAFE OVER-THE-COUNTER MEDICATIONS

- acetaminophen (Tylenol)
- some antacids (Amphojel, Gelusil, Maalox, milk of magnesia)
- throat lozenges (Sucrets)
- some decongestants (Sudafed)
- some cough medicines (Robitussin)

Is it OK for me to take aspirin during my pregnancy?

Almost any medication you take when you are pregnant passes to your baby or has some effect on your pregnancy. Most doctors recommend you avoid aspirin during pregnancy because it can increase bleeding. Discuss aspirin use with your doctor.

Can I take vitamins and minerals while I'm pregnant?

Don't assume these are safe! Discuss with your doctor any vitamins or minerals you take. See page 117 for detailed information on vitamin and mineral usage during pregnancy.

Won't my doctor or the nurses get mad if I call them about every medication I'm thinking of taking?

No. They would rather answer a question about medication use *before* you take something than worry about its effect on your baby after you have taken it.

BIRTH CONTROL

I have an IUD and just learned I'm pregnant. What should I do?

Notify your doctor immediately. You will need to discuss whether the IUD should be removed. Most doctors attempt to remove the IUD, if possible. The risk for miscarriage is higher if your IUD is left in place. The risk for ectopic pregnancy is also higher if you get pregnant with an IUD.

I just found out I'm pregnant, and I'm taking birth-control pills. What should I do?

Stop taking the pills, and notify your doctor. Any method of contraception can fail; the chance of failure with birth-control pills is between 1 and 3%. There is a small increase in problems for the fetus if you take birth-control pills while you're pregnant. It is not cause for great alarm, but discuss it with your doctor.

My partner uses condoms and spermicides, and I just found out I'm pregnant. Will the fact that we have been using spermicides hurt our baby?

Spermicides have not been shown to be harmful to a developing fetus.

IMMUNIZATIONS AND VACCINATIONS

I've heard I should be careful about immunizations and vaccinations during pregnancy. Why?

Some immunizations may harm the developing fetus and should not be received by a pregnant woman. The risk of exposure to various diseases is an important consideration. Not all vaccines harm the fetus. That's why it is very important to discuss this concern with your doctor.

If I do need an immunization, what will my doctor do?

Once your doctor determines you have been exposed to a disease, or exposure is possible, he or she will weigh the risk of the disease against the potential harmful effects of the immunization. Some vaccines are not harmful to a fetus and may be used without problems.

Are there some vaccines that I should never receive if I know I'm pregnant?

Yes. Avoid vaccinations for measles, mumps and rubella (MMR), poliomyelitis and yellow fever. You should receive primary vaccine against polio *only* if your risk of exposure is high, such as if you are traveling to a high-risk area.

Are any vaccines regarded as safe for a pregnant woman?

Vaccines generally regarded as safe during pregnancy are tetanus, diphtheria and rabies. Others may be safe, but we are unsure about them at this time, so avoid them.

How can I know if I should receive a vaccine?

If you are pregnant, ask your doctor. If you don't think you are pregnant, it would still be wise to have a pregnancy test and to be using reliable contraception before receiving a vaccine.

5

Nutrition, Exercise and Weight Management

Nutrition, exercise and weight management are important during pregnancy. Your good nutrition helps give your baby a healthy start in life because the foods you eat can affect your baby's development and growth. Exercise is important to help you stay in good shape during pregnancy. Devel oping strong muscles may help you overcome some problems during pregnancy, such as backaches and muscle cramps. Exercise may also prepare you to do the hard work of labor and delivery. Weight control ensures your developing baby receives the nutrients it needs to build bones and organs. If you gain too much weight, you may have a bigger baby, which could mean a harder labor and delivery for you. Gaining too little weight could mean your baby doesn't receive the nutrients it needs for healthy growth and development.

One study showed 95% of the women who had good-to-excellent diets had babies in good-to-excellent health. Only 8% of those women who ate poor diets (lots of junk food) had babies in good-to-excellent health. One of your main goals in pregnancy is to have the healthiest baby you can. Your nutrition during pregnancy has a great impact on your baby's health. Exercise and weight control add to your overall health and thus the health of your baby.

EATING FOR TWO

I've heard that during pregnancy I'm eating for two. Is this true?

What the old adage "a pregnant woman is eating for two" actually means is that you must be concerned about nutrition for yourself and for your growing baby. However, many women take this to mean they can eat twice as much, which is incorrect! Be smart about your food choices—you must eat wisely for both of you.

Can't I eat all I want during pregnancy?

Only a few lucky women can eat all they want at any time. Some women have the false idea they can eat all they want during pregnancy. Don't fall into this trap. You don't want to gain more weight

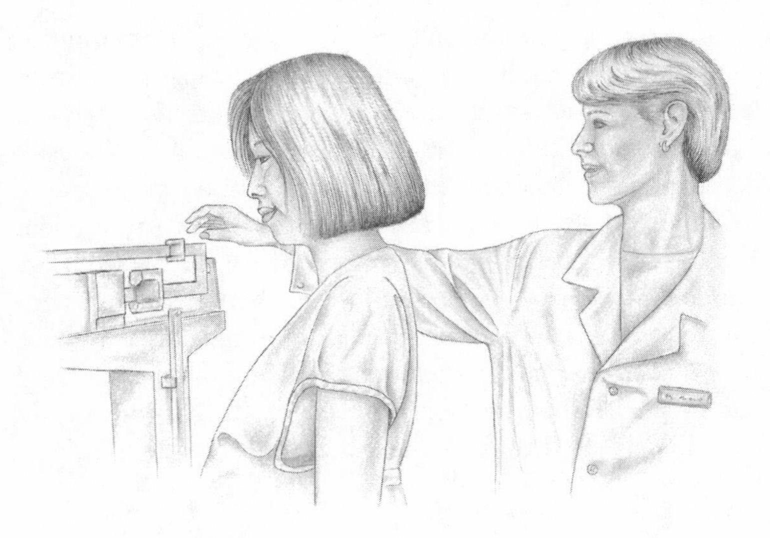

Keeping track of your weight is one way your doctor measures your progress through pregnancy.

than your doctor recommends during your pregnancy—it can make you uncomfortable and it will be harder to lose the extra pounds after your baby is born.

Do I need to increase the number of calories I consume now that I'm pregnant?

Yes. Most experts agree that a normal-weight pregnant woman needs to increase her caloric intake by 300 to 800 calories a day. These extra calories are important for tissue growth in you and your baby. Your baby is using the energy from your calories to create and store protein, fat and carbohydrates, and to provide energy for its own body processes. Expect to gain some weight during your pregnancy—it's natural and normal.

Isn't that a lot of food?

Not really. You can add 300 calories by eating a carton (8 ounces; 240ml) of lowfat yogurt and an apple. Be careful about the calories you consume—you need more food, but not *that* much more.

FOOD CHOICES

What foods should I eat every day?

Eat a variety of foods to supply you with the nutrients you need: dairy products, protein foods, fruits and vegetables, and breads and cereals.

I don't think I eat very many foods with protein in them. Why should I eat protein foods?

During pregnancy, you need protein for growth and development of the fetus, placenta, uterus and breasts. The recommended amount of protein during pregnancy is 6 to 7 ounces (168 to 196g) a day.

How many grams of carbohydrates should I eat daily during pregnancy?

There is no recommended dietary allowance (RDA) for carbohydrate intake during pregnancy. Most physicians believe carbohydrates should make up about 60% of the total number of calories in your diet. If you are eating 2,200 calories a day, you would consume about 1,320 calories as carbohydrate calories.

Do I need to worry about getting enough fat in my diet during pregnancy?

There is rarely concern about inadequate fat intake; usually fat intake is excessive. There is no recommended daily amount for fat intake during pregnancy.

I read that everyone has to have fat in their diet. I shouldn't avoid all fats, should I?

That's a good point. No, you shouldn't avoid all fats, but include them in moderate amounts. Measure how much you use of each, and use them sparingly!

I'm confused about what I should eat every day. Can you recommend a healthful eating plan?

It's a good idea to eat a variety of foods throughout pregnancy. Below is a list of daily servings from six food groups:

- Dairy products—4 to 5 servings a day
- Protein sources—3 to 4 servings a day
- Vegetables—at least 4 servings a day
- Fruits—2 to 4 servings a day
- Breads, cereal, pasta and rice—6 to 11 servings a day
- Fats/flavorings—3 to 5 servings a day

Is there any place I can get more information on nutrition while I'm pregnant?

There is an excellent resource that can provide you with information on all aspects of nutrition, whether or not you are pregnant. The American Dietetic Association's Consumer Nutrition Information Line is a toll-free number that you can call to talk directly with a registered dietician. The number is 1–800–366–1655.

What kinds of foods are dairy products, and how much should I eat of each?

Following are some foods you might choose from this group, and their serving sizes:

- 3/4 cup (336g) cottage cheese
- 2 ounces (56g) processed cheese (such as American cheese)
- 1-1/2 ounces (42g) natural cheese (such as Cheddar)
- 1 ounce (28g) hard cheese (such as Parmesan or Romano)
- 1 cup (240ml) pudding or custard
- 1 8-ounce (240ml) glass of milk
- 1 cup (240ml) yogurt

To keep the fat content low, choose skim milk, lowfat yogurt and lowfat cheese instead of whole milk and ice cream.

What kinds of foods are good sources of protein, and how much should I eat of each?

Following are some you might choose from this group, and their serving sizes:

- 2 tablespoons (30ml) peanut butter
- 1/2 cup (120ml) cooked dried beans
- 2 to 3 ounces (56 to 84g) cooked meat
- 1 egg

Aim for a total of 6 to 7 ounces daily. Poultry, fish, lean cuts of red meat, dry beans, eggs, nuts and seeds are all good sources of protein.

What kinds of foods are in the vegetable group, and how much should I eat of each?

Following are some foods you might choose from this group, and their serving sizes:

- 3/4 cup (180ml) vegetable juice
- 1/2 cup (120ml) broccoli, carrots or other vegetable, cooked or raw
- 1 medium baked potato
- 1 cup (240ml) raw, leafy vegetables (salad greens)

Eating a variety of vegetables gives you a good nutritional balance. Eat at least one vegetable a day that is high in folic acid, such as green leafy vegetables. Be careful about adding alfalfa sprouts to foods you eat. Recent research has found these sprouts may cause salmonella infections in people with weakened immune systems.

What kinds of foods are in the fruit group, and how much should I eat of each?

Following are some foods you might choose from this group, and their serving sizes:

- 1/2 cup (120ml) canned or cooked fruit
- 3/4 cup (180ml) grapes
- 1/2 cup (120ml) fruit juice
- 1 medium banana, orange or apple
- 1/4 cup (60ml) dried fruit

Include one or two servings of a fruit rich in vitamin C, such as orange juice or orange slices. Fresh fruits are also a good source of fiber, which is important during your pregnancy if you suffer from constipation.

What kinds of foods are in the bread-pasta-cereal-rice group, and how much should I eat of each?

Following are some foods you might choose from this group, and their serving sizes:

- 1 large tortilla
- 1/2 cup (120ml) cooked pasta, cereal or rice
- 1 ounce (28g) ready-to-eat cereal
- 1/2 bagel
- 1 slice of bread
- 1 medium roll

What kinds of foods are in the fat/flavorings group, and how much should I eat of each?

Following are some foods you might choose from this group, and their serving sizes:

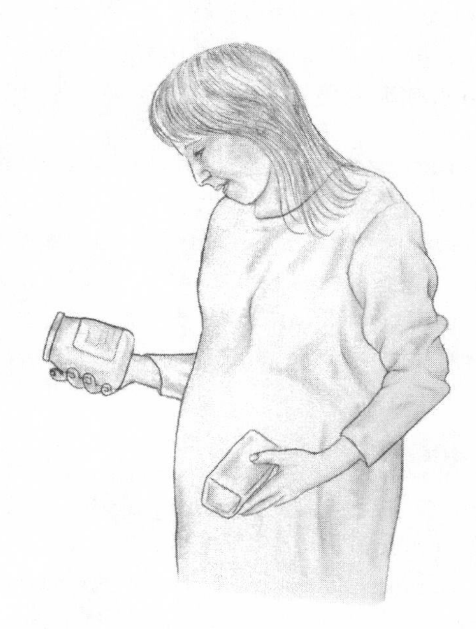

Make healthful food choices for yourself and your baby.

- 1 tablespoon (15ml) sugar or honey
- 1 tablespoon (15ml) olive oil or other type of oil
- 1 pat margarine or butter
- 1 tablespoon (15ml) jelly or jam
- 1 tablespoon (15ml) prepared salad dressing

Be a little more careful in your use of these foods because they can be troublesome if you are trying to control your weight.

I've heard I should eat foods that contain choline and DHA. Why?

Choline and docosahexaenoic acid (DHA) can help build baby's brain cells during fetal development and breastfeeding. Choline can be found in milk, eggs, whole-wheat bread and beef. DHA is found in fish, egg yolks, poultry, meat, canola oil, walnuts and wheat germ. If you eat these foods during pregnancy and while you're breastfeeding, you help your baby obtain these important supplements.

My husband and I eat out a lot because we're tired after work. Are there any foods I should avoid at restaurants?

It's OK to eat out at restaurants; you just need to be a little more careful about what you eat. Avoid any raw meats or raw seafood, such as sushi. Don't eat foods made with raw eggs. Ask about certain foods, such as Hollandaise sauce and Caesar salad. Certain foods may not agree with you, so avoid those foods.

What foods should I choose at a restaurant?

Fish, fresh vegetables and salads are usually your best bets, but be careful with calorie-loaded salad dressings if you're concerned about excessive weight gain. Avoid highly spicy foods or foods that contain a lot of sodium, such as some Chinese food. You may experience water retention after eating these foods.

Foods to Avoid

I have a hard time avoiding foods that are high in sugar and fat. What can I do?

Cookies, chocolate, candy and ice cream have a lot of empty calories. Fill up instead on foods that are high in fiber and low in sugar and fat. Choose fruits and vegetables, legumes and whole-grain crackers and breads.

I really love protein foods that have a lot of fat, like bacon and cheeses. What can I substitute for them?

Choose foods that are high in protein but low in fat, such as skinless chicken and turkey, tuna packed in water, cod, ground turkey and lowfat (1%) or skim milk. If you really love bacon, try soy or turkey bacon.

I know milk products are a good source of calcium for me, but I've heard there are some milk products I should avoid. Is this true?

There are a few foods made from milk you should avoid. These include unpasteurized milk and any foods made from unpasteurized milk. Also avoid soft cheeses, such as Brie, Camembert, feta and Roquefort. These products are a common source of food poisoning called *listeriosis.*

Are there other foods that may contain listeriosis?

Yes: undercooked poultry, undercooked meat, undercooked seafood and undercooked hot dogs can contain listeriosis. Be sure to cook all meat and seafood thoroughly before eating to avoid this problem.

I love junk food. Do I have to give it up completely?

You may have to forgo most junk food while you're pregnant. The foods we consider "junk food" are usually high-calorie, high-fat foods that contain little nutrition for you or your baby. It's probably OK to eat junk food once in a while, but don't make it a regular part of your diet.

I've heard that I shouldn't use artificial sweeteners while I'm pregnant? Is this true?

Aspartame and saccharin are the two most widely used artificial sweeteners. Recently, there has been controversy as to the safety of aspartame. Substitute foods that do not contain the sweetener for products you usually use because at this point we are unsure about its safety for pregnant women and their developing babies.

Pregnant women who suffer from phenylketonuria must follow a low-phenylalanine diet or their babies may be born mentally retarded and suffer from delayed development. The phenylalanine in aspartame contributes to phenylalanine in the diet. Saccharin, although it is not used as much today as in the past, is still found in many foods, beverages and other substances. Saccharin is *not* safe to use during pregnancy.

Sodium Use

I've heard I should be careful with my sodium intake during pregnancy. What is sodium?

Sodium is a chemical that works to maintain the proper amount of fluid in your body. During pregnancy, it can also affect your baby's system. Sodium is found in salty foods (such as potato chips and dill pickles) and in processed foods, from soups to meats. You need some sodium; you just don't need too much of it. Read food labels to discover just how much you're getting!

How much sodium should I take in each day?

During pregnancy, keep your consumption of sodium under 3g (3,000mg) a day.

How can too much sodium hurt me or my baby?

Too much sodium causes water retention, swelling and high blood pressure. Any of these can be a problem for you and therefore for your baby.

I don't know what foods contain sodium. What should I avoid?

You can't avoid something unless you know where to find it. With sodium, that can be tricky. It's in the salt shaker and in salty-tasting foods, such as pretzels, chips and salted nuts. You may be surprised by the amount of sodium in foods that don't taste salty.

Sodium is found in canned and processed products, fast foods, cereals, desserts and even soft drinks and some medications! See the chart on the opposite page for a listing of the sodium content in a variety of foods. Read labels!

SODIUM CONTENT OF SOME FOODS

Fresh or Minimally Prepared Foods	Sodium Content
1 cup apple juice	2mg
3 apricots (fresh)	1mg
1 medium banana	1mg
8 ounces of bluefish	170mg
1 head Boston lettuce	15mg
1 medium carrot	35mg
1 large egg	70mg
1 cup green beans (fresh or frozen)	2mg
3 ounces ground beef	60mg
1 lemon	1mg
1 cup whole milk	120mg
1 cup oatmeal (long-cooked)	10mg
1 cup orange juice	2mg
1 peach	1mg
3 ounces pork	65mg

Prepared Foods	Sodium Content
3 ounces bacon	1,400mg
1 cup baked beans	100mg
1 slice white bread	100mg
1 frozen chicken dinner	1,400mg
1 cup chicken-noodle soup	1,050mg
1 cinnamon roll	630mg
1 tablespoon cooking oil	0mg
3 ounces corned beef	1,500mg
1 cup corn flakes	305mg
1 cup green beans (canned)	320mg
1 cup all-purpose flour	2mg
1 cup self-rising flour	1,565mg
1 tablespoon Italian dressing	250mg
1 tablespoon catsup	155mg
1 olive	165mg
1 dill pickle	1,930mg
1 cup pudding, instant	335mg
1 cup puffed rice	1mg
1 cup tomato juice	640mg

Fast Foods	Sodium Content
1 Arby's turkey sandwich	1,060mg
1 Burger King Whopper	675mg
1 Dairy Queen hotdog	990mg
1 KFC dinner (3 pcs. chicken)	2,285mg
1 Taco Bell enchirito	1,175mg
1 McDonald's Big Mac	1,010mg

EATING PROBLEMS

Cravings

I've been craving certain foods now that I'm pregnant. Is this normal?

For many women, cravings during pregnancy are normal. Cravings for particular foods during pregnancy can be both good and bad. If you crave foods that are nutritious and healthful, eat them in moderate amounts. If you crave foods that are high in sugar and fat, and loaded with empty calories, be very careful about eating them.

Why do I have these cravings now, especially for foods that I don't normally eat?

No one knows for sure, but many believe it is because of the hormonal changes and emotional changes that occur during pregnancy.

I've found that I want to eat late at night, even though I've never felt hungry at night before. Should I eat late at night?

Late-night nutritious snacks are beneficial for some women, especially if they must eat many small meals a day. However, many women should not snack at night because they don't need the extra calories. Food in the stomach late at night may also cause more distress if heartburn or nausea and vomiting are problems.

Nausea

Some foods I normally love make me sick to my stomach now. Why?

This is normal and very common during pregnancy. The hormones of pregnancy have a significant impact on the gastrointestinal tract, which can affect your reaction to certain foods.

I feel so nauseous that I can't eat anything. Is this dangerous?

Nausea, also called *morning sickness,* is usually not dangerous because it doesn't last too long. It becomes dangerous when you are unable to eat an adequate amount of food or drink enough fluid.

Nausea is typically the worst during the beginning of pregnancy. It usually lessens and disappears after the 1st trimester, and you'll feel better for the rest of your pregnancy. See page 29 for further information about nausea and morning sickness.

Cholesterol

I'm 11 weeks' pregnant and had my cholesterol checked at the supermarket last week. It was higher than the last time I had it checked. Is that normal?

Yes. Cholesterol levels usually increase during pregnancy and nursing because of hormonal changes, so it's rather pointless to have them tested at this time.

BEVERAGE CHOICES

My doctor told me to drink lots of water every day, but it's hard to do. Do I really need it?

Water is necessary for your body to process nutrients, develop new cells and sustain blood volume. You may also feel better if you drink more fluid than you normally do. Your blood volume increases during pregnancy; drinking extra fluids helps you keep up with this change.

How else can drinking lots of water help me?

Many women who suffer from headaches, uterine cramping and other problems during pregnancy find increasing their fluid intake helps resolve some of their symptoms. It also helps avoid bladder infections.

How much water do I need to drink?

Drink 6 to 8 glasses (64 ounces; 1.9 liters) of liquid every day. Water is the best liquid to choose. When your urine is light yellow to clear, you're getting enough water. Dark yellow urine is a sign that you need to add more fluid to your diet.

If I drink beverages that normally act as diuretics, will it counteract the increase in fluids?

No, it won't.

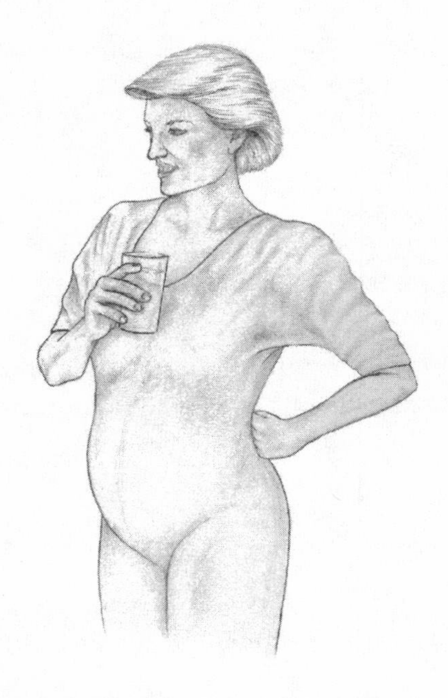

Drinking water is important throughout pregnancy, especially during and after exercise.

How can I possibly drink this much extra fluid?

It's really not that hard. Some women drink water, one glass at a time, throughout the day. (Decrease your intake later in the day so you don't have to go to the bathroom all night long.)

Caffeine

I drink a few cups of coffee and several glasses of diet cola every day. Do I need to worry about caffeine?

Drinking as few as 4 cups of coffee a day (800mg of caffeine) by a pregnant woman has been associated with decreased birthweight and a smaller head size in newborns. That same amount of caffeine may also affect your baby's developing respiratory system. One study showed this exposure before birth might be linked to sudden infant death syndrome (SIDS). Although an exact toxic amount for caffeine has not been determined, it makes sense to limit your caffeine intake.

What foods contain caffeine?

Caffeine is found in many beverages and foods, including coffee, tea, cola drinks and chocolate. Some medications, such as cough medicines and headache medicines, also contain a lot of caffeine. It's important to read labels.

Why is caffeine a problem?

Caffeine is a central-nervous-system stimulant. There are no known benefits for you or your unborn fetus from caffeine. Caffeine can also affect calcium metabolism in both you and your baby.

What do you suggest about caffeine intake during pregnancy?

Limit your caffeine intake during pregnancy and breastfeeding. Read labels on foods, beverages and over-the-counter medications to find out about caffeine content. Eliminate as much caffeine from your diet as possible.

VITAMINS AND MINERALS

Prenatal Vitamins

How important is it for me to take prenatal vitamins?

It's very important to take prenatal vitamins for your *entire* pregnancy. Sometimes late in pregnancy a woman stops taking them—she gets tired of taking them or she decides they aren't necessary. The vitamins and iron in prenatal vitamins are essential to the well-being of your baby, so be sure you take them until your baby is born.

I usually take a lot of vitamins, but my doctor advised me to take only a prenatal vitamin during pregnancy. Why?

Too much of a good thing can be harmful. Some vitamins accumulate in your body's tissues when taken in megadoses and can have

How are prenatal vitamins different from other vitamins?

The main difference is that prenatal vitamins also contain iron and folic-acid supplements.

an adverse effect on you and your baby. Megadoses of vitamin A can cause birth defects when taken during pregnancy. Vitamins D, E and K in megadoses may also be harmful. Follow your doctor's advice, take a prenatal vitamin and eat nutritious, well-balanced meals to get the vitamins and minerals you and your baby need.

Folic Acid

My friend is pregnant, and she's taking folic acid in addition to her prenatal vitamins. Is that something I need to do?

Most women don't need to take extra folic acid during pregnancy. (Folic acid, also called *folate,* is found naturally in green leafy veg-

INGREDIENTS IN A PRENATAL VITAMIN

A typical prenatal vitamin contains the following:

- calcium to build baby's teeth and bones and to help strengthen yours
- copper to help prevent anemia and to aid in bone formation
- folic acid to reduce the risk of neural-tube defects and to aid red blood cell production
- iodine to help control metabolism
- iron to prevent anemia and to help baby's blood development
- vitamins A, B_1, B_2, B_3, B_6 and E for general health and body metabolism
- vitamin B_{12} to promote formation of blood
- vitamin C to aid in your body's absorption of iron
- vitamin D to strengthen baby's bones and teeth and to help your body use phosphorus and calcium
- zinc to help balance fluids in your body and to aid nerve and muscle function

etables.) A deficiency in folate can result in a type of anemia called *megaloblastic anemia*. Additional folate may be necessary when requirements are unusually high, such as in a woman carrying multiple fetuses or suffering from alcoholism or Crohn's disease. Prenatal vitamins have 0.8 to 1mg of folic acid in each pill, which should be sufficient for a normal pregnancy.

Is it true that some foods are fortified with folic acid?

Yes. Many bread and cereal products are fortified with folic acid. Read labels of products you normally buy.

I've read that if a woman has a baby with spina bifida, she needs extra folic acid in later pregnancies. Is that true?

Studies indicate a women who has had a baby with a neural-tube defect, such as spina bifida, may be able to reduce her chances of having another baby with the same problems if she takes extra folic acid before pregnancy and through early pregnancy.

Other Minerals

Do I need mineral supplements during my pregnancy?

The only mineral supplement you need during pregnancy is iron. The average woman's diet seldom contains enough iron to meet the increased demands of pregnancy. Your blood volume increases by 50% in a normal pregnancy, and iron is an important part of blood production in your body.

Does it really make a difference if I don't take an iron supplement?

Prenatal vitamins contain some iron but you may need to take extra iron. One of the first tests your doctor does is for anemia. If he or she determines that you need an iron supplement, you must take it for your health and that of your baby.

Won't iron make me constipated?

Constipation can be a side effect of taking iron. Work with your doctor to find the correct amount of iron to avoid side effects.

Will my baby have healthier teeth (when she gets them!) if I take extra fluoride during my pregnancy?

The use of fluoride and fluoride supplementation during pregnancy is controversial. Some researchers believe fluoride supplementation during pregnancy results in improved teeth in your child, but not everyone agrees. However, no harm to the baby has been shown from fluoride supplementation in a pregnant woman. Some prenatal vitamins contain fluoride.

EXERCISE

I love to exercise and don't want to stop while I'm pregnant. Do I have to?

Experts agree that exercise during pregnancy is safe and beneficial for most pregnant women, if done properly. This is definitely an area to discuss with your doctor at the beginning of your pregnancy!

Exercise is beneficial during pregnancy and can be more enjoyable if you do it with a friend.

I don't really like to exercise, but I do it. Are there benefits to continuing my exercise program during my pregnancy?

Regular, moderate exercise during pregnancy can be beneficial for you in many ways. See the box below.

BENEFITS OF EXERCISE DURING PREGNANCY

Regular exercise is good for you in many ways:

- relieves backache
- prevents constipation and varicose veins
- strengthens muscles needed for delivery
- leaves you in better shape after delivery
- helps you control your weight

What should my exercise goals be during pregnancy?

The goal of exercising during pregnancy is overall good health. It can make you feel better physically, and it can give you an emotional boost.

My mother told me I shouldn't exercise during pregnancy; she was warned not to when she was pregnant with me. Why the change now?

Exercise was not always approved for a pregnant woman. In the past, doctors were concerned about the redirection of blood flow from the fetus to the mother-to-be's muscles during exercise. This does occur to a small degree, but it is not harmful to the fetus in a normal pregnancy.

I've never exercised before, but I'd like to begin now. Can I?

Some women become interested in exercising during pregnancy to help them feel better. If you've never exercised before, you must discuss it with your doctor before you begin. If you don't have any problems with your pregnancy, you should be able to exercise as long as you're comfortable. The key is not to try to do too much too fast. The best exercises for you are walking and swimming. Pregnancy is *not* the time to begin a vigorous exercise program.

What kind of exercises will my doctor recommend?

If you've never exercised before, walking and swimming are excellent forms of exercise. Riding a stationary bike or walking on a treadmill can also be enjoyable and beneficial.

I want to exercise, but it scares me that I might do something to hurt my baby. Should I be scared?

No. It's a good idea to exercise when you're pregnant. If you're fit, you'll do better with weight gain during pregnancy, be able to do the work of labor and delivery better, and feel better after the birth.

Most experts recommend reducing your exercise to 70 to 80% of your prepregnancy level. If you have problems with bleeding or cramping, or have had problem pregnancies before, you must modify your exercise according to your doctor's advice.

Someone told me exercising can cause early labor. Should I believe her?

It was once believed that exercise could cause preterm labor because there is a temporary increase in uterine activity following exercise. However, in a normal pregnancy, this does not cause a problem.

I read that my baby's heart rate increases when mine does during exercise. Can this cause a problem?

The fetal heart rate increases somewhat during and immediately after exercise, but it stays within the normal fetal range of 120 to 160 beats a minute. This should not cause any problems for you or the baby.

My aerobics instructor said my heart rate changes during pregnancy. Why?

During pregnancy, your heart rate is higher; you don't have to exercise as vigorously to reach your target heart rate. Be careful not to stress your cardiovascular system.

HOW TO CHECK YOUR PULSE

While you're pregnant, your pulse rate should not exceed 140 beats a minute for more than 15 minutes during a workout. Check your pulse with the following steps.

- Use a clock or watch with a second hand.
- Place the index and middle fingers of one hand on the side of your neck where you can feel your pulse.
- After finding your pulse, watch the second hand until it reaches the 12.
- Begin counting the pulse beats until the second hand reaches the 2 (10 seconds).
- Multiply that number by 6 to find your heart rate.

What if my heart rate is too high?

If it's too high, slow down but don't stop exercising completely. Continue exercising but at a more moderate rate.

What if my pulse rate is too low?

If you don't feel too winded, pick up the pace a bit, but don't overdo it. Check your pulse rate again in a few minutes to make sure you aren't overexerting yourself.

How often should I check my pulse rate?

You should do this fairly often when you exercise. It will surprise you how fast your pulse can increase during a pregnancy workout.

When should I consult my doctor about exercising during pregnancy?

Discuss it with him or her at your first prenatal visit. If you decide later to start or change your exercise program, consult your doctor before you begin.

WHEN *NOT* TO EXERCISE

Some women should not exercise during pregnancy. If any of the following applies to you, do not exercise during your pregnancy:

- a history of an incompetent cervix, preterm labor or repeated miscarriages
- high blood pressure early in pregnancy
- multiple fetuses
- diagnosed heart disease
- pre-eclampsia
- vaginal bleeding

Will I have to change my exercise program during pregnancy?

Changes in your body due to pregnancy will cause you to change the way you exercise. Your center of gravity changes, so you will need to adjust your exercise for that. As your abdomen grows larger, you won't be able to do some activities very comfortably and you may have to stop other activities all together.

I feel out of breath more quickly now that I'm pregnant. Is something wrong with me?

Your growing abdomen can put a strain on your respiratory system, causing you to feel out of breath sooner than normal. When you exercise, don't work to the point that you have trouble breathing and can't talk. This indicates you're working too strenuously; cut back on your workout.

I feel a lot hotter when I exercise during pregnancy. Is this normal?

When you're pregnant, you normally feel warmer than usual. You'll feel warmer, too, when you exercise, so try to avoid becoming overheated during workouts. Work out in a well-ventilated room, and drink lots of water while you exercise.

Can I play competitive sports during pregnancy?

If you are used to playing a competitive sport, such as tennis, you should be able to continue, but expect to reduce the level of competition. The point to remember is not to get carried away or to overwork yourself.

SAFE EXERCISE CHOICES

The activities listed below are generally considered safe for a normal, low-risk pregnancy.

- walking
- swimming
- low-impact aerobics, especially those designed for pregnant women
- water aerobics
- stationary bicycling
- regular cycling (if you're experienced)
- jogging (if you jogged before pregnancy)
- tennis (played moderately)
- walking on a treadmill
- using a stair stepper or stair climber
- riding a recumbent bike
- using a Nordic Track ski machine

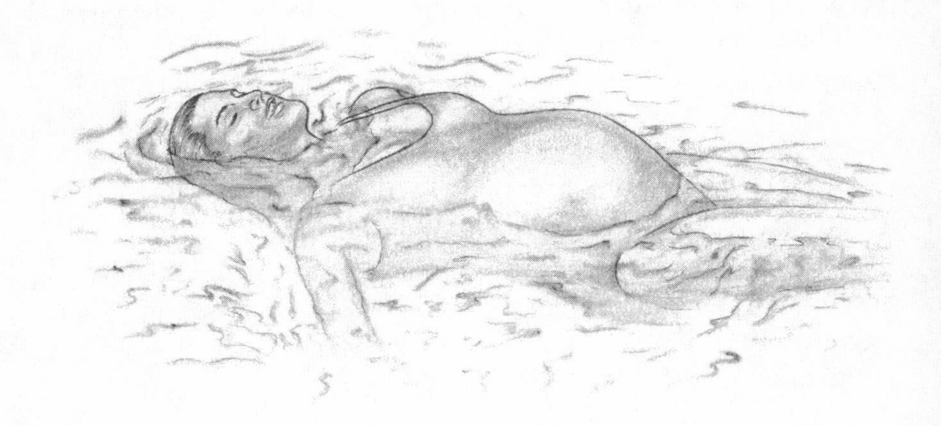

Swimming is an excellent way to exercise when you're pregnant. You'll feel a lot lighter in the water, too.

What sports should I avoid during pregnancy?

Avoid the sports listed below during pregnancy because of the potential problems associated with each:

- scuba diving
- water skiing
- surfing
- horseback riding
- downhill or cross-country skiing
- any contact sport

My health club offers aerobics classes for pregnant women. Are these better than regular aerobics classes?

Aerobics classes specifically designed for pregnant women are a good choice. They concentrate on the unique needs of the pregnant woman, such as strengthening abdominal muscles and improving posture. When choosing a class, be sure the instructor has proper training and the class meets the exercise guidelines developed by the American College of Obstetricians and Gynecologists. To obtain a copy of the guidelines, check out their website (www.acog.org) or e-mail Pamela Van Hine (pvanhine@acog.org) and include your name,

EXERCISE GUIDELINES

Consult your doctor before you begin any exercise program during pregnancy.

Following are general guidelines to help you stay healthy and in good shape.

- Exercise at least 3 times a week for 20 to 30 minutes each time.
- Start your exercise routine with a 5-minute warmup and end with a 5-minute cool-down period.
- Wear comfortable clothes, a support bra and good athletic shoes.
- Drink plenty of water during exercise.
- Don't exercise strenuously for more than 15 to 20 minutes.
- Check your pulse rate; keep it below 140 beats a minute.
- Be careful about exercising in hot, humid weather.
- After 16 weeks of pregnancy, avoid exercises that require you to lie on your back.
- Never allow your body temperature to rise above 100.4F (38C).
- Stop immediately and consult your physician if you experience any problems.

e-mail address, mailing address and the title and code for the pamphlet ("Exercise during Pregnancy," publication code AP119). Or write to ACOG, 409 12th Street, SW, P.O. Box 96920, Washington, DC 20090–6920.

If I exercise, do I need to eat more?

Your nutrition needs increase during pregnancy, and you burn extra calories during exercise, so eat enough calories to ensure a balanced diet. A woman who is normal weight before pregnancy needs to eat between 300 and 800 extra calories a day during pregnancy. Exercising may increase your needs.

Will exercise during pregnancy make labor and delivery easier?

Exercise during pregnancy should help you have an easier time with your labor and delivery.

Will exercise help me recover more quickly after my baby is born?

Many believe that women who exercise during pregnancy have a shorter recovery time after birth. Exercise keeps you fit so you can get back into shape more quickly.

What kind of problems should I watch out for while I'm exercising?

Be aware of any unusual occurrences. Report any of the following to your doctor immediately:

- pain
- bleeding
- dizziness
- extreme shortness of breath
- heart palpitations
- faintness
- abnormally rapid heart rate
- back pain
- pubic pain
- difficulty walking

WEIGHT MANAGEMENT

I'm in good shape; I exercise regularly and my weight is about where it should be. How much weight should I gain during my pregnancy?

Normal weight gain during pregnancy is 25 to 35 pounds (11.25 to 15kg). This may sound like a lot, but if you add up weight for the baby, placenta, amniotic fluid and changes in you, it really isn't that much. See the chart on the opposite page for general weight-gain guidelines.

THE AMOUNT OF EXERCISE NEEDED TO BURN OFF CERTAIN FOODS

Food (Calories)	Minutes Walking	Minutes Biking
Cheeseburger, small (600)	120	100
1/2 chicken breast, no skin (160)	32	26
Fat-free sandwich cookies, 4 medium (220)	44	35
French fries, regular order (260)	53	42
Skim milk, 8 ounces (85)	17	14
Potato chips, plain, about 15 (150)	30	25
Yogurt, plain and lowfat, 8 ounces (150)	30	24

GENERAL WEIGHT-GAIN GUIDELINES FOR PREGNANCY

Current Weight	Acceptable Gain
Underweight	28 to 40 pounds (12.6 to 18 kg)
Normal weight	25 to 35 pounds (11.25 to 15.75 kg)
Overweight	15 to 25 pounds (6.75 to 11.25 kg)

How am I supposed to watch my weight gain and still eat 300 to 800 calories more a day?

Not every woman needs to increase her food intake by 300 to 800 calories; that's just a *general* guideline. Look at your individual case. If you're underweight when you begin pregnancy, you may have to eat more than 800 extra calories each day. If you're overweight when you get pregnant, you may have less need for extra calories.

The key to good nutrition and weight management is to eat a balanced diet throughout your entire pregnancy. Eat the foods you need to help your baby grow and develop, but choose wisely. For example, if you're overweight, avoid peanut butter and other nuts as a protein source; choose water-packed tuna or lowfat cheeses instead. If you're underweight, select ice cream and milkshakes as sources of dairy foods.

I have such a fear of getting fat during pregnancy, I know it's going to cause me a lot of problems. What can I do about it?

You must be prepared to gain weight while you're pregnant. It is a normal part of pregnancy, and it is necessary for your baby's health! Getting on the scale and seeing your weight increase can be hard for some women, especially those who have to watch their weight closely. You must decide at the beginning of your pregnancy that it's all right to gain weight—it's for the health of your baby. You can control your weight gain by eating carefully and nutritiously. You don't have to gain an extra 50 pounds, but you must gain enough weight to meet the needs of pregnancy.

When my mother was pregnant with me, she was allowed to gain just 13 pounds (5.85kg) for her entire pregnancy. Was that normal 30 years ago?

Yes, it was fairly normal then. We realize today that it is permissible and advisable for a woman to gain a sufficient amount of weight during pregnancy. Today the normal weight gain during pregnancy (25 to 35 pounds; 11.25 to 15.75kg) is quite a change from 13 pounds (5.85kg)!

I'm pregnant and know I'm underweight. How much should I gain during my pregnancy?

If you start your pregnancy underweight, the normal weight gain is 28 to 40 pounds (12.6 to 18kg). It's important for you to eat regularly and nutritiously, even if you are not used to doing this.

Can an eating disorder affect pregnancy?

If you believe you have an eating disorder, try to deal with it *before* you get pregnant! Problems associated with an eating disorder during pregnancy include the following:

- not enough weight gain during pregnancy
- a low birthweight baby
- increased chance of fetal death
- low 5-minute Apgar scores
- intrauterine-growth restriction
- baby in breech presentation
- high blood pressure in mother-to-be
- birth defects
- higher rate of substance abuse in mother-to-be
- decreased plasma volume and electrolyte problems in mother-to-be

I'm overweight, and I just found out I'm pregnant. How much weight should I gain while I'm pregnant?

If you're overweight before pregnancy, you probably should not gain as much as other women during your pregnancy. Acceptable weight gain is 15 to 25 pounds (6.75 to 11.25kg). Try to gain this weight *slowly.* Aim for a weight gain of 2 to 4 pounds (0.9 to 1.8kg) the 1st trimester, 5 to 7 pounds (2.25 to 3.15kg) the 2nd trimester and 8 to 14 pounds (3.6 to 6.3kg) the 3rd trimester.

This is an individual situation to discuss with your doctor. It is important for you to eat nutritious, well-balanced meals during your pregnancy. *Do not diet!*

How much should I gain each week during pregnancy?

As an average for a normal-weight woman, many doctors suggest 2/3 of a pound (10 ounces; 300g) a week until 20 weeks, then 1 pound (0.45kg) a week from 20 to 40 weeks. However, this varies for each woman. If you're concerned, talk with your doctor about it.

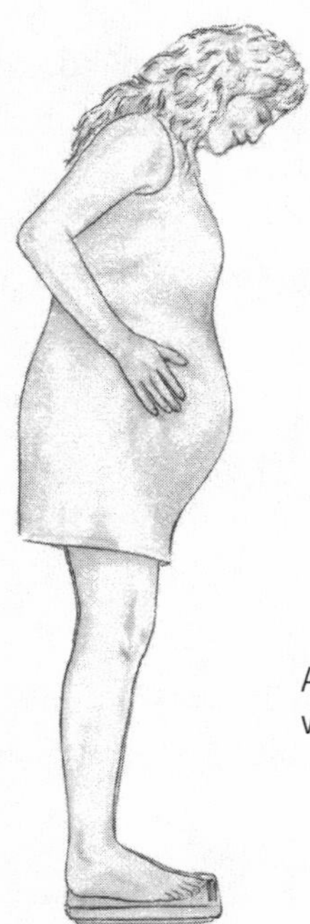

As much as you may dislike it, keeping track of your weight is important during pregnancy.

I'm 7 weeks' pregnant and haven't gained any weight; I think I may have even lost 2 or 3 pounds. Is that OK?

It isn't unusual not to gain weight or even to lose a little weight early in pregnancy. Your doctor will keep track of your weight change during your pregnancy.

My doctor said I must get weighed each time I come in. Can't I just weigh myself at home before I come in and tell the doctor or nurse my weight?

It's best to be weighed at the office. It's one way your doctor can tell that everything is progressing normally with your pregnancy. Although you may be shy about being weighed, it's an important part of your visit to the doctor. Your healthcare team is doing it to make sure everything is OK with your pregnancy.

You say I should gain 25 to 30 pounds (11.25 to 15.7 kg) during my pregnancy. That sounds like a lot to me when the baby only weighs about 7 pounds (3.15kg). Where does all that weight go?

The weight you gain is distributed as shown in the chart below. As you can see, you lose some weight during the birth process. You often lose more weight as your body readjusts to its nonpregnant state.

DISTRIBUTION OF WEIGHT GAIN DURING PREGNANCY

Weight	Location
7-1/2 pounds (3.38kg)	Baby
7 to 10 pounds (3.15 to 4.5kg)	Maternal stores (fat, protein and other nutrients)
4 pounds (1.8kg)	Increased fluid volume
2 pounds (0.9kg)	Uterus
2 pounds (0.9kg)	Amniotic fluid
2 pounds (0.9kg)	Breast enlargement
1-1/2 pounds (0.68kg)	Placenta

6

Fatigue, Work and Pregnancy

Nearly every pregnant woman experiences fatigue during her pregnancy. It is usually worse at the beginning, when hormone levels are increasing and shifting to support the growing baby. As your pregnancy progresses, fatigue usually eases. Rest and relax when you can to help you through this time. Eat right, take your prenatal vitamins and ask your partner for help doing jobs around the house. Avoid sugar and caffeine, which can make fatigue worse.

You may also feel concern about working while you're pregnant. In the past, women were told they couldn't work, but that's changed. With so many women working outside the home, we've been able to study how this activity affects a pregnancy. Studies show that working under normal circumstances, with an uncomplicated pregnancy, does not cause harm to the developing baby, as long as you don't have a job that causes you to stand for exceptionally long periods of time or that requires you to lift or to carry heavy objects. If you have any questions at all about your work, discuss them with your doctor.

FATIGUE

I seem to need more sleep than I ever did before. Is this normal?

Pregnant women need more sleep than they do when they're not pregnant. In most cases, 8 to 10 hours of sleep a night will help you feel better. When you see your doctor, one of the first tests he or she

GETTING A GOOD NIGHT'S SLEEP

You can get a good night's sleep if you prepare for it. Try the following suggestions.

- Go to bed and wake up at the same times each day.
- Don't drink too much fluid at night. Decrease fluid intake after 6 P.M.
- Avoid caffeine after late afternoon.
- Get regular exercise.
- Sleep in a cool bedroom: 70F (21.1C) is the highest temperature for comfortable sleeping.
- If you experience heartburn at night, sleep sitting up or in a semireclining position.

will do is a hematocrit to check for anemia, which can also be a reason for feeling tired.

I usually lie on my stomach when I sleep. Will I be able to do this as I get bigger?

Lying directly on your stomach isn't a good idea. It puts a lot of pressure on your growing uterus, which will be a comfort problem later. The bigger you get, the harder it is to lie on your stomach.

My sister said it's not good for me to lie on my back during pregnancy. Does she know what she's talking about?

After 16 weeks (about 4 months) of pregnancy, it's best not to lie on your back when you sleep or rest. Lying on your back can place the uterus on top of important blood vessels (inferior vena cava and aorta) that run down the back of your abdomen. This can decrease circulation to your baby and to parts of your body. It may also be harder for you to breathe when you lie on your back.

What is the best position for sleeping?

Learn to sleep on your side—you'll be glad you did as you get bigger. Use some extra pillows to support your back so you don't lie flat on your back. Rest your top leg on another pillow. A "pregnancy pillow" that provides support for your entire body may help. See the illustration below.

A pregnancy pillow can relieve stress points and help you feel more comfortable resting or sleeping.

I can't sleep enough at night to make me feel better. How do I get the rest I need?

Try napping during the day. If you can't nap, sit down and relax—listen to music or read, if that helps. When you relax, prop your feet above your chest, if possible, to help with any swelling and to ease any discomfort in your legs.

STRESS

I've been under a lot of stress during my pregnancy. Is there anything I can do to help manage stress?

The following breathing exercise can help you relax when you feel stressed.

- Inhale slowly as you count to 4. Push your abdomen out as you breathe in.
- Let your shoulders and neck relax as you slowly exhale while counting to 6.
- Repeat as often as you need to.

Hint: Play gentle, soothing music as you practice this exercise.

What else can help relieve my stress?

One exercise is to relax each muscle group with each deep breath. Start with the feet and work up through the legs, hands, arms, torso, shoulders, neck and face. Continue for 10 to 20 minutes. This exercise also works when you're having trouble getting to sleep.

WORKING DURING PREGNANCY

My mother told me I shouldn't work during pregnancy. Is this true?

In the past, women were encouraged, or even forced, to stop working when they were pregnant. Today, many women work until they deliver their baby. Whether you work your entire pregnancy depends on your particular circumstances. If you are concerned about it, discuss it with your doctor.

My partner is concerned about my working during pregnancy. Should he be?

More than half of all women work outside the home; many pregnant women work and do well. If you are concerned about whether your job is safe for your pregnancy, discuss your particular situation with your doctor. It may be difficult to know the specific risk of a particular job—the goal is to minimize the risk to you and your baby while still enabling you to work. A normal, healthy woman should be able to work at most jobs throughout her pregnancy.

WORK HAZARDS

Certain factors may increase your risk of problems while working during your pregnancy. If your job includes two or more of the following, talk to your doctor:

- prolonged standing (more than 3 hours a day)
- work on an industrial machine, especially if it vibrates a lot or requires strenuous effort to operate it
- strenuous physical tasks, such as heavy lifting or heavy cleaning
- repetitious, tedious work, such as assembly line jobs
- environmental factors, such as high noise levels or extreme temperatures
- long working hours
- shift changes

I don't want to stop working while I'm pregnant. What precautions should I take?

You will probably have to slow down if you continue to work. You may also have to take it a little easier; you may not be able to do some of the things you do when you are not pregnant. It may also be necessary to ask for help with some of the tasks you are required to perform.

Should I try to rest during my work day?

If possible, try to lie down during breaks or on your lunch hour. Even sitting down in a quiet place can be beneficial. Ten or 15 minutes of rest can make you feel better and restore your energy.

A co-worker who just had a baby said her doctor told her she should exercise her legs and feet often during the day while she was pregnant. Should I do the same?

Yes. Try to do some leg-stretching foot exercises several times each hour. Remove your shoes before doing the following exercise: Extend your legs in front, then point your toes and flex your feet. Repeat this 4 or 5 times. It helps circulation in your feet and may prevent some swelling in your legs.

I've heard I should wear maternity stockings to work. Why?

Whether you sit or stand at work, maternity stockings provide support for your legs. They can be helpful even if you don't work. Maternity stockings may be preferable to regular support stockings because they don't constrict your waist or abdomen.

My job requires me to stand all day. Will that be a problem?

Studies show that women who stand all day have smaller babies. If you stand a lot, you may have problems at the end of your pregnancy with swelling of your feet and ankles. It may be necessary for you to modify your work, lie down a couple of times during the day or work fewer hours.

I have to climb a lot in my job. Should I talk to my supervisor about it?

It's probably best to avoid activities that involve climbing and balance in your job, especially during the 3rd trimester. Talk with your supervisor about eliminating these activities.

I seem to have terrible mood swings while I'm at the office. Is this normal?

Elevated hormones and the stress of being pregnant can trigger mood swings. You may also find you're more tired; it's normal. Take a break if any situation becomes more than you can bear.

It's important to lift boxes, cartons and packages correctly. Always bend your knees, squat and lift with your legs. Don't bend over and lift!

I know my center of gravity is changing. What's the best way for me to lift an object?

Do most of your lifting with your legs. Bend your knees to lift; don't bend at the waist. As your abdomen grows larger, don't lift anything over 30 pounds (13.6kg), including your older children.

I work at a computer terminal all day. Can this harm my baby?

To date, we have no evidence that working at a computer terminal can harm a growing baby. However, if you work at a computer terminal, you should be aware of how long you sit and the way you sit. See the next question.

I have a job that keeps me sitting behind a desk all day. Is there anything I need to be concerned about?

Get up and move around regularly to stimulate your circulation—about once every 15 minutes. Take short walks frequently. Sit in a chair that offers good support for your back and legs. Don't slouch or cross your legs while sitting.

Software you can load onto your computer to help you keep in shape is now available. The program, StretchWare, is available from Shelter Publications and can lead you through many different rou-

Research has found few problems in pregnant women who work at computer terminals.

tines. You can focus on your hands, shoulders, lower back, legs or neck—each routine is fast and easy.

I read that some substances or conditions in the workplace can harm a developing baby. What are they?

Some substances can cause harm to a developing fetus. The chart on the following page describes various agents, their sources and the possible effects they may have on a growing baby.

Is there a danger that my partner or I could bring home traces of substances we are exposed to at work?

Yes. You and your family may bring substances into your home on your work clothes. If you think you may be exposed to hazardous substances, be sure to discuss it with your doctor.

Work, Pregnancy and the Law

I work full time and worry about how people at my job will treat me if I have problems or need time off during my pregnancy. Is there anything I can do?

The U.S. Pregnancy Discrimination Act of 1978 prohibits job discrimination on the basis of pregnancy, childbirth or related disabili-

WORKPLACE HAZARDS AND POSSIBLE EFFECTS ON THE FETUS

Agent	Sources	Possible Effects
Cytomegalovirus	Hospitals, day-care centers	Congenital malformation
Cytotoxic drugs	Hospital or pharmacy preparation of chemotherapeutic drugs	Miscarriage
Ethylene oxide	Surgical-instrument sterilization	Miscarriage
Ionizing radiation	X-rays and radiation treatments, radioactive implants, nuclear power plants	In very high doses, birth defects; lower doses may increase childhood cancer risk
Lead	House, automotive and art paints made before 1980; battery manufacturing plants and radiator repair shops; ceramics and glass manufacturers	Preterm birth, delayed cognitive development
Organic solvents	Paint thinners, lacquers, adhesives; electronics and printing plants	Congenital malformation
PCBs	Electronic capacitors and transformers; hazardous waste industry	Delayed cognitive development
Rubella virus	Day-care centers, schools	Congenital malformation
Toxoplasmosis	Veterinary clinics, animal shelters, meat-packing operations	Congenital malformation

THE U.S. PREGNANCY DISCRIMINATION ACT

If you work in a company that employs 15 or more people, the following may apply to you.

- You must be granted the same health, disability and sick-leave benefits as any other employee for any other medical condition.
- You must be given modified tasks, alternate assignments, disability leave or leave without pay (depending on your company's policy).
- You are allowed to work as long as you can perform your job.
- You are guaranteed job security while you're on leave.
- You continue to accrue seniority and vacation, and you remain eligible for pay increases and benefits.

ty. It guarantees equal treatment of all disabilities, including pregnancy, birth or related medical conditions, by companies that employ 15 or more people. If you have problems, ask your doctor for help. Most will encourage you to work, if working isn't harmful to you or your baby.

Wasn't another law passed more recently that also affects pregnant women?

The Family and Medical Leave Act was passed in 1993. It allows you or your husband to take up to 12 weeks of unpaid leave in any 12-month period for the birth of your baby. You can take this leave intermittently or all at the same time. You must be restored to an equivalent position with equal benefits when you return. However, the act applies only to companies that employ 50 or more people within a 75-mile radius. States may allow an employer to deny job restoration to those in the top 10% compensation bracket. Check with your state's labor office.

It's important to continue working during pregnancy if you want to. As a working pregnant woman, you have many rights. Ask your personnel director for further information.

If you qualify for leave under the Family Medical Leave Act, you can take up to 12 unpaid weeks off in a year to take care of family or personal problems. However, any time you take off *before* the birth of your baby is counted toward the total 12 weeks you are entitled to in any given year.

If morning sickness is causing you to be absent from your job, you may be interested to know that the Family Medical Leave Act (FMLA) states you do *not* need a doctor's note verifying the problem. Nausea or vomiting from pregnancy is classified as a "chronic condition" and may require you be out occasionally, but you don't need a doctor's treatment.

For information on the Family Medical Leave Act, call their hotline at 800–522–0925.

I heard on the radio the other day that there is a fact sheet about discrimination in the workplace during pregnancy. Do you know anything about it?

One excellent fact sheet available from the Equal Employment Opportunity Commission is "Facts about Pregnancy Discrimination." Call 202–663–4900 for a free copy or visit their website: www.eeoc.gov.

What about my state's employment laws; do they affect me as a pregnant woman?

State laws differ, so check with your state's labor office. You may also receive a summary of state laws on family leave from the U.S. Department of Labor:

Women's Bureau
U.S. Department of Labor
Box EX
200 Constitution Avenue NW
Washington, DC 20210
800-827-5335

7

Expecting Two or More Babies

According to statistics, more women today are giving birth to more than one baby in a pregnancy. It's not uncommon to hear of a woman having twins, and the occurrence of triplets is also on the rise. The media report when women deliver many babies, but no one seems to raise an eyebrow anymore when quintuplets and quadruplets are born. It almost seems "normal" for a woman to have more than one baby.

Multiple births occur for many reasons:

- the use of fertility drugs
- the use of in vitro fertilization
- women having babies later in life
- some women having more children

What does this mean for the normal woman? If you're older, it can increase your chances of having more than one baby. Having in vitro fertilization or using fertility drugs can also increase these chances. The more children you have, the greater your chances of having twins, or more.

No matter how it occurs, being pregnant with two or more babies can affect you in many ways. In this chapter, we discuss what changes you may have to make in pregnancy and what adjustments you may need to deal with. These may be necessary for your health and the health of your babies. If this happy event occurs in your life, work with your doctor and other healthcare professionals to help ensure your pregnancy is healthy and safe.

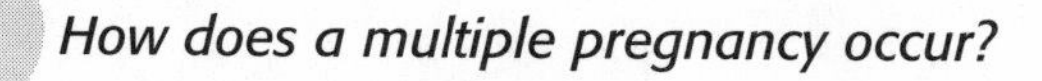

How does a multiple pregnancy occur?

The babies may come from a single egg that divides after fertilization, or more than one egg may be fertilized.

CAUSES OF MULTIPLE PREGNANCY

How do fertility drugs cause an increase in the rate of multiple births?

Fertility drugs can stimulate the ovaries to release more than one egg, increasing the chance of a multiple pregnancy.

Why are multiple fetuses more common with in vitro fertilization?

With in vitro fertilization, multiple embryos are placed in the uterine cavity in hopes that at least one will implant and grow to maturity.

Do older women really have a greater chance of having multiples?

Yes. The incidence of twins is highest among women between ages 35 and 39. This increase has been attributed to higher levels of gonadotropin, the hormone that stimulates the ovaries to develop and release eggs. As a woman gets older, the level of gonadotropin increases, and she is more likely to produce two (or more) eggs during one menstrual cycle.

I read that the more children a woman has, the more likely she is to have more than one baby. Is this true?

Yes, it is. Research shows that a woman has a greater chance of having twins the more pregnancies she has. We know of one mother who had three single births, then twins, then triplets!

My doctor told me he thinks I may be carrying triplets. How common are they?

Triplets are not common; they occur only once in every 8,000 deliveries. Many doctors never deliver a set of triplets in their entire career!

TWIN PREGNANCY

FREQUENCY OF TWIN BIRTHS

Twins from one egg occur about once in every 250 births around the world. The incidence of twins also varies among ethnicities:

- white women: 1 out of every 100 births
- black women: 1 out of 79 births (In certain areas in Africa, twins occur once in every 20 births!)
- Asian women: 1 in every 150 births

Is it true that Hispanic women also have a higher incidence of twins and multiple births?

Some studies have shown this is true.

What is the difference between identical and fraternal twins?

Identical (monozygotic) twins develop from a single egg that divides after being fertilized. Babies are always the same sex, and they look alike. When two eggs are fertilized, the babies will be as different in appearance as any other brothers and sisters. They are called *fraternal (dizygotic)* twins.

Are most twins born to older women fraternal twins?

Usually that is the case. Because babies are born from two different eggs, they are fraternal (not identical).

Parenting twins can be challenging and rewarding.

I've heard that twin births can run in families. Is this true?

Yes, on the *mother's* side. One study showed that if a woman was a twin, the chance of her giving birth to twins was about 1 in 58! If a woman is the daughter of a twin, she also has a higher chance of having twins. Another study reported that 1 out of 24 twins' mothers (4%) was also a twin, but only 1 out of 60 (1.7%) of the fathers was a twin.

I heard the incidence of multiple births is on the increase. Why is that?

Researchers believe two factors are responsible for this increase. One is the wider use of fertility drugs or in vitro fertilization, which can result in multiple births. The second is the growing number of women who are having babies at an older age. We know the chance of twins increases as a woman gets older.

A friend told me about her sister-in-law, who was told early in pregnancy she was going to have twins. Then some time later, one of the twins disappeared. Is she making this up?

No, this happens. Early ultrasound exams reveal two babies; later ultrasounds of the same woman show one baby has disappeared, but the other baby is OK. We believe one of the fetuses may die, then be absorbed in the mother's body. This is one reason many doctors prefer not to predict a twin birth before 10 weeks of pregnancy.

DIAGNOSING A MULTIPLE PREGNANCY

When is a multiple pregnancy most often discovered?

A multiple pregnancy is usually found during the 2nd trimester because the woman is larger than expected and growth seems to be too fast.

What's the best way to diagnose a multiple pregnancy?

Ultrasound is the best way to determine if a woman is carrying more than one baby.

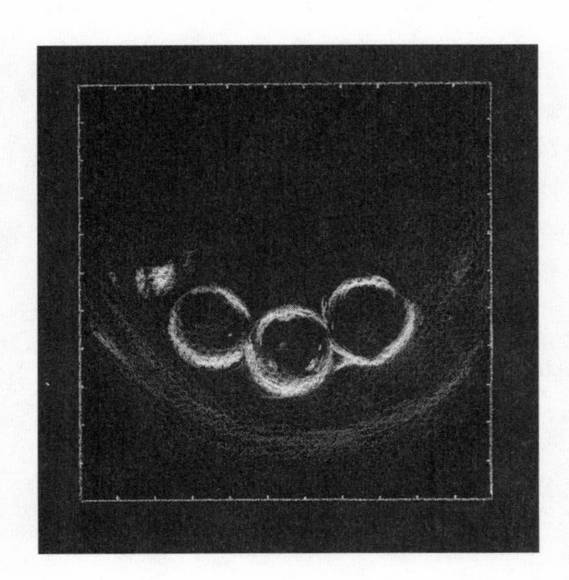

Ultrasound of three fetuses (triplets) early in pregnancy.

SPECIAL CONSIDERATIONS

I'm expecting more than one baby; what do I have to keep in mind during my pregnancy?

One of the most important things you must remember with a multiple pregnancy is to take things more slowly, from the beginning of your pregnancy until delivery. Taking care of yourself is the best way to take care of your developing babies.

Nutrition and Exercise

Is it true that a woman who is carrying more than one baby needs to eat more?

It is necessary for a woman who is carrying multiples to eat more—at least 300 more calories per baby each day than in a single pregnancy! A woman needs more protein, minerals, vitamins and essential fatty acids. Iron supplementation is also necessary.

Will I have a greater chance of having iron-deficiency anemia if I have twins?

Often women who are pregnant with more than one baby have iron-deficiency anemia. A multiple pregnancy is more stressful to your body than a single pregnancy, and your needs increase in many areas.

I'd like to try to keep in shape during pregnancy. Are there any exercises I can do?

Walking and swimming *may* be permissible for you while you're pregnant with multiples. Check out any exercise program with your doctor *before* you begin. Don't do any strenuous exercises, and stop immediately if you feel overexerted. As much as you want to stay in shape, you may have to forgo all exercise until after your babies are safely delivered.

Is it true I'll put on a lot more weight with multiples?

You are more likely to put on extra weight with multiple fetuses. For a normal-weight woman, a weight gain of 35 to 45 pounds (15.75 to 20.25kg) for a twin birth is recommended. However, some women do not gain as much weight because of the added stress on their bodies.

Potential Problems and Discomforts

If a woman is pregnant with multiples, is she likely to have more problems during pregnancy?

The possibility of problems increases slightly when a woman is carrying more than one baby.

These problems may include any of the following:

- miscarriage
- fetal malformations
- low birthweight or intrauterine-growth restriction
- pre-eclampsia
- maternal anemia
- problems with the placenta
- maternal bleeding or hemorrhage
- problems with the umbilical cords
- hydramnios or polyhydramnios (too much fluid in the bag of waters)
- labor complicated by breech or transverse presentation
- premature labor and premature delivery

Is it true that a woman expecting more than one baby has more heartburn than other pregnant women?

This is often the case. It is caused by the larger uterus encroaching on the space the stomach usually enjoys by itself.

I've heard that most complications in a multiple-fetus pregnancy arise in the last trimester. Is this true?

Yes; as the babies grow larger, the mother-to-be may experience more problems. The biggest problem is premature labor and premature delivery. You get bigger earlier, and you get larger than with a single pregnancy. This can cause problems, such as difficulty breathing, back pain, hemorrhoids, varicose veins, pelvic pressure and pelvic pain, even early in a pregnancy.

I recently read an article that mentioned conjoined twins. What are they?

Conjoined twins, once called *Siamese twins*, are twins whose bodies are connected. It is a very serious complication of pregnancy because these babies may share important internal organs, such as the heart, lungs or liver. Sometimes they can be separated; often they cannot.

How are conjoined twins delivered?

It is usually necessary to deliver conjoined twins by Cesarean section.

Does the birth of conjoined twins occur very often?

No, it is very rare.

PREPARING FOR MULTIPLES

A mother of twins at my doctor's office said she waited too long to buy the things she needed for her babies. What did she mean?

Many expectant mothers wait until they are close to the delivery date of their baby to buy nursery items. However, the expectant

mother of multiples shouldn't wait this long—your 2nd trimester is not too early to buy the things you'll need. Buy these things while you can get around easily instead of waiting until after your babies are born.

A friend who had twins told me her doctor advised her to begin her maternity leave from work early. Is this normal?

Often a physician will advise a woman expecting multiples to stop working 8 to 12 weeks before her due date. Ideally, a woman should stop working at 28 weeks with a twin pregnancy, 24 weeks if her job requires standing or physical exertion.

What kind of support would you recommend when my babies are born?

Your time of greatest need will be after you bring your babies home. Ask for help from family, neighbors and friends for the first 4 to 6 weeks. You may be fairly exhausted yourself, so it's helpful to have extra pairs of hands available until you all settle into a routine.

My husband and I want to take childbirth-education classes. Can we when we're expecting twins?

It's an excellent idea to take these classes for any pregnancy! Schedule your classes to begin at least 3 months before your due date. If you have time, a brief course in Cesarean birth might also be worthwhile, if you can find one in your area.

DELIVERY

I've heard that multiple fetuses are usually delivered early. What is the average length of pregnancy with more than one baby?

We try to delay delivery of twins until about the 37th week of pregnancy, and triplets until about the 35th week. In most cases, these pregnancies deliver earlier. The average for twins is about 36 weeks; for triplets, the average is about 33 weeks.

How are multiple fetuses usually delivered?

This depends on how the babies are lying in the uterus. All possible combinations of fetal positions can occur. Some doctors believe two or more babies should always be delivered by Cesarean section. When twins are both head first, a vaginal delivery may be attempted. However, one baby may be delivered vaginally, with the second requiring a C-section if it turns, if the cord comes out first or if the second baby is distressed after the first baby is born.

BREASTFEEDING MORE THAN ONE BABY

I'm expecting twins, and I want to breastfeed. Can I?

Yes, you can. It may be more demanding, but many women successfully breastfeed twins.

I've heard breast milk and breastfeeding are good for twins. Why?

We know that breast milk is especially valuable for small or premature infants; often twins are both. For this reason, if you want to breastfeed, try it.

We're going to have triplets. Is it possible to breastfeed triplets?

You'll find it very challenging, but try it if you want to. One way you may be able to do it is to let each baby breastfeed for a bit at a feeding, then supplement with formula. You can also express your milk, and divide it between the three of them. Because triplets are usually small and premature, your breast milk is valuable to them.

I have a friend who had triplets born 10 weeks early. Her breast milk never came in. Is this common?

No, this is not common. Usually a mother produces breast milk without complications.

8

Changes in Your Developing Baby

*The changes a developing baby goes through during a preg-*nancy are truly miraculous. At conception, your baby is only a few cells. During your 9 months of pregnancy, these few cells grow into a fully developed baby that can live on its own. Your body changes very slowly; you probably won't notice a great deal of growth until the second half of your pregnancy. But by that time, all of your baby's organs are developed, its heart is beating and it is moving inside you!

This chapter attempts to give you an idea of some of the fascinating things that occur as your baby grows and develops. After reading it, you may agree that the growth of your baby is truly a wondrous event.

DUE DATE

Why is a due date important?

A due date is important in pregnancy because it helps your doctor determine when to perform certain tests or procedures. It also helps estimate baby's growth and may indicate whether you are overdue or in premature labor.

I'm confused about how my doctor determines when my baby is due. Can you explain it so I can understand it?

Most women don't know the exact date their baby was conceived, but they often know the day their last menstrual period began. The doctor adds 2 weeks to the date of the last period as an estimate of when conception occurred. Your estimated due date is 38 weeks after the date of conception (40 weeks after the first day of your last period).

Is there any other way to determine when my baby is due?

Yes. Add 7 days to the date of the beginning of your last menstrual period, then subtract 3 months. This gives you the *approximate* date of delivery. For example, if your last period began on January 20, your estimated due date is October 27.

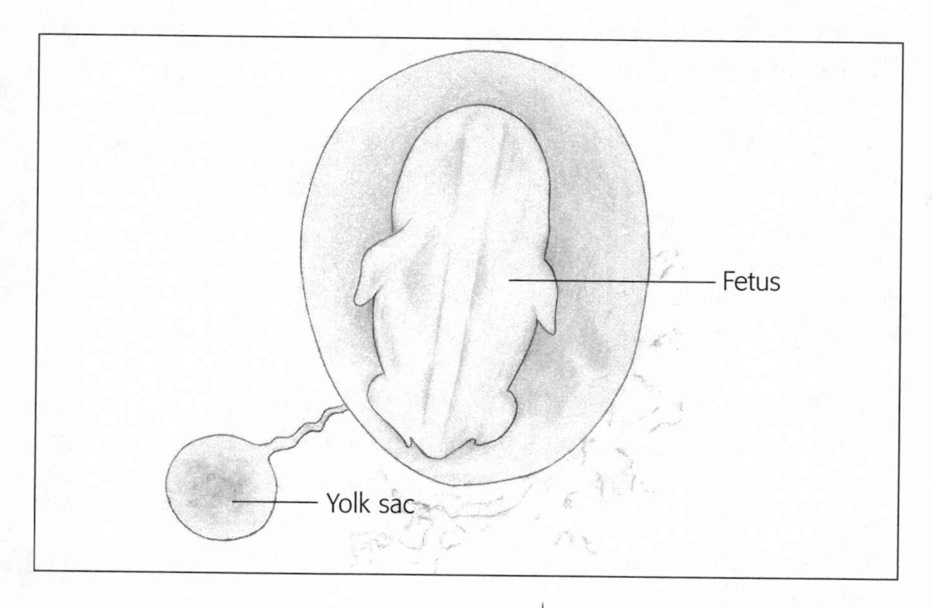

The fetus at 6 weeks looks more like a tadpole than a baby.

My doctor mentioned the gestational age of my baby. What is it?

Gestational age, also called *menstrual age,* dates a pregnancy from the first day of the last menstrual period. It is 2 weeks longer than the fertilization age.

What is the fertilization age?

Fertilization age, also called *ovulatory age,* is 2 weeks shorter than gestational age and dates from the *approximate* date of conception. This is the age of the fetus.

These dating techniques are confusing. When my doctor says I'm 12 weeks' pregnant, how old is my baby?

Most doctors count the time during pregnancy in weeks. If your doctor says you're 12 weeks' pregnant, he or she's referring to the gestational age. Your last menstrual period began 12 weeks ago, but you actually conceived 10 weeks ago, so the fetus is 10 weeks old.

TRIMESTERS

I know my developing baby is going through lots of changes. Can you explain some of them to me?

Your baby grows and changes from a small group of cells to a fully developed baby ready to begin life. Changes are easier to discuss if we look at them in each trimester.

What is a trimester?

Your pregnancy is divided into three trimesters, each about 13 weeks long.

How does my baby change during the 1st trimester?

This trimester is the one of greatest change for a developing fetus. In the first 13 weeks of development, your baby grows from a collection of cells the size of the head of a pin to a fetus the size of a softball. Organs begin developing, and your baby begins to look more normal.

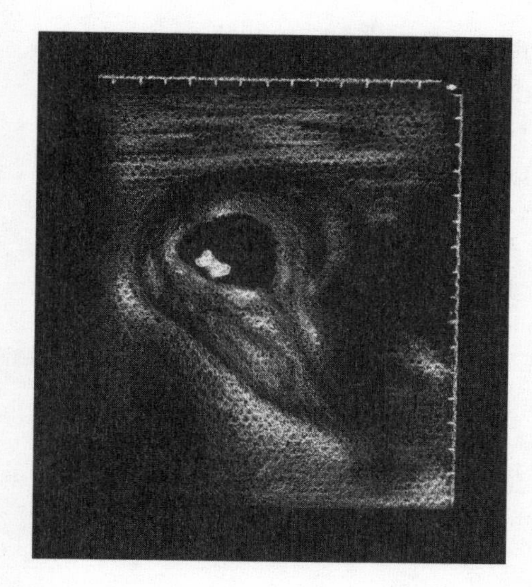

Ultrasound at 6 weeks.

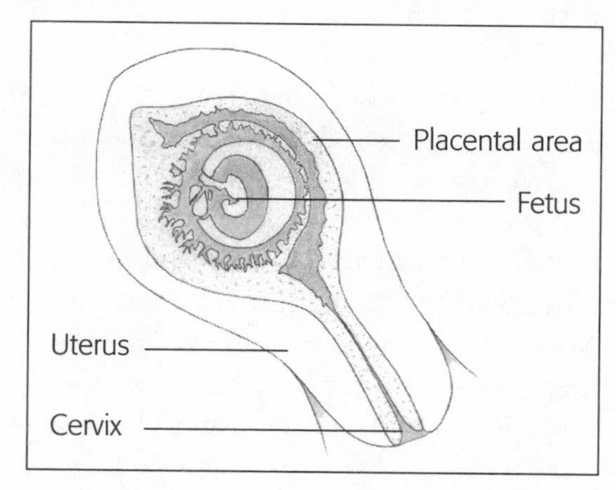

Illustration of what ultrasound at 6 weeks shows.

How does my baby change during the 2nd trimester?

At the beginning of the 2nd trimester (14th week), your baby weighs less than 1 ounce (28g) and is only about 4 inches (10cm) long. By the end of this trimester, your baby is almost 9 inches (22cm) long and weighs close to 1-1/2 pounds (0.7kg).

How does my baby change during the 3rd trimester?

Your baby weighs about 1-1/2 pounds (0.7kg) at the beginning of this trimester (27th week), and its crown-to-rump length is under 9 inches (22cm). When it is delivered, your baby weighs close to 7-1/2 pounds (3.4kg) and is about 21 inches (53cm) long.

What is the difference between an embryo and a fetus?

The designation between "embryo" and "fetus" is somewhat arbitrary. During the first 8 weeks of development (10 weeks of gestation), the developing baby is called an *embryo.* From 8 weeks of development until delivery, it is called a *fetus.*

I read recently that the baby doesn't change very much after about the 12th week of pregnancy. What does this mean?

Very few, if any, structures in the fetus are *formed* after the 12th week of pregnancy. This means your baby forms all of its major organ systems by the end of the 1st trimester. However, these structures continue to grow and to develop until your baby is born.

BABY'S SIZE

How big are most babies when they are born?

The weight varies greatly from baby to baby. However, the average weight of a baby at term is 7 to 7-1/2 pounds (2.6 to 3kg).

Is there any way to estimate from my size how big my baby will be?

It's very hard to estimate the weight of any baby before birth. Many doctors will guess and give a range of a couple pounds. It's not uncommon to estimate a baby will weigh 8-1/2 (3.4kg) pounds and find it's only a 7-pound (2.6kg) baby when it's born.

My doctor said that ultrasound can be used to gauge a baby's weight. Is that true?

Ultrasound is sometimes used to estimate fetal weight, but errors do occur. However, the accuracy of predicting fetal weight with ultrasound is improving.

How does ultrasound measure a baby's weight?

A formula has been established to help estimate fetal weight with ultrasound. Several measurements are used, including the diameter of the baby's head, circumference of the baby's abdomen and length of the femur (thighbone) of the baby's leg. Occasionally, other fetal measurements are taken.

How accurate is ultrasound in measuring a baby's weight before birth?

It is the test of choice to estimate fetal weight. However, estimates may vary as much as half a pound (225g) in either direction.

I'm 13 weeks' pregnant and read that my baby's head is about half or 50% of its body length. Can this be true?

Yes, at this point the head is about half the crown-to-rump length (measurement from top of the head to the baby's buttocks). In 2 months, when you are 21 weeks' pregnant, the head will be about 1/3 of the fetal body. At birth, your baby's head will be 1/4 the size of its body.

BABY'S HEARTBEAT

My doctor told me that my baby's heart starts beating very early. When does this happen?

By the 6th week of pregnancy (age of fetus is 4 weeks), the heart tubes fuse and contractions of the heart begin. This can be seen on ultrasound.

When will I be able to hear my baby's heartbeat?

With doppler ultrasound, it is possible to hear the heartbeat as early as 12 weeks of pregnancy. It may be possible to hear your baby's heartbeat with a stethoscope at around 20 weeks. If you can't hear it, don't worry. It's not always easy, even for a doctor who does this on a regular basis.

While I was listening to my baby's heartbeat the other day at my doctor's office, I heard it skip a beat. Is this serious?

An irregular heartbeat is called an *arrhythmia*. Arrhythmias in a fetus are not unusual, so don't be overly concerned about it. The equipment could also be faulty, or there may be some other problem transmitting the sound.

If my baby has an arrhythmia, what can be done about it?

Arrhythmias are not usually serious in a baby before birth; many disappear after the baby is born. If an arrhythmia is discovered before labor and delivery, you may require fetal heart-rate monitoring during pregnancy. When an arrhythmia is discovered during labor, you may need a pediatrician present when the baby is born.

OTHER INTERESTING FACTS ABOUT YOUR BABY

What determines whether I will have a boy or a girl?

The sex of the baby is determined at the time of fertilization. If a sperm carrying a Y chromosome fertilizes the egg, it results in a male child; a sperm carrying an X chromosome results in a female child. It's all determined by the father's sperm when it fertilizes the egg.

When I had my ultrasound last week, it looked like my baby had its mouth open. Is that possible?

Yes, it is. In addition to opening and closing its mouth, the fetus may also suck its thumb or finger.

I've heard a developing baby swallows amniotic fluid. Is that true?

By 21 weeks, the fetal digestive system has developed enough to allow the fetus to swallow amniotic fluid. The fetus absorbs much of the water in the swallowed fluid. Hydrochloric acid and adult digestive enzymes are present in small amounts in the fetal digestive system at 21 weeks.

Why does my baby swallow amniotic fluid?

Researchers believe swallowing amniotic fluid may help growth and development of the fetal digestive system. It may also condition the digestive system to function after birth.

How much fluid does my baby swallow?

By the time a baby is born, it may swallow large amounts of amniotic fluid, as much as 17 ounces (500ml) of amniotic fluid in a 24-hour period.

Does my baby open its eyes inside my uterus?

Eyelids cover the eyes and are fused or connected around 11 to 12 weeks. They remain fused until about 27 to 28 weeks, when they open.

A friend told me a baby can hear inside the womb. Is this true?

Yes. Life inside the womb may be like living near a busy freeway. The developing baby hears a constant background of digestive noises and the maternal heartbeat. The fetus also hears the mother-to-be's voice, although it may not hear higher-pitched tones.

Does my growing baby respond to sounds?

There is evidence that by the 3rd trimester, the fetus responds to sounds it hears. Researchers have noted fetal heart-rate increases in response to tones it hears through the mother's abdomen.

Will my baby know my voice after birth?

Studies show newborns prefer their mother's voice to a stranger's, which suggests they recognize her voice. They also prefer their mother's native language and respond strongly to a recording of an intrauterine heartbeat.

POTENTIAL PROBLEMS FOR THE DEVELOPING FETUS

An article I read said early pregnancy is the time the fetus is most susceptible to malformations. What does this mean, exactly?

The first 10 weeks of pregnancy (8 weeks of fetal development), called the *embryonic period*, is a time of extremely important development in the baby. The embryo is most susceptible during this time to factors that can interfere with its development. Most birth defects occur during this period.

What is the chance of my baby having a major birth defect?

Every pregnant couple worries about birth defects. The risk of a birth defect is very low, about 1 to 2%.

I was reading a book that mentioned teratology. What is that?

Teratology is the study of abnormal fetal development. When a birth defect occurs, we want to know why it happened. This can be frustrating because we are often unable to determine a cause. A substance that causes birth defects is called a *teratogen* or is said to be *teratogenic.* Some things may have a bad effect (be teratogenic) at one point in pregnancy, then be safe at others.

The most critical time of fetal development appears to be early in pregnancy, during the 1st trimester (first 13 weeks). An example is rubella (German measles). If the fetus is infected during the 1st trimester, abnormalities such as heart defects can occur. If infection happens later, problems are often less serious.

What is a neural-tube defect?

A neural-tube defect is an abnormality in the bone surrounding the spinal cord, in the brain stem or in the brain itself. One of the most common neural-tube defects is *spina bifida*—an absence of vertebral arches, which allows the spinal membrane to protrude. Another abnormality is *anencephaly*—the brain develops only a rudimentary brain stem and only traces of basal ganglia.

Do all medications I take affect my baby? I thought some were safe.

Medications can be grouped into three main groups—safe, unsafe and unsure. It's best to avoid any medication during pregnancy unless you discuss it with your doctor before you take it. Some medications, such as thyroid medication, are necessary and important during pregnancy.

It's easier and safer to discuss medication use with your doctor before you take a medicine. For a chart on how some medications can affect the developing fetus, see page 96.

I know some medications are more harmful than others. What are they?

The medications in the chart on page 96 are the most harmful, but other medications are also unsafe. If you take any of those listed below during your pregnancy, don't panic! Exposure alone does *not* mean absolute harm to the fetus. Effect on a developing fetus depends on when you took the medication, the amount you took and how long you took it. Talk to your doctor if you believe you took any of the medications listed below:

- angiotensin-converting enzyme (ACE) inhibitors
- aminopterin
- anticonvulsants
- benzodiazepines
- ethanol
- etretinate
- live vaccine
- methimazole
- penicillamine (not penicillin)
- ribavirin
- vitamin A (in excessively large doses)

I read about a baby born with cataracts. I thought that only happened to older people—is it possible?

Congenital (present-at-birth) cataracts rarely occur and are usually genetic. With cataracts, the lens of the eye is not transparent. Children whose mothers had German measles (rubella) around the 6th or 7th week of pregnancy may be born with cataracts.

We live in an area with lots of air pollution. Can my exposure to smog and bad air affect my baby?

This is rarely a problem and would be very hard to prove. Your lungs and airways filter the air you breathe, which protects your baby.

Premature Birth

I'm 25 weeks' pregnant. If my baby was born now, would it be OK?

It is hard to believe, but many babies born at 25 weeks survive. Some of the greatest advances in medicine have been in the care of premature babies. However, don't start wishing for delivery now; babies born this early are in the hospital a long time and often have serious problems.

Why is it risky for the baby to be born early?

Premature birth increases the risk of physical and mental impairment in the baby. It also increases the risk of fetal death.

How early is too early?

It depends on your particular situation. In many cases, 1 or 2 weeks is not going to make much difference in your baby—the baby may be only slightly smaller. However, the earlier the baby is born, the greater the risks.

I've heard that more premature babies are surviving today. Is that true?

Yes, it is. Because of advances in technology, today fewer than 10 deaths per 1,000 are reported in premature births.

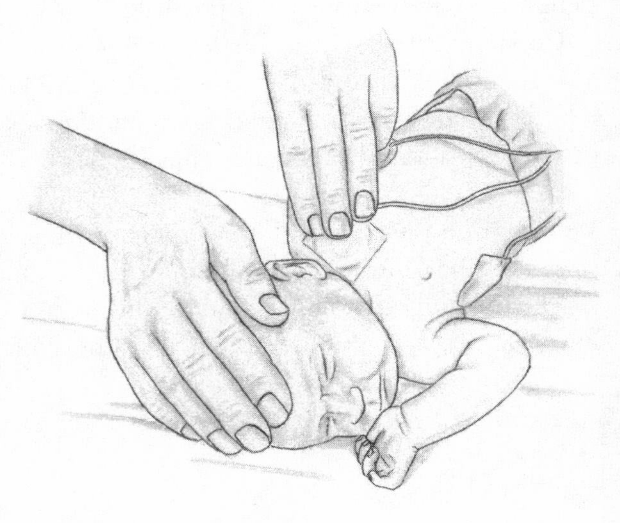

A baby born prematurely is usually very small and needs a great deal more hospital care than a full-term infant.

HELP PREVENT PREMATURE LABOR

We know that some activities may increase your risk of going into premature labor. Taking the following precautions may help reduce your risk of giving birth too early.

- Sit whenever you can. Standing may cause contractions as the body attempts to restore circulation to the uterine area.
- Don't lift and carry heavy objects. When you lift or carry something heavy, you cause abdominal muscles to tighten, which increases pressure on the uterus.
- Don't smoke. Research shows that women who smoke during pregnancy have a 20 to 50% higher risk of premature labor.
- Don't drink alcohol. Alcohol, even in small amounts, may harm the placenta.
- Gain enough weight. Underweight women who do not gain enough weight have a higher risk of having a baby born too early.
- Get enough rest. Resting, especially on your left side, improves circulation to your body and your baby.
- Don't exercise too strenuously. If you exercise too intensely or for too long, it can draw blood away from the uterus to your muscles.
- Don't stoop, bend or climb stairs when you can avoid it. These activities raise your blood pressure and draw blood away from your uterus. Or they can cause irritability of the uterus, resulting in contractions.
- Limit caffeine intake. You might increase your risk of premature labor if you drink 5 or more cups of coffee a day.
- Keep all prenatal appointments. Routine appointments with your doctor can help identify problems early so they are easier to treat.

Is it true that premature babies have long hospital stays?

The average hospital stay for a premature baby ranges from 50 to more than 100 days.

How are these premature babies affected?

In babies born extremely early, there is an increased rate of physical and mental handicaps, some of them severe. This is the reason your doctor attempts to prolong your pregnancy as long as possible.

Hydrocephalus

What is hydrocephalus?

Hydrocephalus is a problem that causes an enlargement of the head. It occurs in about 1 in 1,000 babies in the United States and is responsible for about 12% of all severe fetal malformations found at birth.

How does hydrocephalus happen?

The organization and development of the brain and central nervous system of the baby begin early. Spinal fluid circulates around the brain and spinal cord and must be able to flow without restriction. If openings are blocked and the flow of fluid is restricted, it can cause hydrocephalus (sometimes called *water on the brain*). The fluid accumulates and causes the baby's head to enlarge.

If my baby has hydrocephalus, can anything be done?

Hydrocephalus is a symptom and can have several causes, including spina bifida, meningomyelocele and omphalocele. Sometimes intrauterine therapy—while the fetus is still in the uterus—can be performed.

How is hydrocephalus treated in utero (before the baby is born)?

There are two ways of treating hydrocephalus inside the uterus. In one method, a needle is passed through the mother's abdomen into the affected area of the baby's brain to remove fluid. In the other method, a small plastic tube is placed into the area of fluid in the fetal brain. This tube is left in place to drain fluid continuously from the baby's brain.

The Presence of Meconium

A couple of friends of mine who've had babies were discussing meconium. What is it?

The term *meconium* refers to undigested debris from swallowed amniotic fluid in the fetal digestive system. It is a dark substance that your baby may pass from its bowels into amniotic fluid. This may happen before delivery, at the time of delivery or after the birth.

Is meconium important?

The presence of meconium can be important at the time of delivery. If a baby has a bowel movement and meconium is in the amniotic fluid, the infant may swallow the fluid before birth or at the time of birth. Meconium inhaled into the lungs may cause pneumonia or pneumonitis.

Is there any way to know about meconium ahead of time?

It is detected when your water breaks. Before this time, the only way to know about it is through amniocentesis.

If there is meconium present when I'm in labor, what can be done?

It is removed from the baby's mouth and throat after delivery with a small suction tube so the baby won't swallow it.

What causes meconium in the amniotic fluid?

It may be caused by fetal distress. Meconium doesn't always mean distress, but the possibility must be considered.

Intrauterine-Growth Restriction

A friend of mine was telling me her doctor was concerned about intrauterine-growth restriction. It sounds very serious; what is it?

Intrauterine-growth restriction (IUGR) means a newborn baby is small for its age. By medical definition, the baby's weight is below the 10th percentile for the baby's gestational age. This means that 9 out of 10 babies of the same gestational age are larger.

In the past, the term "retardation" was used instead of "restriction." Because retardation in this sense does not apply to the development or function of the baby's brain, the American College of Obstetricians and Gynecologists decided to change the term to reflect more accurately what happens to the baby. Today, *intrauterine-growth restriction* is the acceptable medical term.

Why is IUGR serious?

When the baby's weight is low, the risk of problems increases.

What causes intrauterine-growth restriction?

There are many conditions that increase the chance of IUGR:

- maternal anemia
- smoking during pregnancy
- poor weight gain during pregnancy
- vascular disease in the mother-to-be, including high blood pressure
- kidney disease in the mother-to-be
- alcoholism or drug abuse by the pregnant woman
- multiple fetuses
- infections in the fetus
- abnormalities in the umbilical cord or the placenta
- small size of mother-to-be (probably not a cause for alarm)

WAYS TO PREVENT A LOW BIRTHWEIGHT

To help avoid giving birth to a low-birthweight baby, consider the following.

- Gain enough weight during pregnancy. This may mean changing your body image and your eating habits.
- Quit smoking before pregnancy, and avoid secondhand smoke during pregnancy.
- Get prenatal care as soon as you discover you're pregnant. Keep all your prenatal appointments.
- Follow your doctor's suggestions and instructions during your pregnancy.
- If you're considering fertility treatment, understand the *risks* as well as the benefits of ART and multiple births.
- Ask your doctor about screening for lower-genital-tract infections early in pregnancy.
- Wait at least 18 months between delivery of one baby and conception of the next.

If a woman has one baby with IUGR, will her next baby be affected?

Research has shown that a previous delivery of a growth-restricted infant indicates it may happen in subsequent pregnancies.

How will my doctor know if my baby is too small?

Your doctor will usually find the problem by watching the growth of your uterus, using measurements of your uterus, weighing you and using ultrasound. If there is no change, IUGR is suspected. If you measure 10.8 inches (27.4cm) at 27 weeks of pregnancy and at 31 weeks, you measure only 11 inches (28cm), your doctor might become concerned about IUGR. This is one reason to keep all your prenatal appointments.

If IUGR is diagnosed, what can I do?

Your doctor will advise you to avoid anything that can make it worse. Stop smoking. Stop using drugs or alcohol. Eat nutritiously. You may need bed rest. This allows your baby to receive the best blood flow from you and thus the best nutrition.

What is the most serious risk to a baby with IUGR?

The greatest risk is stillbirth (death of the baby before delivery). To avoid this, it may be necessary to deliver the baby before full term.

If I have a baby with IUGR, will I have a C-section?

You may. Infants with IUGR may not tolerate labor well, so the possibility of a C-section increases due to fetal distress. The baby may be safer outside the uterus than inside, where there is a problem.

Umbilical-Cord Problems

My friend's baby had knots in his umbilical cord. What causes this?

We believe umbilical-cord knots form as the baby moves around early in pregnancy. A loop forms in the umbilical cord; when the baby moves through the loop, a knot forms.

I've heard that the baby can get tangled up in the umbilical cord. Is this true?

In some cases this is true, but it usually isn't a problem. There is nothing you can do to prevent this from happening.

Could a tangled cord hurt my baby?

It isn't necessarily a problem. It only becomes a problem if the cord is stretched tightly around the neck or another part of the body, or in a tight knot.

Is there anything I can do to keep my baby from getting a knot in its umbilical cord?

No, there is nothing you can do to prevent it. Be reassured that these knots do not occur often.

9

Changes in You

You won't notice a great deal of change in your body until the second half of your pregnancy. You may experience fatigue or morning sickness at the beginning of pregnancy, but these both usually disappear by the end of the 1st trimester (13 weeks). You will begin to gain more weight in the last trimester. Slowly you will see your abdomen grow larger. Your breasts will get bigger, you may add some weight to your hips and thighs, and you may experience some swelling in hands and feet. These changes are normal in pregnancy. We hope that by knowing about them, and other changes you may experience, you will be more comfortable with what happens to you.

It may be a while before you realize you're pregnant! You shouldn't gain much weight during the 1st trimester—probably no more than 5 pounds (2.25kg) for the first few months. Your abdomen will grow a little, but even though you want to, you won't feel the baby move during this time.

By about the 4th month, you'll begin showing; people will be able to tell you're pregnant. One of the most exciting things in your pregnancy will happen soon—you'll begin to feel your baby move!

During the last part of your pregnancy, you will notice many changes. Your baby will be growing quite a bit and gaining a great deal of weight during this time.

HOW YOUR BODY CHANGES EACH TRIMESTER

What changes will I see during the 1st trimester?

You will see very little change in yourself, although your baby is growing and changing quite rapidly. You may not even realize you are pregnant until the middle or close to the end of this trimester! You will experience very little weight gain during this time—probably no more than 5 pounds (2.25kg) for the entire 13 weeks. Your abdomen will grow a little—you may be able to feel your uterus about 3 inches (7.6cm) below your bellybutton. You won't feel the fetus move during this time.

What changes will I see during the 2nd trimester?

Others will be able to tell you are pregnant during this trimester. You will be able to feel your uterus about 3 inches (7.6cm) below your bellybutton at the beginning of this trimester. By the end of this trimester, you will feel your uterus about 3 inches (7.6cm) above your bellybutton.

Average weight gain for the 2nd trimester is a total (including weight from the 1st trimester) of 17 to 24 pounds (7.65 to 10.8kg). You will also begin to feel your baby move during this time.

What changes will I see during the 3rd trimester?

You will experience a great deal of change because your baby is growing so much. You will be able to feel your uterus about 3 inches (7.6cm) above your bellybutton at the beginning of this trimester. By delivery, your uterus is 6-1/2 to 8 inches (16.5 to 20.3cm) above your bellybutton.

Your baby gains a lot of weight during this time, even though you may not. Total weight gain by delivery is 25 to 35 pounds (11.25 to 15.75kg) for the average woman.

What can I do about the changes I go through during pregnancy?

The most important thing you can do for yourself is to get good prenatal care. Keep all your prenatal appointments and establish good communication with your doctor. Follow his or her recommendations about nutrition, medication and exercise. Ask any questions you have, and discuss any situation you are concerned about.

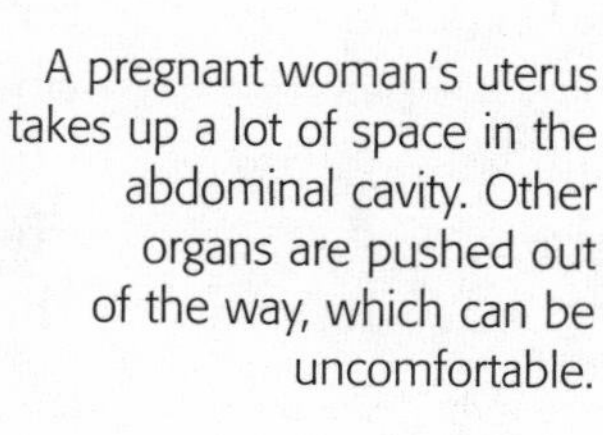

A pregnant woman's uterus takes up a lot of space in the abdominal cavity. Other organs are pushed out of the way, which can be uncomfortable.

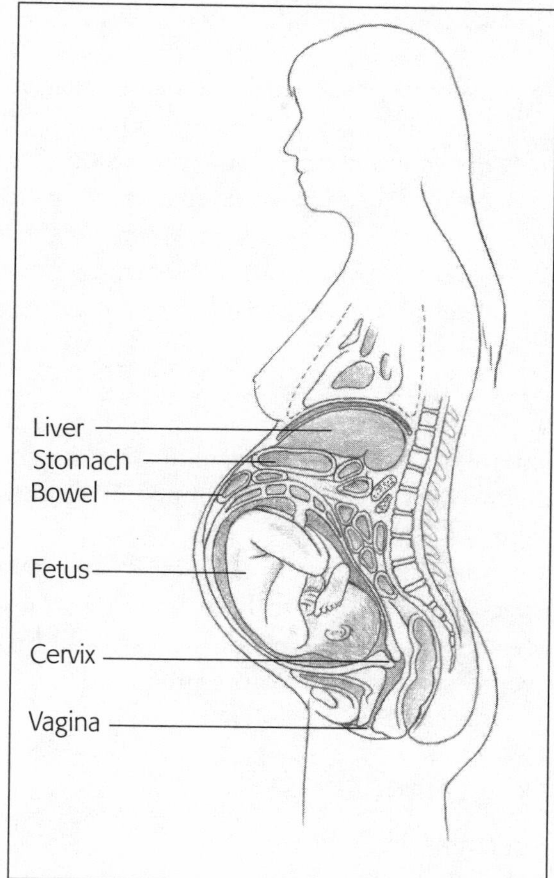

My cousin said that with her second and third pregnancies, her body started to change much earlier than with her first pregnancy. Why?

The way a woman's body responds to pregnancy is influenced by her previous pregnancies. Skin and muscles stretch to accommodate the enlarged uterus, placenta and baby. Stretched muscles and stretched skin are never exactly the same again. They may give way faster to accommodate the growing uterus and baby with subsequent pregnancies, which causes a woman to show sooner and to feel bigger.

I'm 11 weeks' pregnant, but I don't even show yet. Should I be concerned?

No. A lot has been happening with the development of your baby's organs and organ systems. However, friends are probably not

Everyone tells me I'm too big. What's wrong?

Before you become overly concerned, discuss it with your doctor. Friends may tell you that you are too big or too small; probably nothing is wrong. Women and babies are different sizes and grow at different rates. The continual change and continual growth of the fetus are most important.

yet able to tell you're pregnant. You may be able to feel your uterus down by your pubic bone or your clothes may be getting a little snug.

If this is your first pregnancy, it often takes longer to see a change in your tummy. If you have had other pregnancies, you will probably show sooner. Don't despair—you'll be getting larger soon, then everyone will know you're pregnant!

SKIN CHANGES

Stretch Marks

What are stretch marks?

Stretch marks, also called *striae distensae,* are areas of stretched skin that may be discolored. They usually occur on the abdomen as

Is there anything I can do to avoid getting stretch marks?

No one has found a reliable way of avoiding stretch marks. Women have tried many kinds of lotions with little success. There is no harm in trying lotion products, but they probably won't help much.

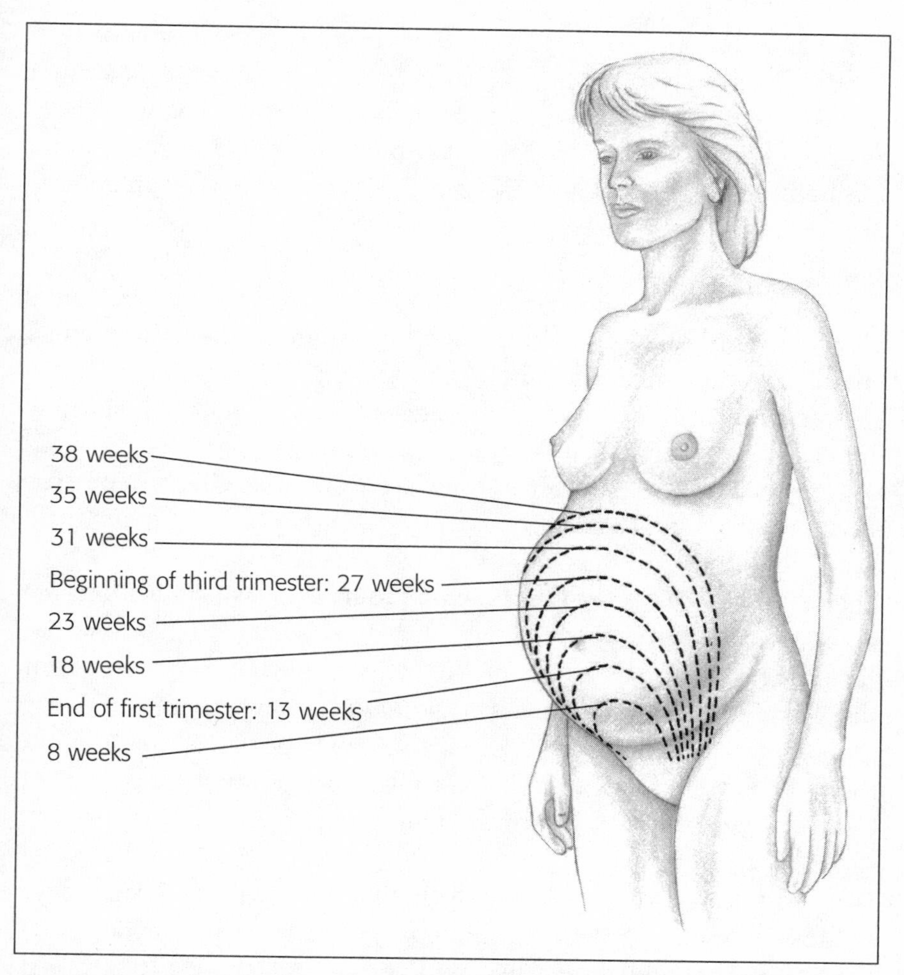

This illustration shows how a woman's uterus grows during pregnancy. The dotted lines represent growth from about 8 weeks through the end of the 3rd trimester (about 38 weeks).

your growing uterus stretches the skin. They can also occur on the breasts, hips or buttocks.

Will my stretch marks go away after my pregnancy?

Stretch marks usually fade and won't be as noticeable after your pregnancy, but they won't go away completely. Some new treatments seem to help a lot. Retin-A or Renova in combination with glycolic acid is fairly effective. You need a prescription for Retin-A and

Renova, but you can get glycolic acid from your dermatologist. Cellex-C, with glycolic acid, also improves the appearance of stretch marks. The most effective treatment, but the most costly, is laser treatment. This is often done in combination with the medication methods described above. These treatments are done *after* pregnancy.

Other Skin Changes

I have a mole that seems to be getting larger. Is this something I should be concerned about?

Pregnancy can cause many changes in your skin. Moles may appear for the first time, or existing moles may grow larger and darken during pregnancy. If you have a mole that changes, be sure to have your doctor check it.

I have little pieces of skin that seemed to have grown since I became pregnant. What are they?

Skin tags are small lumps or bumps of skin that may appear for the first time during pregnancy. If you already have them, they may grow larger while you are pregnant. Don't worry too much about them. If they are in an area that is rubbed frequently, you may want to talk to your doctor about removing them.

I've had flareups of pimples lately. Is this related to my pregnancy?

Most women experience some changes in their skin while pregnant. Some women find their skin breaks out more often. Some lucky women find their skin becomes less oily and softer. These changes are due to the hormones of pregnancy; your skin will probably return to normal after your baby is born.

My dermatologist just told me I have a couple of precancerous spots on my face. I've had them before and usually get them removed. Can I do this during pregnancy, or should I wait until after the baby is born?

Yes, you can have these spots removed. This is usually done in the doctor's office and is not a problem.

A dark vertical line has appeared on my abdomen. What is it?

It is called the *linea nigra* and appears on many women during pregnancy.

Will this line disappear after pregnancy?

It often fades markedly after pregnancy, but it may never fully disappear.

I've got brown patches on my face that I never had before. What are they?

These patches are called *chloasma* or *mask of pregnancy* and are believed to be caused by the hormonal changes brought about during pregnancy. Usually these dark patches disappear completely or get lighter after your baby is born. (Oral contraceptives often cause similar pigmentation changes.)

My sister-in-law had red palms all during her pregnancy. Is this common?

The condition you're referring to is palmar erythema; it is not uncommon. It occurs in 65% of pregnant white women and 35% of pregnant black women. It is probably caused by increased estrogen in the system and usually doesn't cause any problems. It's OK to use lotions, but the redness of your palms may not disappear until after you deliver.

Since I got pregnant, I've noticed some small red elevations on the skin of my neck and upper chest. What causes this?

During pregnancy, you may experience vascular changes in your skin. These small red elevations, with branches extending outward, are called *vascular spiders, telangiectasias* or *angiomas.* They usually occur on the face, neck, upper chest and arms, and disappear after delivery.

Do vascular spiders and red palms occur together?

Yes, they often occur together. Symptoms are temporary and disappear shortly after delivery.

I've noticed since I've been pregnant that my skin feels itchy, and I scratch a lot. Does this indicate a problem?

Itching, also called *pruritis gravidarum,* is a common symptom during pregnancy. It usually occurs later in pregnancy, and about 20% of all pregnant women suffer from it. Itching does not indicate any problem in your pregnancy.

The skin over my abdomen itches the worst. What causes this?

As your uterus grows and fills your pelvis, abdominal skin and muscles must stretch to accommodate it. Stretching of the skin causes abdominal itching in many women.

What can I do about this itching?

If you scratch the skin, it can make it worse, so try not to scratch. There are lotions available to help reduce the itching. You may be able to use cortisone creams occasionally. Ask your doctor about relief.

VARICOSE VEINS

My mother had varicose veins during her pregnancies. Will I?

Varicose veins, also called *varicosities* or *varices,* occur to some degree in most pregnant women. If your mother had varicose veins, you have a greater chance of having them.

What causes varicose veins?

Varicose veins are dilated blood vessels that fill with blood. They usually occur in the legs but also in the birth canal and in the vulva. They may appear as hemorrhoids. Pressure from the uterus and change in blood flow make varices worse.

What do varicose veins look like?

Symptoms vary. For some women, varicose veins are only a blemish or purple-blue spot on the legs. They cause little or no discomfort, except in the evening. For other women, varices are bulging veins that require elevation of the legs at the end of the day and compression stockings during the day; they can be very uncomfortable.

Will varicose veins get worse during pregnancy?

They may. In most cases, they become more noticeable and more painful as pregnancy progresses. Increasing weight (from your growing baby), clothing that constricts at the waist or legs, and standing a great deal cause them to worsen.

If I have varicose veins, what can I do?

Many women wear medical maternity support hose; there are various types available. Also try the following:

- Clothes that don't restrict circulation at the knee or groin may help.
- Spend as little time as possible on your feet.
- Elevate your feet above the level of your heart, or lie on your side when possible to allow drainage of the veins.
- Wear flat shoes.
- Don't cross your legs when you sit down.
- If you continue to have problems after your pregnancy, you may need surgery.

PREVENT VARICOSE VEINS

There are several things you can do to help prevent varicose veins. Some of these suggestions work well to relieve varices if you already have them.

- Exercise.
- Don't cross your legs at the knee.
- Don't stand for long periods of time.
- If you must stand, bounce gently on the balls of your feet every few minutes.
- Lie on your side several times a day (left side is best).
- Keep your total pregnancy weight gain in the normal range—from 25 to 35 pounds (11.25 to 15.75kg) for a normal-weight woman.

Friends who have varicose veins say wearing medical maternity support hose works great, but they are almost impossible to get on. Do you have any suggestions?

Medical maternity support hose, also called *compression hose,* are not the everyday support hose you buy at the store. They are fitted for you by a specialist. There are a couple of tricks that can help you get them on more easily. First, turn stockings inside out. Starting at the toe, unroll the stockings up your legs. Second, put your support hose on before you get out of bed in the morning—your legs may tend to swell as soon as you get up.

EMOTIONAL CHANGES

Now that I'm pregnant, I'm not as excited as I thought I'd be. Is this normal?

If you aren't immediately thrilled about pregnancy, don't feel alone. A common feeling and response to pregnancy is to question your condition. Some of this may be because you're not sure of what lies ahead.

When will I begin to think of the fetus as my baby?

This is different for everyone. Some women begin to feel this way as soon as they know they are pregnant. For others, it occurs when they hear their baby's heartbeat, around 12 or 13 weeks, or when they first feel their baby move, between 16 and 20 weeks.

I seem to cry at the least little thing. Why does this happen?

Crying easily, mood swings, energy lows and fatigue are all normal aspects of pregnancy. During the 1st trimester of pregnancy, hormones increase to support the pregnancy. Some women are more sensitive to these changes, especially those who are sensitive to a similar hormonal shift before menstruation. If you become weepy or edgy around your menstrual period, you may experience similar emotions as your body adjusts to pregnancy.

Will these emotional swings continue during my pregnancy?

They continue to some degree throughout pregnancy. These swings are caused by the changing hormones in your body. Explain to your partner and other family members that you may experience these swings.

I am experiencing conflicting feelings about my pregnancy. Is this normal?

It is very normal. Your feelings arise from your adjustment to your pregnancy—you are taking the first steps toward an incredible role change that will involve many aspects of your life. Your feelings of conflict come from your attempts to deal with all the questions and concerns you have.

I've been very depressed during my pregnancy. Should I ask my doctor for an antidepressant?

Antidepressant medication is not usually prescribed during pregnancy. However, if it is necessary, there are medications considered safe; familiar ones include Prozac and Zoloft. Treatment must be done on an individualized basis. Your doctor and possibly a psychiatrist or psychologist will discuss the situation with you.

I'm in my 3rd trimester and I'm more emotional than ever. Is there anything wrong with me?

No, you're normal. You may be getting a little anxious about the upcoming labor and delivery. You may find mood swings occur more frequently, and you may be more irritable. Relax and don't focus on your feelings. Talk to your partner about how you're feeling and what you're experiencing.

SOME PREGNANCY CONCERNS

I have terrible morning sickness. When will it end?

By the end of the 1st trimester, most women experience an improvement in morning sickness. For more information on morning sickness, see pages 29–32.

Is it unusual to experience pain in the uterus during pregnancy?

As your uterus grows during pregnancy, you may feel slight cramping or even pain in your lower abdominal area on your sides. Your uterus tightens or contracts throughout your pregnancy. If you don't feel this, don't worry. However, if contractions are accompanied by bleeding from the vagina, call your doctor immediately!

A friend mentioned Braxton-Hicks contractions. What are they?

They are painless, nonrhythmical contractions you may feel when you place your hands on your abdomen. You may also feel them in the uterus itself. These contractions may begin early in your pregnancy and are felt at irregular intervals. They are not signs of true labor.

I have a weird feeling in my pelvic area—sort of a "pins and needles" feeling. Is there something wrong?

Not usually. This is another feeling associated with increased pressure as the baby moves lower in the birth canal. Tingling, pressure and numbness are common at this time.

Can I do anything to alleviate any of this pressure?

Lie on your side to help decrease pressure in your pelvis and on the nerves, veins and arteries in your pelvic area.

Round-Ligament Pain

When I move or get up, it hurts on the lower part of my sides. Should I worry?

What you are describing is usually called *round-ligament pain.* There are ligaments on either side of the uterus; as your uterus gets bigger, these ligaments stretch and get longer and thicker. Quick movements can stretch the ligaments, and that hurts. This is not harmful to you or your baby, but it can be uncomfortable.

What can I do for round-ligament pain?

Be careful about quick movements. If you experience discomfort, you may feel better if you lie down and rest. Most doctors recommend shifting or changing your position, or taking acetaminophen (Tylenol) if the pain still bothers you. Tell your doctor if it gets worse.

Sciatic-Nerve Pain

What is sciatic-nerve pain?

Sciatic-nerve pain is an occasional excruciating pain in your buttocks and down the back or the side of your leg. You may experience it as your pregnancy progresses. The sciatic nerve runs behind the uterus in the pelvis to your legs. We believe pain is caused by pressure on the nerve from the growing uterus.

What can I do about sciatic-nerve pain?

The best remedy is to lie on your opposite side. It helps relieve pressure on the nerve. Don't do any heavy lifting. If you have to stand for any length of time, rest the toes of one foot on some object that is 3 to 4 inches off the ground, such as a thick book (the phone book or a dictionary works great!) to relieve pressure on the sciatic nerve. Heat (or cold) may help. Mild pain relievers, such as acetaminophen, are also OK.

Backaches

I've heard that backaches are a normal part of pregnancy. What causes them?

Nearly every woman experiences backache at some time during pregnancy. It usually occurs as you get bigger. You may also experience backache after walking, bending, lifting, standing or excessive exercise. Be careful about lifting and bending. Do it correctly: Squat and lift with your legs.

How do I take care of problems with my back?

You can treat backache with heat, rest and analgesics, such as acetaminophen (Tylenol). Special maternity girdles can provide some support. Keep your weight under control, and participate in mild exercise, such as swimming, walking or stationary-bike riding. Lie on your side when resting or sleeping.

Should I be concerned about lower-back pain?

Lower-back pain is common during pregnancy, but it could be an indication of a more serious problem, such as pyelonephritis or a kidney stone. If pain becomes constant or more severe, call your doctor.

WAYS TO AVOID BACKACHES

If you experience backaches, try the following suggestions to help prevent them.

- Exercise to strengthen stomach, arm and thigh muscles.
- Do your Kegel exercises (ask your doctor for more information).
- Stand correctly—tuck your pelvis under and hold your shoulders back.
- Lift correctly—place feet shoulder-width apart, under your buttocks. Bend at the knees; lift with arms and legs, *not* your back!
- Get up and move around often. Don't stand or sit in the same place for a long time.
- Stretch muscles to keep them limber.
- Be sure your mattress supports you correctly.
- Sleep on your left side with a pillow between your knees to align legs. Many pillows on the market are designed especially for this purpose.
- Get out of bed slowly, swinging both legs to the floor and pushing up with your arms. Don't twist.
- Take a warm (*not* hot) bath.
- Get a massage.

Swelling

Will my hands and feet swell during my pregnancy?

Swelling during pregnancy is caused by your body producing as much as 50% more blood and fluids to meet your baby's needs.

Some of this extra fluid leaks into your body tissues. When your enlarging uterus pushes on pelvic veins, it partially blocks blood flow in the lower part of your body. This pushes fluid into your legs and feet, causing swelling.

If your hands swell and it's uncomfortable to wear your rings, put them on a pretty chain and wear them around your neck, or put them on a bracelet.

My feet are huge—I can't wear any of my shoes. What can I do?

Some swelling in your feet is normal during pregnancy. Wear sneakers, flats or shoes with low heels (no higher than 2 inches). If swelling becomes extreme, especially during the last trimester, consult your doctor; it could be a sign of problems. Rest lying down on your side as frequently as possible. A woman's feet may increase half a shoe size during pregnancy, so you may need to buy larger shoes.

I've heard that lying on my side in the 3rd trimester will help with swelling. Is this true?

Yes, it is. By the 3rd trimester, your uterus is quite large and puts a lot of pressure on your blood vessels, which blocks their flow. Lying or sleeping or your side during the 3rd trimester helps relieve this pressure.

Urinary Concerns

I just found out I'm 9 weeks' pregnant, and I have to go to the bathroom all the time. Does this last all through pregnancy?

One of the first symptoms of early pregnancy is frequent urination. This problem continues off and on throughout pregnancy; you may have to get up to go to the bathroom at night when you never did before. It usually lessens during the 2nd trimester, then returns during the 3rd trimester, when the growing baby puts pressure on the bladder.

My friend, who is also pregnant, told me she has a urinary-tract infection. She said it's common in pregnancy. Is it?

It is more common to get urinary-tract infections during pregnancy. They are also called *bladder infections, cystitis* and *UTIs*.

How will I know if I have a urinary-tract infection?

Symptoms include painful urination, a burning during urination, the feeling of urgency to urinate, blood in the urine and frequent urination.

Can a urinary-tract infection harm my baby?

It may be a cause of premature labor and low-birthweight infants. If you think you have an infection, call your doctor. If you do have an infection, take the entire prescription of antibiotics prescribed for you.

WAYS TO PREVENT A URINARY-TRACT INFECTION

- Don't hold your urine.
- Empty your bladder as soon as you feel you need to.
- Drink plenty of fluids.
- Cranberry juice helps acidify your urine (kills bacteria) and may help you avoid infections.
- For some women, it helps to urinate after having intercourse.

Vaginal Discharge

Ever since I got pregnant, I've noticed I have more vaginal discharge. Is this a sign of a problem?

No, it's normal to have an increase in vaginal discharge or vaginal secretion during pregnancy. It is called *leukorrhea*. The discharge is usually white or yellow and fairly thick. It is unlikely to be an infection if it is not irritating.

What causes the increase in vaginal secretions?

We believe it is caused by the increased blood flow to the skin and muscles around the vagina, which also causes Chadwick's sign in early pregnancy. This symptom is visible to your doctor as a violet or blue coloration of your vagina when he or she does a pelvic exam.

How do I treat this vaginal discharge?

Do *not* douche if you have a heavy vaginal discharge during pregnancy. Wear sanitary pads for protection. Avoid wearing pantyhose and nylon underwear—choose cotton underwear or underwear with a cotton crotch.

How will I know if the vaginal discharge is caused by an infection?

The discharge that accompanies a vaginal infection is often foul smelling, is green or yellow, and causes itching or irritation around or inside the vagina. If you have any of these symptoms, notify your doctor. Many creams and ointments are safe to use during pregnancy to treat this problem.

Constipation

I've never had problems with constipation before. Why do I have it now?

It is common during pregnancy for bowel habits to change. Most women notice an increase in constipation, often accompanied by irregular bowel habits and an increased occurrence of hemorrhoids. These problems are usually the result of a slowdown in the movement of food through the gastrointestinal system and iron supplements or iron in prenatal vitamins.

What can I do to relieve constipation?

Increase your fluid intake, and exercise 3 to 4 times a week. Many doctors suggest prune or apple juice or a mild laxative, such as milk of magnesia. Eat foods that are high in fiber, such as bran and prunes; they increase the bulk in your diet and may help relieve constipation.

Can I take laxatives to relieve the constipation?

Do not use laxatives, other than those mentioned above, without consulting your doctor. If your constipation is a continuing problem, discuss it at a prenatal visit.

FEELING YOUR BABY MOVE

My friend was talking about quickening. What is it?

Quickening is feeling your baby move. It usually occurs between 16 and 20 weeks of pregnancy.

I'm 15 weeks' pregnant and felt my baby move already. Is there something wrong?

The first time a woman feels her baby move is different for every woman. It can also be different from one pregnancy to another. One baby may be more active than another, so you feel movement sooner.

I thought I felt my baby move when I was 11 weeks' pregnant, but my doctor said it probably was gas. How will I know that what I feel is my baby moving?

Many women describe the first feelings of movement from their baby as a gas bubble or fluttering in their abdomen. It may be something you notice for a few days before you realize what it is. Movements will be more common and occur fairly frequently—that's how you'll know that what you're feeling is your baby moving. The movement will be below your bellybutton. If it's your first baby, it may be 19 or 20 weeks before you are sure you feel movement.

I'm in the early part of my second trimester, and I haven't felt my baby move yet. Is that OK?

Yes, it's all right. The normal time to feel movement is between 16 and 20 weeks.

Taking care of yourself is important during pregnancy. Get enough rest, eat healthful meals and exercise. Plan some quiet time for yourself every day.

I just felt my baby move for the first time last week but haven't felt it for a couple of days. What's wrong?

Probably nothing. It is normal not to feel it every day at first. As your baby grows, movements become stronger and more regular.

A pregnant friend complains that her baby moves all the time. My baby doesn't move that much. Should I be worried?

This is a hard question to answer. Your sensation of your baby moving is different from your friend's, and the movement of every baby is different. It isn't unusual for one baby to move less than another. If your baby has been very active, then is very quiet for a while, you may want to discuss it with your doctor, who will determine if there is any concern.

My baby is extremely active during the night, and it keeps me awake. Is there anything I can do about it?

There really isn't much you can do about this. Try changing your position in bed. Avoid exercising just before bed—it may cause your baby to move more. If these tips don't work, you may have to be patient and just endure it until your baby is born.

My baby kicks a lot, and it hurts. Is there anything I can do to make it stop?

Try changing your position, or lie on your side. It still may be uncomfortable. Taking acetaminophen or relaxing in a warm (not hot) bath may also help.

I get a sort of pain under my ribs sometimes when my baby is active. Can I do anything about it?

Try lying on your opposite side. For example, if you feel pressure under your right ribs, lie on your left side.

A friend of mine is 26 weeks' pregnant. Her doctor wants her to keep track of her baby's movements. Why?

A doctor may have a mother-to-be monitor her baby's movements around this time if she has had a difficult pregnancy, if she had a previous stillbirth or if she has a medical condition, such as diabetes. Recording movements at certain times each day may provide the doctor with additional information about the status of the fetus. Between 20 and 32 weeks of pregnancy, the fetus can move between 200 and 500 times a day, including kicking, rolling or wiggling.

My doctor said my baby is floating. What did he mean?

This means the baby can be felt at the beginning of the birth canal, but it has not dropped into the birth canal. That is, the baby is not engaged (fixed) in the birth canal at this time. The baby may even move away from your doctor's fingers when you are examined.

I feel as though my baby is going to fall out. This can't happen, can it?

No, it can't. What you are probably experiencing is the pressure of your baby as it moves lower in the birth canal. Bring it to your doctor's attention. He or she may want to do a pelvic exam to check how low the baby's head is.

TAKING CARE OF YOUR TEETH

I've always heard that a woman should avoid any dental treatment when she is pregnant. Is this true?

No! You should have regular dental checkups during your pregnancy. They are very important to your overall health. Recent research has shown that women with gum disease are 7 times more likely to deliver a premature baby. Take care of any tooth or gum problems you may experience during pregnancy.

My gums bleed more now that I'm pregnant. Should I be concerned?

Hormonal changes of pregnancy can cause sore, bleeding, swollen gums. Your gums are more susceptible to irritation and may bleed more often when you floss or brush your teeth.

Will my gums get better after pregnancy?

Yes. The condition usually clears up after the baby is born. Talk to your dentist if the problem becomes too uncomfortable.

Should I tell my dentist I'm pregnant?

Yes. If you need any dental treatment, advise your dentist you are pregnant before he or she does anything. Some dental anesthetics might harm your baby. In most cases, a pregnant woman should not have a general anesthetic.

I have a small nodule on my gum that bleeds when I brush it. What is it?

This is called a *pyogenic granuloma* or *pregnancy tumor* and may bleed when you brush your teeth or eat. This condition usually clears up after pregnancy, but don't ignore it if it causes you problems.

I was scheduled to have cosmetic bonding done to my teeth, then I found out I was pregnant. Should I cancel my appointment?

Wait until after the baby is born to have any elective dental procedure. However, if you have a dental trauma, such as an abscess or a broken tooth, take care of it immediately!

GOOD DENTAL CARE DURING PREGNANCY

- Brush your teeth after every meal.
- Floss at least once a day.
- Have at least one checkup and dental cleaning during pregnancy, preferably after the 1st trimester.
- Watch your diet. Eat foods rich in vitamin C (good for gums) and calcium (to keep teeth healthy).
- If you have morning sickness, brush or rinse teeth thoroughly after vomiting.

I usually have X-rays at my dental checkups. Should I have them now?

Tell your dentist you're pregnant *before* you begin your exam. In most cases, avoid dental X-rays. If there is a particular need for them, discuss the problem with your dentist and your doctor before proceeding any further. If you must have an X-ray, shield your abdomen with a lead apron.

I had a root canal last year and had to take antibiotics before the procedure. If I have the same kind of problem while I'm pregnant, should I take antibiotics?

You must discuss this situation with your dentist and your doctor. They will be able to decide the best course of action. Taking care of this kind of problem is important—an infection in you might harm your baby. Together, your dentist and doctor will plan the safest course of treatment for you and your baby.

BREAST CHANGES

I'm 13 weeks' pregnant, and my breasts are getting bigger. Isn't this a little early?

Many changes occur in your breasts during pregnancy. After about 8 weeks, it's normal for your breasts to start getting larger. You may even notice they are lumpy or nodular. These are all normal changes in pregnancy.

I've heard that a woman gains a lot of weight in her breasts during pregnancy. Is that true?

Most women gain between 1 and 1-1/2 pounds in each breast.

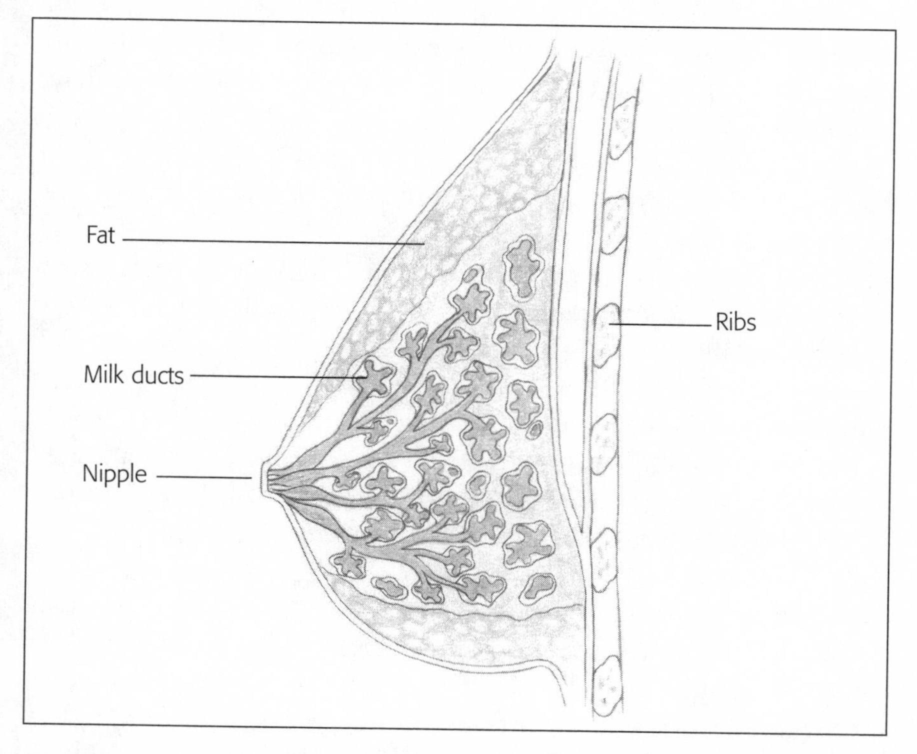

A pregnant woman's breasts change a lot during pregnancy. One of the greatest changes is the increase in the number of milk ducts, which prepares the breast for nursing.

My breasts are very tender and sore. Is this normal?

Tenderness, tingling or soreness of your breasts early in pregnancy is common.

The area around my nipples is getting darker. Should I be concerned?

No, this is normal. The nipple is surrounded by the *areola*. Before pregnancy the areola is usually pink but turns brown or red-brown and may get larger during pregnancy and lactation (when you produce milk).

I've noticed some fluid coming from my breasts, staining my clothes. I'm only about halfway through my pregnancy. Is this breast milk already?

No, it isn't. During the 2nd trimester, a thin yellow fluid called *colostrum* is formed; it is the precursor to breast milk. Sometimes it will leak from the breasts or can be expressed by squeezing the nipples. Don't try to express the fluid. Wear breast pads if you have problems with leakage.

I've heard about inverted nipples but don't know what they are. Can you tell me more about them?

Inverted nipples are flat or retract (invert) into the breast. Women with inverted nipples may find it more difficult to breastfeed. Talk to your doctor about it.

How can I tell if I have inverted nipples?

Place your thumb and index finger on the areola, the dark area surrounding the nipple. Gently compress the base of the nipple. If it flattens or retracts into the breast, you have inverted nipples.

Can I do anything about inverted nipples?

Yes. Breast shields can help prepare your breasts for nursing. You can wear them during the last few weeks of pregnancy. You wear these plastic shells under your bra to create a slight pressure at the base of the nipple. This pressure helps draw the nipple out, making it easier for you to breastfeed your baby.

OTHER CHANGES

I've noticed that my hair has been growing faster and feels thicker now that I'm pregnant. Is this common?

Changes in your hair are often triggered by pregnancy hormones. You may also notice less hair loss than usual. Unfortunately, after your baby is born, the hair you have retained during pregnancy is lost. Don't worry if it happens to you—you're not going bald!

My nails, which have always been soft and hard to grow, are now long and grow very fast. Will they always be like this?

The same hormones that cause your hair to grow also influence your nails. You may have problems keeping your nails filed to a practical length! Enjoy them while you're pregnant.

I seem to be getting more facial hair now that I'm pregnant. Why?

Usually it's not a problem, but check with your doctor if it worries you. Facial hair will probably disappear or decrease after pregnancy, so wait before making any decisions about permanent hair removal.

I feel hot all the time since I've been pregnant. Why do I feel this way?

During pregnancy, your metabolism increases; your body uses more energy when you're pregnant. This may cause you to feel overheated.

I've been perspiring so much during my pregnancy. Why?

Pregnancy hormones elevate your body temperature, which may lead to greater perspiration. Use absorbent powder to keep dry because excess moisture can result in a heat rash. Don't get overheated, and wear layers of clothing to peel off if you have to. If you perspire heavily, keep up your fluid intake to avoid dehydration.

When I'm lying down and look at my stomach, there's a bulge there I didn't have before (not the baby). Is this the sign of a problem?

Abdominal muscles are stretched and pushed apart as your baby grows. Muscles that are attached to the lower portion of your ribs may separate in the midline, which is called a *diastasis recti*. It isn't painful, and it does not harm the baby.

Will this go away after pregnancy?

It may still be present after the birth of your baby, but the separation won't be as noticeable. Exercising can strengthen the muscles, but you may still have a small bulge or gap.

Every time I go to the doctor, my stomach is measured with a tape measure. Why?

As you progress in your pregnancy, your doctor needs a point of reference to measure how much your uterus is growing. Some measure from the bellybutton to the top of the uterus. Others measure from the pubis symphysis, the place where pubic bones meet in the middle-lower part of your abdomen, to the top of the uterus.

What do these measurements reveal?

These measurements can reveal a great deal. If at 20 weeks, you measure 11.2 inches (28cm), your doctor may be concerned about the possibility of twins or an incorrect due date. If you measure 6 inches (15cm) at this point, your due date may be wrong or there may be a concern about intrauterine-growth restriction or some other problem. If there is a question, your doctor may have you further evaluated by ultrasound.

I'm due in a couple of weeks, and I've noticed a change in the shape of my abdomen—it seems lower. Should I be concerned?

Often a few weeks before labor begins or at the beginning of labor, the head of your baby begins to enter the birth canal, and your uterus seems to drop a bit. This is called *lightening*. Don't be concerned if this occurs.

A friend told me that when her baby dropped, she felt better. Why?

One benefit is an increase in space in your upper abdomen, which gives you more room to breathe. However, as your baby descends, you may notice more pressure in your pelvis, bladder and rectum, which may make you uncomfortable.

Someone told me that my center of gravity changes during pregnancy. How does this affect me?

When your uterus grows, it grows out in front of you, and your center of gravity moves forward over your legs. Joints are also looser, and it may feel as if they are slipping. These changes may affect your posture and cause backaches.

I'm 19 weeks' pregnant and have gained only 4 pounds (1.8kg). Should I be concerned?

Weight gain can vary a great deal. If you were sick a lot or had nausea during the first few months, you may have lost weight at first and may be a little behind in gaining weight. If you were overweight before you got pregnant, you may not have gained as much. At this point, you should be gaining weight regularly. Discuss it with your doctor if you are concerned.

10

Your Partner and Your Pregnancy

Usually pregnancy involves three people—you, your growing baby and your partner. Your partner's support during pregnancy can be important to you. At times you may be emotional; having someone to discuss your concerns with can be reassuring. And it's wonderful to share your happiness during this time of change. Together, you can dream and plan for your future as a family.

Your pregnancy may cause some nervousness or anxiety in your partner. It's probably important to your partner to be able to share his feelings and concerns with you, too. Be supportive of him; encourage him to share his thoughts and ideas with you. It may help him feel part of your pregnancy.

Encourage him to go to your prenatal appointments with you. It will give him the opportunity to ask questions that are important to him. Often a man will ask whether it is safe to have sex during pregnancy. In a normal pregnancy, this isn't usually a problem. As we all know, sexual intimacy is a wonderful way to express our love for each other. In most cases, pregnancy doesn't mean this form of closeness has to stop. In some situations, you will need to be cautious. We suggest the two of you discuss this matter with your doctor, who knows your pregnancy situation.

Your pregnancy is the beginning of big changes in your life. After the birth of your baby, you will be a family, with a future to look forward to. You will have many wonderful times to share, and maybe hard times to weather. Knowing you can count on one another helps when everything seems overwhelming. Establishing communication and caring for each other during this time can strengthen the bonds of your relationship and will help you in your future together.

How much should my partner be involved in my pregnancy?

Your partner can be an important source of support for you. Involve him as much as he is willing to be involved. Make him feel he's part of what's going on.

How can I involve my partner more in my pregnancy?

Because you are the focus during pregnancy, your partner may feel left out. Educate him so he understands what you and the baby are going through. Share with him this book and our other books and information you receive. Take him with you to see the doctor. Go to childbirth-education classes together.

SEX DURING PREGNANCY

My partner and I are concerned about sexual activity during pregnancy. What should we do?

Discuss it with your doctor. You need to rule out complications and ask for individual advice. Most doctors agree sex can be a part of a normal pregnancy.

After my partner and I have sex, I feel the baby move a lot. Is this because we had sex?

Your baby moves a lot, no matter what you are doing. If you feel it move more after sexual intercourse, it doesn't mean it was disturbed, uncomfortable or in danger.

My partner is scared to have sex with me because he's afraid it will hurt the baby. What can I tell him?

Sexual activity doesn't usually harm a growing baby. Neither intercourse nor orgasm should be a problem if you have a healthy pregnancy. The baby is well protected by the amniotic sac and amniotic fluid. Uterine muscles are strong and protect the baby, and a thick mucus plug seals the cervix, which helps protect against infection. Often it's the man who asks about sex during pregnancy. You might want to discuss this with your doctor if your partner goes with you to your appointments.

My partner and I enjoy sex a lot. Is this bad for me or the baby?

Frequent sexual activity should not be harmful to a healthy pregnancy. Usually a couple can continue the level of sexual activity they are used to. If you are concerned, discuss it at a prenatal appointment.

I read that some women have a greater desire for sex during pregnancy. Is this true?

Researchers report that pregnancy does enhance the sex drive for some women. Some women may experience orgasms or multiple orgasms for the first time during pregnancy. This is due to heightened hormonal activity and increased blood flow to the pelvic area.

Physically, I don't feel very much like having sex. Why?

During the 1st trimester, you may have experienced fatigue and nausea. During the 3rd trimester, your weight gain, enlarging abdomen, tender breasts and other problems may make you desire sex less. This is normal. Tell your partner how you're feeling, and try to work out a solution that is satisfactory for both of you.

I don't feel very sexy now that I'm pregnant. Is this normal?

You may feel less attractive, but many men find a pregnant woman very attractive. If you experience these feelings, discuss them with your partner.

Isn't there some happy medium to my feelings about sex during pregnancy?

According to research, women generally experience one of two sex-drive patterns. The first is a lessening of desire in the 1st and 3rd trimesters, with an increase in the 2nd trimester. The second is a gradual decrease in desire for sex as pregnancy progresses. Sex is individual; you're not going to fit any pattern perfectly. Discuss your feelings with your partner. Tenderness and understanding can help you both.

I feel physically uncomfortable having sex. What can we do about it?

You may find new positions for lovemaking are necessary. Your larger abdomen may make some positions more uncomfortable than others. In addition, physicians advise a woman not to lie flat on her back after the 16th week of pregnancy. The weight of the uterus restricts circulation. Lie on your side or with you on top.

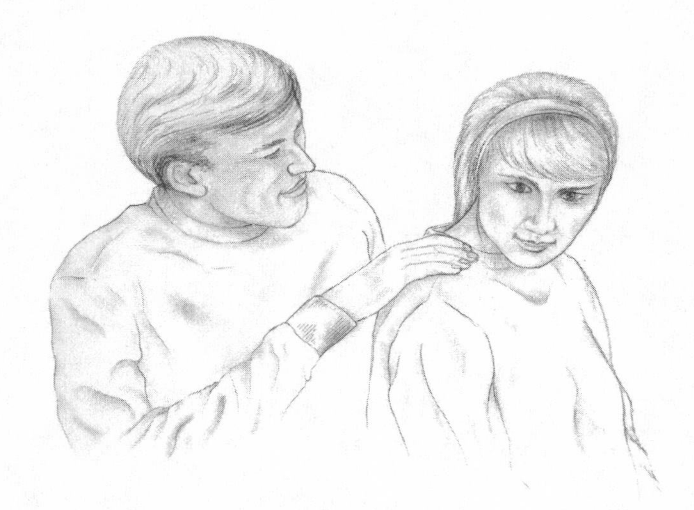

What should I do if I have problems or concerns?

Discuss any complications and concerns with your doctor throughout pregnancy. If you have any unusual symptoms during or following sexual activity, discuss them before resuming sex.

What about sex and miscarriage?

If you have a history of miscarriage, your doctor may caution you against sex and orgasm. However, there is no data that actually links sexual intercourse and miscarriage.

My friend told me that having sex can cause me to go into labor early. Is this true?

Orgasm causes mild uterine contractions, so if you have a history of early labor, your doctor may advise against intercourse and orgasm. Chemicals in semen may also stimulate contractions, so it may not be advisable for a woman's partner to ejaculate inside her. However, in a normal pregnancy, even one near delivery, this is usually not a problem.

What should we avoid during sex now that I'm pregnant?

Don't insert any object into the vagina that could cause injury or infection. Blowing air into the vagina is also dangerous because it can force a potentially fatal air bubble into the woman's bloodstream. Nipple stimulation releases oxytocin, which causes uterine contractions. You might want to discuss this with your doctor.

Are there times we should avoid sex during pregnancy?

Avoid sexual activity if you have any of the following problems or conditions:

- placenta previa or a low-lying placenta
- incompetent cervix
- premature labor
- multiple fetuses
- ruptured bag of waters
- pain
- unexplained vaginal bleeding or discharge
- you can't find a comfortable position
- either partner has an unhealed herpes lesion
- you believe labor has begun

YOUR PARTNER'S FEELINGS

My partner isn't as enthusiastic as I am about the upcoming birth of our first baby. Is this normal?

Not all expectant fathers are as excited about the impending birth as the mother-to-be is. You are directly involved in the pregnancy because you are carrying the baby. Your partner is less involved, so you may have to adjust your expectations somewhat. You may need to take an active role in encouraging your partner to become more involved, such as asking him to accompany you to a prenatal visit. Discuss with him his feelings about the pregnancy. He may have fears and uncertainties he hasn't voiced to you. Be open and direct with each other about your feelings—it will help both of you.

Is it OK for my partner to go to my prenatal appointments with me?

It's a great idea for him to accompany you! It helps him realize what is happening to you and may help him feel more like he's a

part of the pregnancy. It's also good for your partner and your doctor to meet before labor begins.

My partner seems very anxious about my pregnancy. Is this normal?
Your partner may feel increased anxiety as your pregnancy progresses. He may be concerned about your health, the health of the baby, sex, labor and delivery, and his ability to be a good father. Share your own concerns with him. It may help calm his anxieties.

YOUR PARTNER'S INVOLVEMENT IN THE PREGNANCY

My partner wants to know how he can make our pregnancy easier for me. What can I tell him?
A man can help his pregnant partner in many ways:

- Keep stress to a minimum.
- Communicate with you about his feelings and concerns.
- Be patient and supportive.
- Promote good nutrition.

- Encourage exercise.
- Help around the house and do chores.
- Attend prenatal checkups when possible.
- Plan for the baby's arrival.
- Learn about the birth process.

YOUR PARTNER'S PHYSICAL HEALTH

Can a man can suffer from morning sickness when his wife is pregnant?

Many fathers-to-be experience some sort of physical problem during their wife's pregnancy. The condition is called *couvade* and was first noted in a Carib Indian tribe in which every expectant father

WAYS DAD CAN BOND WITH BABY

The baby's father can begin bonding with the baby *before* birth and continue after the baby is born. Encourage your partner to try the following suggestions.

- Talk to the baby while it is in the uterus.
- Talk to the baby soon after birth. Babies bond to sound very quickly.
- Hold the baby close and make eye contact; a baby relates to people through sight and smell.
- Feed the baby with a bottle of formula or expressed breast milk.
- Help with daily baby chores, such as changing diapers, holding the baby when he or she is restless and dressing and bathing the baby.
- Take turns getting up at night with the baby.

engages in rituals that enable him to understand what his wife is experiencing. In our culture, a father-to-be may experience nausea, headache, back and muscle aches, insomnia, fatigue and depression.

I recently read that reproduction and fetal development may be affected if a man is exposed to various chemicals. Is this true?

Yes. Exposure by the father-to-be to alcohol, cigarettes, certain drugs and some environmental hazards could harm the unborn baby. It could also affect the man's ability to father a child or affect the quality of his sperm.

What kind of problems can be caused by a man's exposure to these substances?

Problems include miscarriage, stillbirth, birth defects, low-birthweight babies, a greater risk of childhood cancer and even subtle learning disabilities.

When is this exposure the most important?

Usually male exposure is harmful if it occurs before and around the time of conception.

I've heard that my partner's use of alcohol before my pregnancy may affect the baby. How?

Some researchers believe heavy alcohol consumption by the baby's father may produce fetal alcohol syndrome (FAS) or fetal alcohol exposure (FAE) in the baby. (See page 214 for further information on FAS and FAE.) Alcohol intake by the father has also been linked to intrauterine-growth restriction.

My partner uses recreational drugs occasionally; I think he was using them when I got pregnant. Can this cause any problems?

Your partner's drug habits may have an effect on your pregnancy. The best thing to do is to discuss it with your doctor and see if there is anything he or she can do to reassure you about the well-being of your baby.

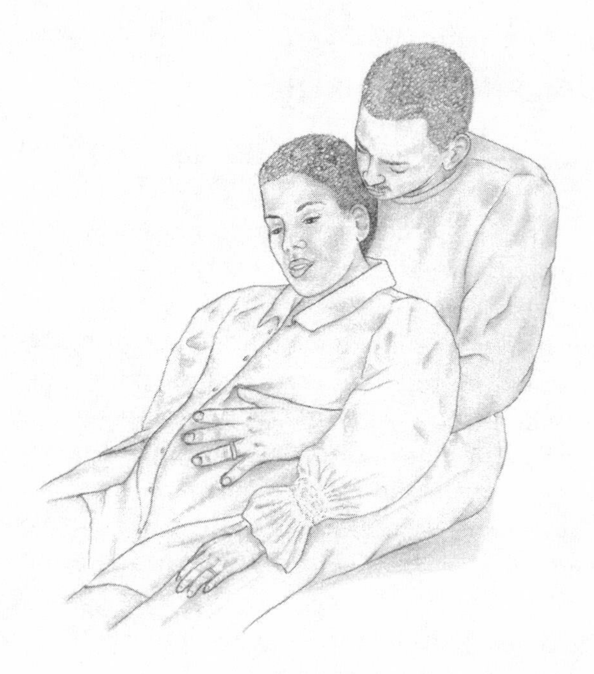

Is it true I need to be concerned about substances my partner is exposed to at work?

Yes. Your partner may bring substances into your home on his work clothes. If you think you may be exposed to hazardous substances in this manner, discuss it with your partner and your doctor.

I don't smoke, but my partner does. Should I try to get him to stop now that I'm pregnant?

When a nonsmoking pregnant woman and her unborn baby are exposed to secondhand smoke, both are exposed to harmful chemicals. Ask your partner to stop smoking during your pregnancy or at least not to smoke inside your home or your car. You can also avoid exposure by not going to public places that allow smoking.

My partner is 53. Can his age cause problems for me or my baby?

We have information indicating the age and health of the father does make a difference in the health of your baby. Some researchers believe there may be a slight increase in the risk of Down syndrome and other problems if the baby's father is over 50.

YOUR PARTNER'S INVOLVEMENT DURING AND AFTER THE BIRTH

Will the doctor let my partner cut the umbilical cord after the birth?

Cutting the cord is something many men enjoy doing. Talk to your doctor about your partner's participation in the delivery.

I'm afraid I'm going to feel exhausted dealing with the baby after we get home. How can I get my partner to help me?

It's better when both partners share the responsibilities and chores of parenthood. Form an equal-parenthood partnership, and encourage him to take equal responsibility for parenting your new baby. He'll enjoy being a father much more if he is actively involved in the care and decision making for his new daughter or son.

My doctor said my partner can be very important to me during labor and delivery. How?

He can help prepare you for childbirth, and he can support you as you labor. He can share in the joy of the delivery of your baby. He can also support you emotionally, which can be important to you both.

11

Lifestyle Changes

Your lifestyle can have a great impact on your baby. Everything you eat, drink or take into your body (such as cigarette smoke or alcohol) may pass to your developing baby. We address medications and various other substances in chapter 4. In this chapter, we cover some harmful substances your lifestyle may expose you to. They can be harmful to *any* pregnant woman.

We also discuss the harm smoking, alcohol use and various types of drug use can cause for you and the baby. Many people are unaware of how destructive even the occasional use of some of these things can be. It's important to think about the health and safety of you and your baby. Your baby depends on you for the best start in life you can give him or her.

How can my lifestyle affect my developing baby?

Some substances that you can use safely may have adverse effects on a developing fetus. Other substances are bad for both you and your baby. It's never too early to start thinking about how your actions affect the baby growing inside you.

What kind of activities can affect my baby?

Just about anything you are exposed to can affect your baby. Cigarette smoke, alcohol, drugs, tranquilizers, even caffeine can affect a fetus. (For a discussion of caffeine, see page 116.)

How do researchers know these substances affect a developing baby?

Information about the effects of specific substances on a human pregnancy often comes from cases of exposure before a pregnancy is discovered. These cases help researchers understand possible harmful effects, but they don't help us understand the picture completely. For this reason, we often cannot make exact statements about particular substances and their effects on the mother or developing baby.

CIGARETTE SMOKING

I smoke cigarettes every day. Should I stop?

Yes! A pregnant woman who smokes one pack of cigarettes a day (20 cigarettes) inhales tobacco smoke more than 11,000 times during an average pregnancy! Tobacco smoke inhaled by the mother can affect a growing baby.

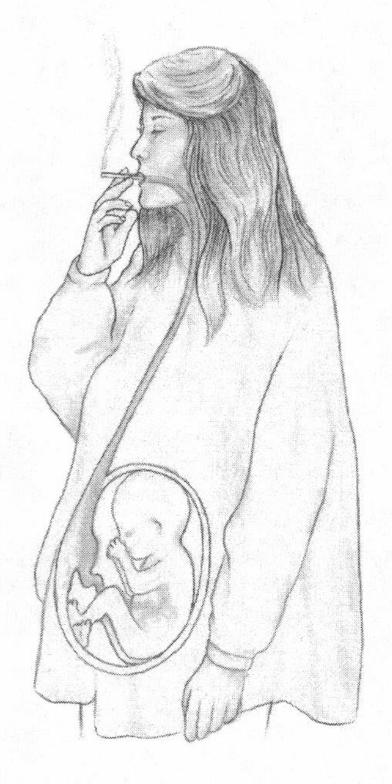

Smoking by a mother-to-be directly affects her growing baby. Smoke inhaled by the mother passes through the placenta to the fetus.

RISKS OF CIGARETTE SMOKING

A mother-to-be who smokes puts herself and her baby at risk. Consider the following facts.

- The risk of developing placental abruption increases almost 25% in moderate smokers and 65% in heavy smokers.
- Placenta previa occurs 25% more often in moderate smokers and 90% more often in heavy smokers.
- Miscarriage, death of the fetus or death of a baby soon after birth are risks directly related to the number of cigarettes a woman smokes each day. Risk can increase as much as 35% for a woman who smokes more than a pack of cigarettes a day.
- Infants born to mothers who smoke weigh less than other babies. This can cause problems for the baby.
- Lower IQ scores and increased incidence of reading disorders have been noted in children born to mothers who smoked during pregnancy.
- Hyperactivity is higher in children whose mothers smoked while pregnant.
- Research has shown that smoking during pregnancy interferes with the woman's absorption of vitamins B and C and folic acid.
- A recent study linked cigarette smoking by a mother-to-be with mental retardation in her baby.
- Newborns of mothers who smoke may have nicotine deprivation. Adults who suffer from nicotine deprivation exhibit symptoms such as cravings, nervousness and irritability.

Why is cigarette smoking so harmful?

Tobacco smoke contains many harmful substances, including nicotine, carbon monoxide, hydrogen cyanide, tars, resins and some cancer-causing agents. When a pregnant woman inhales cigarette smoke, these chemicals pass through the placenta to the developing baby.

I want to quit smoking. Is it OK for me to use the Nicoderm patch or Nicorette gum while I'm pregnant?

The stop-smoking patches and gum contain many of the same substances that cigarettes do. The specific effects of Nicoderm and Nicorette on fetal development are unknown. However, if you are pregnant, researchers advise not using either of these stop-smoking systems because you and your baby might be exposed to the harmful substances you are trying to avoid.

What can I do if I smoke?

The best way you can help yourself is to quit smoking completely before and during your pregnancy. If you can't do this—it's hard to quit cold turkey—reduce the number of cigarettes you smoke. It may help reduce your risks.

I don't smoke, but my husband does. Will this hurt me or the baby?

Some research indicates a nonsmoker and her unborn baby are exposed to carboxyhemoglobin and nicotine through secondary smoke. These substances may harm you and your baby. Ask your husband to stop smoking while you are pregnant. If he's receptive to the idea, you might suggest he quit smoking altogether. Secondhand smoke isn't good *after* your baby is born, either!

ALCOHOL USE

What is fetal alcohol syndrome?

Fetal alcohol syndrome (FAS) is a collection of problems that affect children born to women who drink excessive amounts of alcohol during pregnancy. It is characterized by growth restriction before and after birth. Defects in the heart and limbs, and unusual facial characteristics, such as a short, upturned nose, a flat upper jawbone and "different" eyes, have also been seen in FAS children. These children may also have behavioral problems, impaired speech and impaired use of joints and muscles.

Is FAE the same as FAS?

Let's begin by explaining about diagnosis of FAS. To have a definite diagnosis of fetal alcohol syndrome, specific criteria must be met. The mother-to-be must have a history of alcohol consumption during pregnancy. The baby must exhibit three medical criteria—abnormalities of the face or skull, growth restriction and damage to the central nervous system, usually a mental deficiency. If the mother's consumption of alcohol cannot be proved, we generally refer to the condition as *FAE* or *fetal alcohol exposure.* A baby with a mild birth defect may be diagnosed with FAE if the mother had *anything* to drink during pregnancy.

How much alcohol is too much?

At this time, we believe *any* amount of alcohol is too much. Most studies indicate four to five, or more, drinks a day are required to cause FAS, but mild abnormalities have been associated with as little as two drinks a day (1 ounce of alcohol). It's best to avoid alcohol completely while you're pregnant.

Is it all right to drink alcohol while I'm pregnant?

Alcohol use by a pregnant woman carries considerable risk. Even moderate use of alcohol has been linked to an increase in the chance of miscarriage. Excessive alcohol consumption during pregnancy can result in abnormalities in the baby. Chronic use of alcohol during pregnancy can lead to fetal alcohol syndrome (FAS).

I don't drink much. Can't I drink socially while I'm pregnant?

There is a lot of disagreement about this because we don't know what is a "safe" level of alcohol consumption during pregnancy. Why take the risk of harming your baby? Avoid alcohol during pregnancy.

Is this the reason alcoholic beverages carry warning labels?

Yes. The warning advises women to avoid alcohol during pregnancy because of the possibility of causing problems in the fetus, including FAS and FAE. Unfortunately, a study in 1995 found that pregnant women in North America ignored the advice to avoid alcohol during pregnancy. In that study, 4 times as many women said they drank alcohol during pregnancy than those who had been interviewed in 1991. Don't put your baby at risk! Pass up *all* alcohol during your pregnancy.

What about recipes that call for alcohol? Should I avoid them?

A good rule of thumb is it's probably OK to eat a food that contains alcohol if it has been baked or simmered for at least 1 hour. Cooking for that length of time cooks out nearly all of the alcohol content.

What about drinking nonalcoholic wine and beer during pregnancy?

Even though they are labeled "no alcohol," these beverages contain *some* alcohol—about 0.5%. Because we don't know what alcohol-intake level is safe for the fetus, it's a good idea to avoid all of them.

Can I drink before pregnancy, while I'm trying to get pregnant?

If you're trying to get pregnant, you probably won't know exactly when you do conceive. Why take chances? Stop drinking while you're trying to conceive—that way you'll avoid any problems.

I've heard taking drugs with alcohol can cause more problems. How is that?

Taking drugs with alcohol increases the chance of damaging the fetus. Drugs that cause the greatest concern include analgesics, antidepressants and anticonvulsants.

I read somewhere that my partner's use of alcohol before my pregnancy may affect the fetus. Is this true?

Some researchers believe heavy alcohol consumption by the baby's father may produce FAS in the baby. Alcohol intake by the father has also been linked to intrauterine-growth restriction.

What other precautions should I take with regard to alcohol?

Be very careful about substances you use that may contain alcohol. Over-the-counter cough medicines and cold remedies often contain alcohol—as much as 25%!

DRUG USE

How do you define drug abuse?

Drug abuse usually refers to drugs prohibited by law, but it can also include use of legal substances, such as alcohol, caffeine, tobacco and prescription medications. Abuse of these substances means not using them as they were prescribed or using them to excess.

What is physical dependence?

Physical dependence implies the drug must be taken to avoid unpleasant withdrawal symptoms—it does not always mean addiction or drug abuse. For example, many caffeine users develop withdrawal symptoms if they stop drinking coffee, but they are not considered drug abusers or drug addicts.

What is psychological dependence?

Psychological dependence means the user has developed an emotional need for a drug or medication. This need may be more compelling than a physical need and can provide the stimulus for continued drug use.

Can drug use affect my pregnancy?

Yes! Certain drugs damage the developing fetus. In addition, a woman who abuses drugs may have more complications of pregnancy because of her lifestyle.

What kind of problems do you mean?

Nutritional deficiencies may be more common. Anemia and intrauterine-growth restriction can also occur. A pregnant woman may have an increased chance of pre-eclampsia. (See page 273 for a detailed discussion of pre-eclampsia.)

Prescription Medications

How do amphetamines affect the baby?

Research has shown that use of central-nervous-system stimulants, such as amphetamines, during pregnancy is associated with an increase in cardiovascular defects in babies.

Are barbiturates harmful during pregnancy?

Barbiturate use may be associated with birth defects, although this has not yet been proved definitely. We have seen withdrawal, poor feeding, seizures and other problems in babies born to mothers who abused barbiturates during pregnancy.

Can other tranquilizers affect a pregnant woman?

Tranquilizing agents include benzodiazepines (Valium and Librium) and other, newer agents, such as Xanax. Several studies have related the use of these drugs to an increase in birth defects.

What are opioids?

Opioids are derived from opium and synthetic compounds with similar actions. They produce euphoria, drowsiness or sleepiness, and decreased sensitivity to pain. Habitual use can lead to physical dependence.

What common drugs are opioids?

Opioids include morphine, Demerol, heroin and codeine.

What kind of problems can opioids cause?

These drugs are associated with a variety of congenital abnormalities and complications of pregnancy. Women who use opioids during pregnancy are often at high risk for premature labor, intrauterine-growth restriction in the baby and pre-eclampsia.

What can happen to a baby if the mother uses opioids?

The baby may experience withdrawal symptoms after birth.

Are there any other problems associated with using opioids during pregnancy?

If the mother uses the drugs intravenously, other problems may occur, such as AIDS, hepatitis and endocarditis. Any of these is very serious during pregnancy.

Illegal Drugs

What about marijuana use during pregnancy? Can it hurt the baby?

Marijuana contains tetrahydrocannabinol (THC). Research has shown use of marijuana by a mother-to-be can cause various problems, including attention deficit, memory problems and impaired decision making in children, which usually appear between the ages of 3 and 12 years.

Can use of hashish hurt a fetus?

Hashish contains tetrahydrocannabinol (THC), just as marijuana does. Avoid using it during pregnancy.

Is the use of hallucinogens declining?

The use of some hallucinogens, such as LSD, mescaline and peyote, is not as common as it was several years ago. However, use of phencyclidine (PCP), a powerful hallucinogen, is growing.

How does use of PCP affect a pregnancy?

PCP, also called *angel dust*, can cause severe mental illness and loss of contact with reality in the user. We believe it can cause abnormal development in a fetus, although it has not been definitely proved.

I know cocaine use is more common today. How does it affect a pregnancy?

Today, cocaine use is a more common cause of complication in pregnancy. Often a user consumes the drug over a long period of time, such as several days. During this time, she may eat or drink very little, which can have serious consequences for a developing fetus.

How does cocaine affect the mother-to-be?

Use of cocaine has been associated with convulsions, arrhythmias, hypertension and hyperthermia in a pregnant woman. Continual use of cocaine can affect maternal nutrition and temperature control, which can harm the fetus. Cocaine use has been linked with miscarriage, placental abruption and congenital defects.

I've heard that use of cocaine during early pregnancy can cause serious problems. Is this true?

If a woman uses cocaine during the first 12 weeks of pregnancy, there is an increased risk of miscarriage. Damage to the developing baby can occur as early as 3 days after conception!

How does cocaine use by the mother-to-be affect the baby?

Infants often have lower IQs and long-term mental deficiencies. Sudden infant death syndrome (SIDS) is also more common in these babies. Many babies are stillborn.

What about crack use?

All that we have stated about cocaine use also applies to crack use.

I know someone who used drugs a few times while she was pregnant. Her baby seems all right. Aren't you exaggerating the dangers?

No. Your friend was lucky. A fetus is totally dependent on the mother-to-be for all of its needs, so everything a woman does can affect her baby. What may seem like a small amount to a woman can have a major effect on the fetus whose organs are still being formed. It is up to you to do all you can to help your baby have the best possible start in life.

SEXUALLY TRANSMITTED DISEASES

I've heard sexually transmitted diseases can harm a growing baby. Is this true?

Yes. If you have a sexually transmitted disease (STD), you must be treated as soon as possible!

What is a sexually transmitted disease?

It is a disease that is contracted during oral, vaginal or anal intercourse.

Yeast Infections

What is monilial vulvovaginitis?

Monilial vulvovaginitis is an infection caused by yeast, or monilia, and usually affects the vagina and vulva. Yeast infections are more common in pregnant women than in nonpregnant women.

COMMON SEXUALLY TRANSMITTED DISEASES

Following are the most common sexually transmitted diseases:

- monilial vulvovaginitis
- trichomonal vaginitis
- condylomata acuminatum (venereal warts)
- genital herpes simplex infection
- chlamydia
- gonorrhea
- syphilis
- HIV/AIDS

What kind of problems can yeast infections cause during pregnancy?

This STD has no major negative effects on pregnancy, but it can cause discomfort for you.

How are yeast infections treated during pregnancy?

Yeast infections may be harder to control when you're pregnant. They may require frequent retreatment or longer treatment (10 to 14 days instead of 3 to 7 days). Vaginal creams or suppositories used for treatment are safe during pregnancy, although most physicians recommend avoiding treatment during the 1st trimester. Your partner does not have to be treated unless he has symptoms.

I've heard of a pill I only have to take once to clear up a yeast infection. Can I take it during pregnancy?

You're talking about Diflucan (fluconazole), an antifungal drug. Unfortunately, we are not recommending it during pregnancy or breastfeeding because it has not yet been proved safe for use in either situation.

If you think you have a sexually transmitted disease, discuss it with your doctor and your partner.

What kinds of problems can a yeast infection cause the baby?

A newborn infant can get thrush (a mouth infection) after passing through a birth canal infected with a yeast infection. Treatment of the newborn with nystatin is effective.

Trichomonal Vaginitis

What is trichomonal vaginitis?

Trichomonal vaginitis is a venereal infection caused by parasites called *trichomonas.* Symptoms include persistent burning and itching of the vulva area accompanied by a frothy white or yellow discharge.

What kind of problems can trichomonal vaginitis cause during pregnancy?

This infection has no major effects on a pregnancy.

Why is treatment of trichomonal vaginitis a concern during pregnancy?

Metronidazole, the drug used to treat trichomonal vaginitis, should not be taken during the 1st trimester of pregnancy. It is prescribed after the 1st trimester. The same recommendation applies to metronidazole in oral form or gel form.

Venereal Warts

What are venereal warts?

They are skin tags or warts that are transmitted by sexual contact. They are also called *condyloma* or *condylomata acuminatum.*

What causes these warts?

They are caused by the human papilloma virus (HPV), which is passed during sexual intercourse.

Why are venereal warts a problem during pregnancy?

Warty skin tags can become enlarged during pregnancy; in rare cases, they block the vagina at the time of delivery. If a woman has

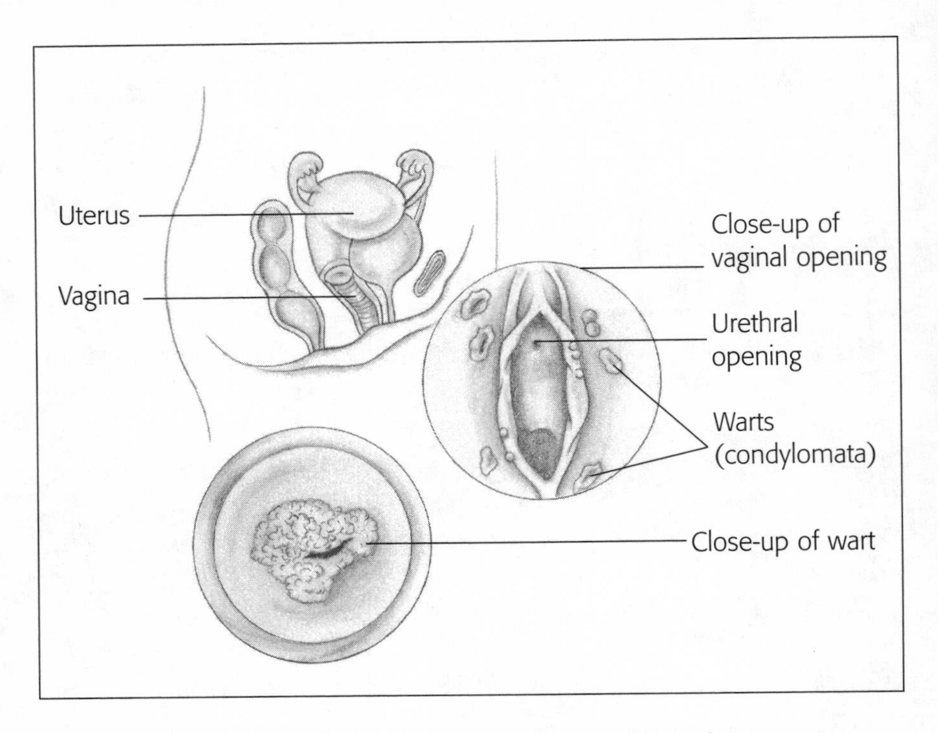

Venereal warts *(condylomata acuminatum)* can cause problems during pregnancy.

extensive venereal warts, a Cesarean delivery may be necessary to avoid heavy bleeding and other complications.

How can venereal warts affect a baby?

Infants delivered through a birth canal infected with venereal warts have been known to get small benign tumors on the vocal cords (laryngeal papillomas) after delivery.

Can venereal warts be treated during pregnancy?

Often they can be. Doctors use several methods to treat them, including freezing the warts off, laser therapy and chemical removal. If warts become large enough to interfere with delivery, your doctor may recommend removing them. With the exception of one chemical irritant, podophyllin, all three treatment methods have been used safely during pregnancy.

Herpes

What is genital herpes simplex infection?

Genital herpes simplex infection is herpes that involves the genital area. It can be significant during pregnancy because of the danger of infecting a newborn with the disease at the time of delivery.

What are the symptoms of genital herpes?

Usually clusters of small blisters appear in the genital area within a week after infection. At first the blisters are itchy, then they become sore and break, leaving painful ulcers. Symptoms can also include aches and pains, fatigue, fever and a vaginal discharge. Symptoms usually disappear within 3 weeks. Subsequent outbreaks can occur at any time but are usually shorter and milder.

What kind of problems can herpes cause a mother-to-be?

Infection early in pregnancy may be associated with an increase in miscarriage or premature delivery.

What kind of problems can herpes cause the baby?

Infection in the mother is associated with low birthweight. We believe an infant can contract the infection when traveling through an infected birth canal. When membranes rupture, the infection may also travel upward to the uterus and infect the baby, resulting in fetal infections. Infected newborns have a mortality rate of 50%.

How can herpes simplex be treated during pregnancy?

There is no effective treatment. Acyclovir may decrease the symptoms, but the safety of acyclovir in pregnancy has not been established.

If I have herpes, can I prevent my baby from becoming infected?

When a woman has an active herpes infection late in pregnancy, she will have a Cesarean section to prevent the infant from traveling through the infected birth canal.

How can I avoid getting genital herpes?

You must know your partner is free from infection. If your partner suspects he has herpes, he should see his doctor for treatment. If your partner has herpes or could have been exposed to it, the best way to avoid the disease is through abstinence from sex during outbreaks and having him wear a condom during intercourse.

Chlamydia

What is chlamydia?

Chlamydia is a common sexually transmitted disease. It is estimated that between 3 and 5 million people are infected each year. Symptoms include vaginal discharge and pelvic pain. However, it can be symptomless—you may not know you have been exposed. Between 20 and 40% of all sexually active women have been exposed at some time.

How can chlamydia affect pregnancy?

One of the most important complications of chlamydia is pelvic inflammatory disease (PID). This is a severe infection of the female organs that can make it more difficult for you to get pregnant. If you have had PID, your chance of having an ectopic pregnancy is greater. During pregnancy, a mother-to-be can pass a chlamydial infection to her baby as it travels through the birth canal. The baby will have a 20 to 50% chance of getting chlamydia.

How does a chlamydial infection affect the baby?

A baby exposed to chlamydia may be born with an eye infection or pneumonia.

If chlamydia is often symptomless, how will I know I have it?

You can have tests, including a pelvic exam and a cervical swab.

How is chlamydia treated?

Treatment usually involves tetracycline, which should *not* be given to a pregnant woman. During pregnancy, erythromycin is the drug of choice.

Gonorrhea

What is gonorrhea?

Gonorrhea is a venereal infection transmitted primarily by sexual intercourse. In a woman, the urethra, vulva, vagina and Fallopian tubes may be involved. However, there may be no symptoms of the disease.

How can gonorrhea affect the baby?

The baby may be infected as it passes through the birth canal, resulting in eye inflammation. Eye drops are routinely used in newborns to prevent this problem. Other infections in the baby may also occur.

How is gonorrhea treated during pregnancy?

Gonorrheal infections are treated with penicillin and other medications that are safe to use during pregnancy.

Syphilis

What is syphilis?

Syphilis is a sexually transmitted disease characterized by lesions that may involve any organ or tissue. The disease may be present for years without symptoms.

How can syphilis affect pregnancy?

Syphilis increases the chance of stillbirth. It can also cause various infections in the newborn. Any stage of syphilis during pregnancy can result in infection in an infant.

How can syphilis be treated during pregnancy?

Syphilis can be treated effectively during pregnancy with penicillin and other medications that are safe to use.

AIDS

I know that AIDS affects more women today. How does pregnancy affect AIDS?

Pregnancy may hide some of the symptoms of AIDS (Acquired Immune Deficiency Syndrome), which can make the disease harder to discover. Some treatments may not be used during pregnancy.

Can a woman infected with AIDS pass it to her baby?

It is possible for a woman to pass HIV, the virus that causes AIDS, to the baby before birth, during birth and, if she breastfeeds, after birth. However, transference of HIV from mother to baby occurs most often during delivery.

How can a woman find out if she has AIDS or is positive for HIV?

Two blood tests are used—the ELISA test and the Western blot test. If the ELISA test is positive, it is confirmed by the Western blot test. Both tests measure antibodies to the virus, not the virus itself. The Western blot test is believed to be 99% sensitive and specific.

Are there any new tests available?

Yes, there are. A test called the *EIA (enzyme isoenzyme assay)* can be done instead of the ELISA test. To confirm the diagnosis of HIV, in addition to the Western blot test, a doctor can now order an *IFA (immunofluorescent assay)*.

I've heard that if a woman is given AZT during pregnancy, the baby almost always will be born without AIDS. Is this true?

Research has shown that AZT treatment can decrease the likelihood that an infected mother will pass the infection to her baby. According to a study released by the National Institutes of Child Health and Human Development, if an HIV-positive woman takes AZT during pregnancy and delivers by Cesarean section, her risk of passing the virus to her baby is almost none. Having a C-section alone cuts the risk of transmission of the disease by 50%.

If you are concerned about HIV and AIDS, discuss it with your doctor. Combinations of medications are being tested with some success.

12

Special Concerns of the Single Mother-to-Be

Today, some women are choosing to have their babies alone; their reasons vary. Many women will have the support of the father-to-be but have decided not to get married. For other women, the baby's father is unable or unwilling to be with them. We provide this information to give you a foundation for seeking answers to questions about your situation. There may be many issues you have not thought about. Questions in this chapter fall into two groups: We answer the first group of questions because we have been asked many of them before.

For the second group of questions, we do not provide any answers because they concern legal matters we aren't qualified to answer. However, we include them because there are many legal ramifications to this decision. Use the questions to help formulate questions about your personal situation to ask your attorney, a patient advocate, a hospital social worker, your doctor or family members.

DEALING WITH OTHER PEOPLE

I'm a single woman who has chosen to have my baby alone. What should I tell people who ask me why I am doing this?

It doesn't matter what people ask you—really it's none of their business. What is important is how you feel about the pregnancy. It's up to you to decide what you want to tell people and how much of an explanation you want to provide.

Some people think I'm crazy to have a baby alone. What should I say to them?

Once your friends understand your situation, they'll support you. If others don't support you, don't talk with them about your pregnancy or your reasons for having your baby alone.

I feel as if I have no one close to share my pregnancy problems and concerns with. What can I do?

Share your problems and concerns with your family and friends. Mothers of young children can identify with your experiences—they have had the same or similar experiences recently. If you have friends or family members who have young children, talk with them. Even if you were married, you would probably share your concerns with all of these people. Try not to let your situation alter this.

My family is against my decision to have my baby alone. Is there anything I can do about this?

If this is a decision you are comfortable with, deal with their discomfort by asking them to talk about the reasons they are against your pregnancy. You will never change some people's minds, so you will have to learn to live with their disapproval or ignore it.

Your doctor is a good person to talk to about your pregnancy concerns. If your doctor can't help you, he or she will be able to direct you to someone who can.

Some people seem very interested in my situation but hesitate to talk to me. Should I encourage them to ask questions?

Only if you are comfortable with their questions. Some people are genuinely concerned about you; others are just nosy. Before you answer, decide if the person's truly interested in you. Then share as much or as little as you are comfortable discussing.

Do you think people will treat me or my baby differently because I am a single mother?

Today, being a single mother isn't that unusual. Many women of all ages have made this decision. Some people may treat you differently; others won't care. Good friends and family members should draw closer to you.

People seem to assume my partner and I are married, but we aren't. What should we do about this?

If you are pregnant and you are together, most people will assume you are married. First, decide if it's important to clear up the misunderstanding. If it's a sales clerk or a waitress, then it probably isn't important to clarify your situation. If it's your doctor, you should let him or her know what is going on.

SPECIAL CONSIDERATIONS

I'm having a lot of trouble emotionally with this pregnancy. Whom should I talk to about it?

Begin by talking with your doctor. Office personnel can direct you to a counselor or a support group, depending on what you need.

Will I have to make special plans for when I go into labor? What should they cover?

Just as any pregnant woman, you must decide who will be with you when you labor and deliver, and who will be there to help afterward. The only special plan to consider is how you will get to the hospital. One woman decided to have her friend drive her, but she couldn't reach her when the time came. Her next option (all part of her plan) was to call a taxi, which got her to the hospital in plenty of time.

What can I do about a labor coach? I don't have a particular person in mind to ask.

Ask a good friend, a relative or someone else who is close to you. Not all women have their partner as their labor coach. Often a woman who has already given birth using the same methods is an excellent labor coach. She will understand your discomfort and be able to identify with your experience.

If I am a single mother, will the nurses treat me differently?

The nurses' job is to provide the best care they possibly can; they pride themselves in taking care of their patients.

How will it be different for me when I take my baby home by myself?

A new baby is always an incredible challenge, in any situation. You will probably need more support from family and friends because you won't have anyone to share the responsibilities with at home. Don't hesitate to ask for assistance. If you have no one you can ask to give of their time, you might consider hiring someone to stay with you at night for the first week or two, to enable you to get back on your feet.

Because I had donor insemination, my baby won't have another set of grandparents, aunts and uncles. Do you think this will be a problem?

Families today are different than they were in the past. Many children don't have a complete set of parents or grandparents, even in the closest family units. In these situations, an older family friend can be just as loving and giving to a child as a grandparent. Encourage older friends to take an active part in your child's life.

Are there support groups for single parents?

Yes, there are. Ask your doctor or pediatrician for the names of groups in your area. (See also the Resources on page 375.)

A single mother-to-be has many additional concerns during pregnancy. Explore every aspect of the situation for your sake and the sake of your baby.

I'm scared that if I get sick, no one will be there to take care of my baby. How can I deal with this problem?

You need to plan ahead for this situation. Find a family member or close friend you can call upon to help out in case this happens. Knowing you have provided for this event should give you peace of mind.

LEGAL QUESTIONS

The following questions are included without answers because they are legal questions to discuss with an attorney who specializes in family law. Use them as a guide to develop questions to ask about your particular situation.

- A friend who's a single mother told me I'd better consider the legal ramifications of this situation. What was she talking about?
- I've heard that in some states, if I'm unmarried I have to get a special birth certificate. Is this true?
- I'm having my baby alone, and I'm concerned about who can make medical decisions for me and my expected baby. Is there anything I can do about this concern?
- I'm not married, but I am deeply involved with my baby's father. Can my partner make medical decisions for me if I have problems during or after the birth?
- If anything happens to me, can my partner make medical decisions for our baby after he or she is born?
- What are the legal rights of my baby's father if we are not married?
- Do my partner's parents also have legal rights in regard to our child (their grandchild)?
- My baby's father and I went our separate ways before I knew I was pregnant. Do I have to tell him about the baby?

- I chose to have donor (artificial) insemination. If anything happens to me during my labor and/or delivery, who can make medical decisions for me?
- Who can make medical decisions for my baby?
- I got pregnant by donor insemination. What do I put on the birth certificate under "father's name"?
- Is there any way I can find out more about my sperm donor's family medical history?
- Will the sperm bank send me updates if medical problems appear in my sperm donor's family?
- I had donor insemination. Does the baby's father have any legal right to be part of my child's life in the future?
- Someone was joking with me that my child could marry its sister or brother some day (because I had donor insemination) and wouldn't even know it. Is this possible?
- As my child grows up, he or she may need some sort of medical help (like a donor kidney) from a sibling. Will the sperm bank give out this kind of information?

13

Other Pregnancy Concerns

In the previous chapters, we have covered the questions about pregnancy we hear most often. But you may have some questions we didn't cover. We realize there are *many* interests and concerns you and your partner may have. We cover various topics in this chapter—introducing your pet to your new baby, choosing a pediatrician, driving and wearing seat belts during pregnancy, traveling while you're pregnant and deciding which type of childbirth-education class is right for you.

Before you despair that we didn't cover your particular question, scan through this chapter. It's sort of a catch-all that covers many different areas about pregnancy that didn't fit anywhere else. You'll find lots of valuable information.

YOUR MATERNITY WARDROBE

Now that I know I'm pregnant, I'm excited about wearing maternity clothes. When will I need them?

It's hard to predict exactly when you'll need to start wearing maternity clothes. You may have some clothes that are loose enough to wear for a while. You might be able to wear some of your partner's shirts. Or use a rubber band to expand the waist of pants and jeans. Hook one loop of the band around the button, pass it through the buttonhole, then hook the other end of the band around the button. Instant waistband expansion!

A rule of thumb to follow is when you become uncomfortable wearing your regular clothes, it's time to start wearing maternity clothes.

Are there any points I should keep in mind when selecting maternity clothes?

Choose natural fabrics when possible—avoid synthetic fabrics. During pregnancy, your metabolic rate increases, and you may feel warmer than usual. Wear fabrics that breathe, such as cotton in the summer, and layer your clothing in winter.

My friend told me that I should wear special maternity underwear while I'm pregnant. What did she mean?

Undergarments that add support to your abdomen, breasts or legs may make you feel more comfortable during pregnancy. These undergarments include maternity bras, nursing bras, maternity panties and maternity support hose. Choose panties and support hose with a cotton crotch.

What are maternity bras?

Maternity bras are designed to provide your enlarging breasts with the extra support they need during pregnancy. They have wider sides

MATERNITY STYLES

You'll find a variety of maternity clothes available to fit your personal taste. Many women find the following styles add to their comfort:

- wide elastic bands or panels that fit under your abdomen to provide support
- wrap-around openings that tie and are easy to adjust
- elastic waists that expand
- button or pleated waistbands that are adjustable
- waistbands that have sliders to adjust fit

and stretchier backs than regular bras. They usually have four sets of hooks on the back, instead of two or three, providing more room for you to grow.

Can't I just wear my normal bra in a larger size?

It's probably better to buy a maternity bra. They can help combat the sagging of your breasts, which is associated with pregnancy.

What is a nursing bra?

A nursing bra has cups that open so you can breastfeed without having to get undressed. Buy a nursing bra only if you plan to breastfeed your baby. You won't need one if you bottlefeed.

When should I buy a nursing bra?

Wait until the final weeks of your pregnancy; don't buy one before the 36th week. It may be difficult to get a correct fit before then.

How will I know a nursing bra will fit correctly?

Choose a nursing bra with about a finger's width of space between any part of the cup and your breast. This allows for the enlargement of your breasts when your milk comes in. Take nursing pads with you when shopping for a nursing bra for a better fit. Choose a bra that is comfortable when fastened on the loosest row of hooks to allow for shrinkage in your ribcage after pregnancy.

What are maternity panties?

These panties provide support for your enlarging abdomen. Some have panels for your abdomen; others have a wide elastic band that fits under your abdomen to provide support. These panties may be most comfortable in the last trimester of pregnancy.

Will I have to wear medical maternity support stockings?

Most women do not have to wear medical maternity support hose (also called *compression hose*) during pregnancy. However, if you have a family history of varicose veins or if you develop them during pregnancy, you may need to wear them. You may not be able to depend on over-the-counter support hose. If you need to visit a vein specialist to have maternity support stockings personally fitted, discuss it with your doctor. See page 180 for additional information on varicose veins and compression hose.

Can I wear regular pantyhose?

If you don't have any problems with varicose veins, regular pantyhose are OK. Choose hose with a stretchy, wide, nonbinding waistband. Wear them over or under your abdomen, whichever is more comfortable. You might also be able to buy maternity pantyhose.

CHOOSING YOUR BABY'S PEDIATRICIAN

My friend told me that I should pick my baby's pediatrician before the baby is born. Is this true?

Yes. You can interview a pediatrician to help you build the right partnership for your child's health and well-being. Talk with the pediatrician about the care of your baby, ask questions about feeding and receive some guidelines about dealing with a new baby.

> *How do I find a pediatrician?*
>
> *Ask your doctor, friends, co-workers and family members for references to pediatricians they know and trust. If you cannot find one that way, contact your local medical society and ask for a reference.*

When should I arrange a visit?

It's usually most beneficial to visit the pediatrician 3 or 4 weeks *before* your due date. If the baby comes early, you will have already made these arrangements.

INTERVIEWING A PEDIATRICIAN

There are many things you and your partner will want to cover in this initial interview. Below is a list of questions that may help you create a dialogue with this important doctor for your child.

- What are your qualifications and training?
- What is your availability?
- What are your office hours?
- Can an acutely ill child be seen the same day?
- How can we reach you in case of an emergency or after office hours?
- Who responds if you're not available?
- Is the office staff cordial, open and easy to talk to?
- Do you return phone calls the same day?
- Are you interested in preventive, developmental and behavioral issues?
- How does your practice operate?
- Does it comply with our insurance?
- What is the nearest (to our home) emergency room or urgent-care center you would send us to?

Should I take the baby's father with me to this visit?

It's a good idea for both of you to visit the pediatrician. Your partner may have some questions. This is the perfect time for the two of you to sit down and discuss your concerns with your baby's doctor.

Why is it important to find a pediatrician before the birth?

It's important to meet this person under calm circumstances, to discuss the doctor's philosophy, to learn his or her schedule and to clarify what you can expect of this physician. When your baby is born, the pediatrician will be notified so he or she can come to the hospital and check the baby. If you select a pediatrician before the birth, your baby will see the same doctor for follow-up visits in the hospital and at the doctor's office.

What other things should we consider when selecting a pediatrician?

Some issues can be resolved only by analyzing your feelings after your visit. Below is a list of questions you and your partner might want to discuss after your visit.

- Are the doctor's philosophies and attitudes acceptable to us, such as use of antibiotics and other medications, childrearing practices or medically related religious beliefs?
- Did the doctor listen to us?
- Was he or she genuinely interested in our concerns?
- Did the physician appear interested in developing a rapport with our expected child?
- Is this a person we feel comfortable with and with whom our child will be comfortable?

What if we belong to an HMO and cannot choose a particular physician?

It's still a good idea to meet your baby's pediatrician before your baby is born. If you have a conflict or don't see eye to eye on important matters, you may be able to choose another pediatrician within the practice. Ask your patient advocate for information and advice.

TRAVELING DURING PREGNANCY

I've got to make a business trip soon, and I'm pregnant. Can I go?

Travel during pregnancy can be fatiguing and frustrating, but if your pregnancy is normal, you should be able to travel during the 1st and 2nd trimesters without too much trouble. Talk with your doctor if you're considering traveling during your 3rd trimester. Always discuss travel with your doctor *before* you make any reservations.

?

What should I keep in mind about traveling while I'm pregnant?

Take frequent breaks to stretch your legs during trips. Don't overdo it—rest when possible. You might want to avoid places where good medical care is not available or where changes in climate, food or altitude could cause you problems.

I'm just finishing my 1st trimester, and we are planning a trip. Is that OK?

Ask your doctor. Most will tell you it's OK to travel during pregnancy, but each situation is different. Some general considerations about traveling during pregnancy include the following.

- Don't plan a trip during your last month of pregnancy.
- If you're having any problems, such as bleeding or cramping, don't travel.
- If you are uncomfortable or have problems with swelling, then traveling, sitting in a car or doing a lot of walking may make things worse (and it probably won't be much fun either).
- If your pregnancy is considered high risk, a trip during pregnancy is not a good idea.
- Avoid long flights, especially nonstop overseas or cross-country flights. It's difficult to make long journeys without being able to move around much.
- When flying, preorder special meals, such as low-sodium or vegetarian, if you want to avoid foods that might cause you problems.
- If you experience nausea when traveling, carry crackers or another bland snack food to nibble on. Prop up your feet when you sit for any length of time.

- Get up and keep moving when you can during a flight. Try to walk at least 10 minutes every hour. Sometimes just standing up helps your circulation. Try to get an aisle seat, close to the bathroom.
- Wear medical support knee-high hose to help prevent swelling. They are not tight at the knee and will improve circulation to your feet.
- Observe seat-belt signs, and stay seated during turbulence. Your balance may not be as good while you're pregnant.
- Be careful of X-ray devices in the airport.
- If you're 36 weeks' pregnant (or more), bring a letter from your doctor saying it is OK for you to fly. Be advised: Even with a letter, a captain has the authority to keep you off the plane, but it doesn't happen very often.
- Remember you are pregnant when you plan a trip. Be sensible in your planning, and take it easy.

What are the greatest risks for me if I decide to travel during my pregnancy?

The biggest risk of traveling during pregnancy is the development of a complication while you are away from home and away from those who have been involved in your pregnancy and know your history. Other concerns include your discomfort or trouble sleeping, especially if you are cooped up in a car for hours or are trying to sleep in a strange bed. Consider these things, and discuss them with your doctor before making plans, making reservations or buying tickets.

I've heard I shouldn't travel during the last month of my pregnancy. Why?

At this point, labor could begin at any time, your water could break or other problems could occur. Your doctor knows what has happened during your pregnancy and has a record of tests done—these things are important. If you check into a hospital in a strange place, they don't know you and you don't know them. Some doctors won't accept you as a patient in this situation, and it can be awkward. It doesn't make sense to take this kind of a chance.

Can't my doctor check me and tell if I will be in labor soon so I'll know if I can go on a trip?

First of all, no one can predict when your labor will begin. No one can guarantee you can go on a trip and not go into labor or have other problems. You can't guarantee it even if you're at home! Plan ahead, and discuss it with your doctor before you make plans or buy airplane tickets.

My husband has to go out of town for a business trip, and I'm due in 3 weeks. Can't my doctor check me and tell if I will go into labor while he's gone?

Your doctor can check you, but this really only tells you where you are at that point in time. Nothing will guarantee your husband won't miss the delivery. The last month of pregnancy isn't a good time for either one of you to be traveling.

DRIVING AND SEAT-BELT USE IN PREGNANCY

Is it safe for me to drive during pregnancy?

Yes. It may become uncomfortable for you to get in and out of the car as pregnancy progresses, but being pregnant should not interfere with your ability to drive.

I always wear a seat belt in the car, but I'm wondering if a seat belt could cause me problems now that I'm pregnant. Should I wear one?

Yes! Many women are confused about wearing seat belts and shoulder harnesses during pregnancy, but don't be misled. These safety restraints are necessary during pregnancy, just as they are necessary when you're not pregnant. Seat-belt use is so important that the National Highway Safety Administration uses a pregnant

Seat-belt use is extremely important during pregnancy. Always buckle up!

dummy in simulated accidents to record how an accident could affect a pregnant woman and her unborn baby.

Will wearing a safety belt hurt my baby?

There is no evidence that the use of safety restraints increases the chance of fetal or uterine injury. You have a better chance of survival in an accident wearing a seat belt than not wearing one.

Is there a proper way for me to wear a seat belt while I'm pregnant?

Yes. Place the lap-belt part of the restraint under your abdomen and across your upper thighs so it's snug and comfortable. Adjust your sitting position so the shoulder harness crosses your shoulder without cutting into your neck. Position the shoulder harness between your breasts; don't slip this belt off your shoulder.

THE COSTS OF HAVING A BABY

What does it cost to have a baby?

It costs a lot to have a baby! Costs vary from one part of the country to another, depending on how long you stay in the hospital and whether you or your baby have complications. Prices can range from $5,000 to $15,000 for a delivery. Total cost depends on how long you and your baby are in the hospital, if you have an epidural and if you deliver vaginally or by Cesarean section.

INSURANCE COVERAGE

Your insurance coverage can vary quite a lot from company to company. Find out what your insurance company covers by asking the following questions.

- What type of coverage do I have?
- Are there maternity benefits? What are they?
- Do maternity benefits cover Cesarean deliveries?
- What kind of coverage is there for a high-risk pregnancy?
- Do I have to pay a deductible? If so, what is it?
- How do I submit claims?
- Is there a cap on total coverage?
- What percentage of my costs is covered?
- Does my coverage restrict the kind of hospital accommodations I may choose, such as a birthing center or a birthing room?
- What procedures must I follow before entering the hospital?
- Does my policy cover a nurse-midwife if I choose to use one?
- Does coverage include medications?
- What tests during pregnancy are covered under the policy?
- What tests during labor and delivery are covered under the policy?
- What types of anesthesia are covered during labor and delivery?
- How long can I stay in the hospital?

- Does payment go directly to my doctor or to me?
- What conditions or services are *not* covered?
- What kind of coverage is there for the baby after it is born?
- How long can the baby stay in the hospital?
- Is there an additional cost to add the baby to the policy?
- How do I add the baby to the policy?
- Can we collect a percentage of a fee from my husband's policy and the rest from mine?

How can I find out more about exactly what it will cost?
You may need to check with the hospital and your insurance company, if you have insurance. Someone in your doctor's office can usually help you with this.

Is it really OK to ask my doctor's office questions about insurance? I don't want to bother them.
Yes, it's OK, so don't be afraid to ask. Most offices have at least one person who deals only with insurance companies. They realize how important this is.

I live in Canada. Is insurance for a baby different here?
Yes, the Canadian healthcare system is very different from the U.S. system. Canadians pay a healthcare premium on a monthly basis, and cost varies depending on the province you live in. The government pays the doctor who delivers your baby.

CHILDBIRTH-EDUCATION CLASSES

When should I register for childbirth-education classes?
Plan ahead. Before you are 20 weeks' pregnant, begin looking into classes that are offered in your area. You and your partner should be

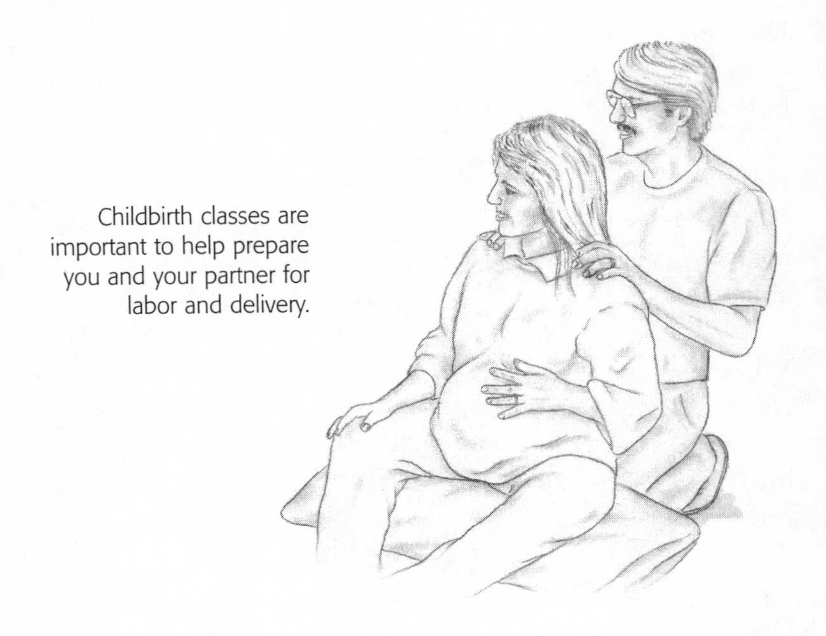

Childbirth classes are important to help prepare you and your partner for labor and delivery.

signed up or just beginning classes by the beginning of the 3rd trimester, or about 27 weeks. It's a good idea to plan to finish the classes at least a few weeks before your due date.

Why should we take these classes?

It's a good way to prepare for this very important and exciting time of your life! You will find that other people have the same concerns you have.

Where are classes held?

Classes are offered in various settings. Most hospitals that deliver babies offer classes. They are often taught by labor-and-delivery nurses or by a midwife. Ask your doctor about which classes would be best for you. Friends can also be good sources, or you might look in your yellow pages under "Childbirth Education."

Are classes only for first-time moms?

No. Classes are recommended if you have a new partner, if it has been a few years since you've had a baby, if you have questions or if you would like a review of labor and delivery.

Do many couples take childbirth-education classes?

Yes. Nearly 90% of all first-time expectant parents take some type of childbirth-education class.

How do these classes help?

Studies have shown that women who have taken classes need less medication, have fewer forceps deliveries and feel more positive about the birth than women who do not take classes.

What kind of things will we learn about in childbirth-education classes?

Classes cover many aspects of labor and delivery, including breathing techniques, vaginal birth, Cesarean delivery, hospital procedures, ways to deal with the discomfort and pain of labor and delivery, and the postpartum or recovery period.

Does insurance cover classes?

Some insurance companies and a few HMOs offer at least partial reimbursement for class fees. Classes are usually reasonably priced.

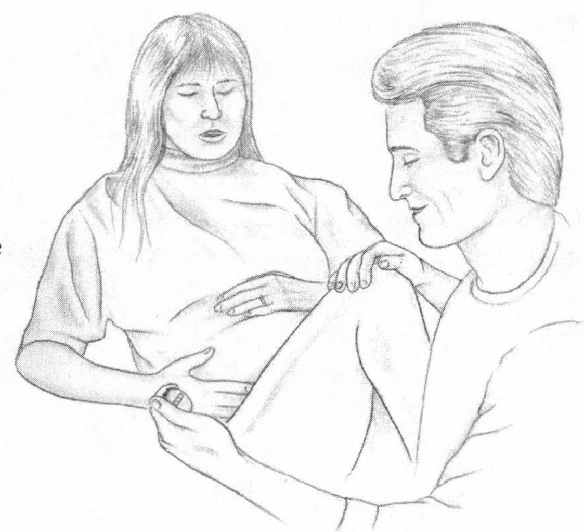

Some childbirth methods teach breathing techniques to help you deal with the pain of labor. If you choose one of these methods, practice your breathing with your labor coach to prepare you for labor and delivery.

CHOOSING A CHILDBIRTH-EDUCATION CLASS

How will you know a class is right for you? There are quite a few ways to evaluate a class.

- Find out what is available in your area.
- Talk to friends and relatives who have taken various classes.
- Decide whether you want a drug-free birth or whether you are willing to consider pain relief if it becomes necessary.
- Learn about the qualifications of the instructors in various programs.
- Visit some classes or talk to the teachers of a class in your area to choose the best one for you.

What are Lamaze classes?

Lamaze is the oldest technique of childbirth preparation. It emphasizes relaxation and breathing during labor and delivery.

What are Bradley classes?

These classes teach the *Bradley method* of relaxation and inward focus, using many types of relaxation. Bradley class members are typically people who have decided they do not want to use any type of medication for labor-pain relief.

What are Grantly Dick-Read classes?

The *Grantly Dick-Read method* attempts to break the fear-tension-pain cycle of labor and delivery. These classes were the first to include fathers in the birth experience.

OTHER PREGNANCY QUESTIONS

I have a couple of friends who got pregnant at about the same time I did, but we all look as if we're at different stages of pregnancy. Is anything wrong?

No, not usually. Every woman's pregnancy is different. A lot of what you look like depends on your size (how tall you are, your weight) and the size of your growing baby. Don't expect to look the same as other women or to have the same experiences as your friends.

I feel upset because there's so much to do before my baby is born. What can I do?

You may start to feel guilty because you can't do everything you want to as your pregnancy progresses. Blaming yourself for things that are out of your control is counterproductive. Take some time to evaluate each situation, do what you can, let the rest go, then relax and enjoy life!

My breasts are really sore. Is this normal?

Changes in your breasts may begin early in your pregnancy; it isn't unusual for them to tingle or to be sore. You may also notice your breasts growing larger, or see a darkening area or an elevation of the glands around the nipple.

It seems like I am always going to the bathroom since I found out I'm pregnant. Is this normal?

More frequent urination is common in pregnancy.

Pets

We have a dog that has been our "baby" for 6 years. Now we are expecting a real baby. Will we have problems with our pet?

When a baby is born to a couple with a dog that has been the center of attention for a long while, problems may arise. Sometimes the dog resents the attention the baby gets and growls at the infant, barks or demands attention. The animal may even revert to unacceptable behavior, such as wetting or tearing things up.

You may discover your animals have a difficult time being replaced by the new baby. There are techniques you can use to help your animal accept the baby when you bring it home.

What can we do to help our dog accept the new baby?

If your dog has never been around children, begin introducing him or her to the sights, sounds and smells of a new baby before your baby is born. When you bring the baby home, give your dog positive attention while introducing him or her to the new baby. Be firm when your dog misbehaves—don't let him or her get away with bad behavior. Be sure your male dog is neutered; unneutered dogs are more apt to growl, snap and bite. Don't isolate your dog when you bring the baby home. Make him or her a part of family interactions. Never leave the dog alone with the baby. Use common sense, and take things slowly.

We have a cat. Should we expect problems with him when we bring the baby home?

Cats are affected in many of the same ways as dogs, and much of the advice on dogs applies to cats. Expect a cat to take longer to adjust to a new baby than a dog does. You may have to train your cat to stay out of the baby's crib.

Dealing with Other People

We've been considering names for our baby; some of them are unusual. Should we discuss our choices with others?

Some couples decide on a name together, but don't tell anyone else until after the baby is born. It's easy for people to criticize a name when you're thinking about it, but few people will tell you they don't like a name when you've already named your baby!

Everybody at work seems to have advice for me. How do I handle this?

Unwelcome advice, unwarranted questions, even physical contact are common during pregnancy. Use humor to deflect some of the questions. You can listen to unasked-for advice, nod wisely and say "thanks," without making any commitment. Try not to let this attention annoy you.

I find it annoying when people (even total strangers) pat my pregnant tummy. How can I keep them from doing this?

Ask people to look and not to touch! When someone reaches out to touch your abdomen, tell them you are uncomfortable with that.

Taking Others to Prenatal Appointments

Would it be all right to take my partner to my appointments with me?

It's a great idea! It will help him realize what is happening to you and to feel a part of the pregnancy. And it's nice for your partner and your doctor to meet before labor begins.

Can I take anyone else with me to my appointments?

It's all right to take your mother or mother-in-law to an appointment with you to hear the baby's heartbeat. Things have really changed since your mother carried you; she might enjoy a visit. If you want to bring anyone else, discuss it with your doctor first.

My kids are curious and ask a lot of questions about my pregnancy. Is it OK to take them with me to my prenatal appointments?

Many offices don't mind if you bring your children with you; other offices ask that you not bring children along. Ask about office policy. If you're having problems and need to talk with your doctor, it can be very difficult to have a discussion if you're also trying to take care of a young child.

BRINGING CHILDREN TO OFFICE VISITS

Some suggestions for bringing children include the following.

- Ask about office policy ahead of time.
- Don't bring them on your first visit, when you will probably have a pelvic exam.
- If you're bringing your children to hear the heartbeat, don't bring them the first time your doctor tries to hear it; wait until after you have heard it first.
- Bring one or two children at a time rather than a large group.
- Bring something to entertain your child in case you have to wait—not all offices have toys or books for kids.
- Be considerate of other patients; don't bring a child who has a cold or is sick. This could be very serious for other pregnant women sitting in the waiting room.
- Don't bring other people's children to your appointment.

SOME PREGNANCY PRECAUTIONS

I don't usually use sunscreen, but a friend suggested it's important during pregnancy. Why?

Sunscreen lessens the likelihood of getting the *mask of pregnancy,* which is a darkening of skin pigment on cheeks, forehead and chin.

Use products with SPF 15 or higher. If you're prone to acne breakouts, use a water-based or oil-free product.

I like to look tan all the time, so I use a tanning booth. This won't harm my baby, will it?

Researchers have not studied the effects on a growing fetus when a pregnant woman lies in a tanning booth. Until we know that there is no reason for concern, avoid this activity while you're pregnant.

Someone said I shouldn't bathe during pregnancy, that it's better to shower. Is this true?

There is no medical reason to choose showering over bathing during pregnancy. In the last few weeks of pregnancy, as you get bigger, you must be careful about slipping in the shower or the tub. If you think your water has broken (ruptured membranes), your doctor may recommend that you don't bathe.

I like to sit in a hot tub after I exercise, but I read I shouldn't while I'm pregnant. Why?

Your baby relies on you to maintain correct body temperature. Research has shown that an elevated temperature for an extended time may harm a developing fetus, so for this reason, avoid hot tubs, saunas, steamrooms and spas during pregnancy.

I've always heard that a pregnant woman shouldn't have her hair colored or get a permanent. Is there any real reason to avoid these?

No. It's probably a good idea to avoid these activities during the 1st trimester, if you have morning sickness. The fumes from the hair dye or the permanent solution could make you feel ill.

I love to have a massage because it relaxes me so much. Can I continue to have massages while I'm pregnant?

It's probably OK to have a massage during pregnancy. You may find it more difficult as your pregnancy progresses and you get bigger. If you want to have a massage when you are further along in your pregnancy, lie on your side instead of on your stomach or back. Always be careful not to get overheated in any activity.

Is it OK to use the microwave during my pregnancy?

We don't know for sure if there is danger to your pregnancy from being around a microwave oven, so follow the directions provided with your microwave. It's a good idea not to stand next to or directly in front of it while it's in use.

Is it all right to douche during pregnancy?

No. Most doctors agree douching can be dangerous during pregnancy.

What's the problem with douching during pregnancy?

Using a douche may cause an infection or bleeding or even break your bag of waters (rupture your membranes). It can cause more serious problems, such as an air embolus. An air embolus results when air gets into your circulation from the pressure of the douche. It is rare but can be a serious problem.

I usually have electrolysis to remove facial hair. Can I have this done during pregnancy?

No one knows for sure whether this procedure is safe. Because no information is available, wait until after your baby is born to have facial hair removed.

To take care of leg hair, I have my legs waxed. Is this permissible while I'm pregnant?

There is probably little risk to you with this procedure. Be sure you don't get overheated while having it done. You shouldn't raise your body temperature above 102F (39C) for more than 15 minutes.

When I was 15, I got a tattoo on my shoulder, but I want to have it removed now. My dermatologist told me to wait till after the baby is born. Why?

Many tattoos are removed using lasers, and we are unsure how safe it might be for you to have this done during pregnancy. Wait until after your baby is born to have it removed.

I just got a gift certificate for an herbal wrap, and I'm 14 weeks' pregnant. Should I wait to have it until after my baby is born?

Definitely wait until after your baby is born to have an herbal wrap. Being wrapped in hot towels will cause your body to become very heated, which is not advisable during pregnancy.

Can I continue to use my electric blanket now that I'm pregnant?

There has been controversy about using electric blankets during pregnancy. At this time, no one knows the answer to this question. Until we know more, the safest thing to do is not to use an electric blanket but to find other ways to stay warm, such as with down comforters or extra blankets.

14

Problems and Warning Signs

It would be unusual if you didn't have some concerns about problems you might experience during your pregnancy. Nearly every woman does. Often these concerns arise because the whole pregnancy experience is new to you. You're normal if you are a little nervous about all the unknowns that can occur during a pregnancy. You're not alone!

By being aware of various problems that might occur, and knowing what signs and symptoms to look for, you can help your doctor treat you more easily. You are part of your medical care. You know your body better than any doctor ever will, so you know when things aren't right. By asking about a concern at one of your prenatal appointments or calling the office when you're concerned about something, you and the healthcare professionals who care for you will be working together to make this a great pregnancy! This helps you deal with any situation before it becomes more serious.

BLEEDING DURING PREGNANCY

I'm 7 weeks' pregnant and started to bleed a little last night. It scares me. What should I do?

Call your doctor about any bleeding; he or she may want you to have an ultrasound. This early in pregnancy, you are probably worrying about having a miscarriage. Be assured that bleeding during

I'm worried that I won't know when to call my doctor if I have any problems during my pregnancy. Are there warning signs I should know about?

If you think there is something to be concerned about, ask for help. General warning signs include the following:

- *vaginal bleeding*
- *painful urination*
- *severe abdominal pain*
- *loss of fluid from the vagina, usually a gushing of fluid but sometimes a trickle or continual wetness*
- *a big change in the movement of the baby or a lack of fetal movement*
- *high fever (more than 101.6F; 38.7C)*
- *chills*
- *severe vomiting or inability to keep food or liquids down*
- *blurring of vision*
- *severe swelling of the face or fingers*
- *a severe headache or a headache that won't go away*
- *an injury or accident serious enough to give you concern about the well-being of your pregnancy, such as a fall or an automobile accident*

pregnancy is not unusual and doesn't always mean a problem. About 1 woman in 5 bleeds sometime in early pregnancy.

What causes the bleeding?

Usually we cannot give a definite answer as to what causes it, but we do know that it is not usually a problem. If you experience any vaginal bleeding during pregnancy, call your doctor.

I called my doctor and told him I had some bleeding, and he told me to rest and not to have intercourse. Isn't there some medicine I can take or something I can do to stop the bleeding and make sure everything is going to be OK?

Your doctor gave you good advice—there isn't any surgery or medicine that will stop the bleeding. If your concern or your doctor's concern is high, he or she may schedule you for an ultrasound. An ultrasound won't stop anything from happening; it may give some reassurance, but you may still bleed. You must discuss a course of treatment or actions to take with your doctor, who knows your past history and individual situation.

If I go to bed with bleeding, will that help?

Contact your doctor before you do anything. Follow his or her instructions. Going to bed and resting may help. Your doctor knows your medical and pregnancy history, so follow his or her advice.

If you have *any* symptoms that worry you, call your doctor.

FALLING WHILE YOU'RE PREGNANT

IF YOU FALL

If you fall during pregnancy, contact your doctor, especially if you experience any of the following:

- bleeding
- a gush of fluid from the vagina, indicating rupture of membranes
- severe abdominal pain

Movement of the baby after a fall is reassuring.

I fell down today. How do I know that my baby wasn't hurt?

A fall is the most frequent cause of minor injury during pregnancy. Fortunately, a fall is usually without serious injury to the fetus or to the mother.

What should I do if I fall?

Call your doctor; you may require attention. If it's a bad fall, he or she may advise monitoring the baby's heartbeat or order an ultrasound for you.

GESTATIONAL DIABETES

I've heard about diabetes that occurs only during pregnancy. What is it?

Some women develop diabetes only during pregnancy; it is called gestational diabetes. It affects about 10% of all pregnancies. After pregnancy, nearly all women with gestational diabetes return to normal, and the problem disappears.

If I have gestational diabetes with this pregnancy, will I have it again?

A woman who develops gestational diabetes in one pregnancy has a good chance of developing it in a subsequent pregnancy.

Who gets gestational diabetes?

Women at greatest risk of developing gestational diabetes are overweight, with family members who have insulin-dependent or diet-controlled diabetes. Occasionally a woman with no known personal or family risk factors develops the problem.

Children of diabetic women are more likely to develop diabetes themselves. Daughters of women who developed gestational diabetes are likely to become diabetic during their own pregnancies. If you know your mother developed gestational diabetes, tell your doctor.

A woman's own weight when she was born may indicate her chances of developing gestational diabetes. One study showed women who were in the *bottom* 10th percentile of weight when they were born were 3 to 4 times *more likely* to develop gestational diabetes during pregnancy.

What causes the problem?

Gestational diabetes is triggered when the hormonal changes of pregnancy, combined with dietary factors, result in higher blood-sugar levels.

How can gestational diabetes affect me?

It can cause several medical complications, including kidney, eye, blood and vascular problems. The condition may cause premature labor because the uterus becomes overdistended. A woman may experience a very long labor because the baby is large. Sometimes a baby cannot fit through the birth canal, and a Cesarean delivery is required. You may experience more infections during pregnancy; the most common involve the kidneys, the bladder, the cervix and the uterus.

How does gestational diabetes affect my baby?

A baby's growth may be exaggerated. In some cases, the baby grows so large it cannot be delivered safely by vaginal birth.

After birth, a baby may also have very low blood sugar, called *hypoglycemia*, because the baby's body now controls its own blood sugar. The baby may also be born with hyperbilirubinemia (severe jaundice). Some babies have weak or high-pitched cries, appear shaky and tire quickly. A baby may be unable to nurse well or for long enough to get adequate nutrition, which can affect his or her growth.

What will my doctor do if I have gestational diabetes?

The best way to treat gestational diabetes is for you to eat properly. Your doctor will probably recommend a six-meal, 2000- to 2500-calorie/day eating plan and may have you see a dietitian.

Getting regular exercise and drinking lots of water every day are also very important in this plan. If you have gestational diabetes, your blood-sugar level may be tested at office visits and by you at home.

If I have pregnancy diabetes, will I get the other kind of diabetes?

More than half of all women who experience diabetes during pregnancy become diabetic later in life.

MISCARRIAGE

This is my first pregnancy, and I'm very nervous about having a miscarriage. What exactly is a miscarriage?

A miscarriage is a loss of a pregnancy before 20 weeks of gestation. An embryo or a fetus is delivered before it can survive outside the womb. This may also be called a *spontaneous abortion*. Loss of the fetus after 20 weeks is a *stillbirth*.

Why do miscarriages occur?

Most of the time we don't know—a miscarriage can happen for many different reasons. The most common finding in early miscarriages is abnormal development of the early embryo. Research indicates that more than half of these miscarriages have chromosomal abnormalities. Outside factors can also cause miscarriage. Maternal factors are also believed to be relevant in some miscarriages.

Do miscarriages occur very often?

Miscarriages occur in 1 out of every 4 pregnancies; about 25% of all pregnancies end in miscarriage.

What kind of outside factors can cause a miscarriage?

Research has shown that radiation and some chemicals (drugs or medications) may cause a miscarriage.

What maternal factors can cause a miscarriage?

There are maternal factors that can increase the chance of miscarriage. These factors include the following:

- Research has shown that unusual infections in the mother-to-be, such as listeriosis, toxoplasmosis and syphilis, may cause miscarriage.
- A deficiency of progesterone is believed by some to be a

cause of early miscarriage; if detected early enough, it may be treatable, but not everyone agrees with this.
- Genital infections have been shown to trigger miscarriage. When an infection is found, the woman and her partner are treated.
- Sometimes a woman's body makes antibodies that attack the fetus or disrupt the function of the placenta.
- Women who smoke have a higher rate of miscarriage.
- Alcohol also has been blamed for an increased rate of miscarriage.

I've heard that sometimes a particular couple can have a high risk of miscarriage. Can you explain this?

This does cause some confusion for many people, but it is fairly easy to understand. When a couple's genes unite upon fertilization of the egg by the sperm, the union can produce genetic abnormalities that can cause a miscarriage. Genetic screening can sometimes reveal this, if this is the problem (see page 66).

Can nutrient deficiency cause a miscarriage?

We have no concrete evidence that deficiency of any particular nutrient or even moderate deficiency of all nutrients can cause a miscarriage.

Can a woman cause a miscarriage to occur?

Not usually, so don't blame yourself if you have a miscarriage. It's a normal reaction to look for a reason for losing a pregnancy and to think you might have done something wrong. Many women try to blame stress, emotional upset or physical activity for causing a miscarriage. These things do not usually cause miscarriages.

I've heard that there are different types of miscarriage. What are they?

Following are the medical descriptions for types of miscarriage:

- threatened miscarriage
- inevitable miscarriage
- incomplete miscarriage

- missed miscarriage
- habitual (recurrent) miscarriage

What is a threatened miscarriage?

A *threatened miscarriage* occurs when there is a bloody discharge from the vagina during the first half of pregnancy. Bleeding may last for days or weeks. There may be cramping and pain—pain may feel like a menstrual cramp or mild backache. Bed rest is about all a woman can do to try to prevent the miscarriage from happening, although being active does not cause miscarriage.

What is an inevitable miscarriage?

An *inevitable miscarriage* occurs with the rupture of membranes, dilatation of the cervix and passage of blood clots and even tissue. Loss of the pregnancy is almost certain under these circumstances. Contraction of the uterus usually occurs, expelling the embryo or products of conception.

What is an incomplete miscarriage?

In an *incomplete miscarriage,* the entire pregnancy is not immediately expelled. Part of the pregnancy may be passed while the rest remains in the uterus. Bleeding may be heavy and continues until the uterus is empty or until a doctor empties it, usually with dilatation and curettage (D&C).

What is a missed miscarriage?

A *missed miscarriage* can occur when an embryo that has died earlier is retained in the uterus. A woman may not bleed or have any other symptoms. The time period between the failure of the pregnancy and the discovery of the miscarriage is usually weeks.

What is a habitual miscarriage?

A *habitual miscarriage* usually refers to three or more consecutive miscarriages. It may also be called *recurrent miscarriage.*

What are the warning signs of a miscarriage?

The first warning sign is bleeding from the vagina, followed by cramping. Call your doctor if you experience these problems! The longer you bleed and cramp, the more likely you are to have a miscarriage.

What can I do if I think I'm having a miscarriage?

Call your doctor. In nearly all instances, there is nothing you can do to stop a miscarriage from happening. There is no surgery that can be done or medicine you can take to stop a miscarriage. Most physicians recommend bed rest and decreased activity. Some recommend use of the hormone progesterone, but not all agree with its use. Ultrasound and blood tests may be used to help determine whether you are going to miscarry, but you may have to wait and see.

What will my doctor do if I am having a miscarriage?

If you expel all of the products of the pregnancy and bleeding stops and cramping goes away, you may be done with it. If everything is not expelled, it will be necessary to perform a D&C to empty the uterus. It is preferable to perform this surgical procedure so you won't bleed for a long time, risking anemia and infection.

I've heard a woman needs to be concerned about Rh-sensitivity if she has a miscarriage. Is this true?

If you're Rh-negative and have a miscarriage, you will need to receive RhoGAM. This applies *only* if you are Rh-negative.

If I have a miscarriage, will there be an embryo or a fetus? What will it look like?

You usually won't see a fetus. What you pass looks like white, gray or red tissue.

If I miscarry, will it be possible to tell if it was a boy or girl?

No, this is not possible.

When my sister had a miscarriage, they told her to save the tissue, but she had already flushed it. Why did they want her to save it?

Some doctors want you to bring the tissue to the lab to verify it was really the pregnancy that was passed and not just a blood clot.

If I am having a miscarriage, will my pregnancy test be positive?

Yes. Hormones will make your pregnancy test positive.

ECTOPIC PREGNANCY

What is an ectopic pregnancy?

Ectopic pregnancy, sometimes called *tubal pregnancy,* occurs about once in every 100 pregnancies. An ectopic pregnancy happens when implantation of the embryo occurs outside the uterine cavity, usually in the Fallopian tube. It can also occur on the ovary, in the entrance to the tube, at the point the tube joins the uterus and at the mouth of the uterus. An ectopic pregnancy is serious because heavy bleeding may result when it ruptures.

I'm 8 weeks' pregnant and have pain on my side where I think my ovary is. Could it be an ectopic pregnancy?

It isn't unusual to have mild pain early in pregnancy from a cyst on the ovary or stretching of the uterus or ligaments. It probably isn't an ectopic pregnancy, but if the pain is bad enough to cause you concern, call your doctor.

What factors increase the risk of having an ectopic pregnancy?

The following factors can increase your risk for an ectopic pregnancy:

- pelvic infections (PID or pelvic inflammatory disease)
- previous ruptured appendix
- previous ectopic pregnancy
- surgery on your Fallopian tubes (such as reversal of a tubal ligation)
- use of an IUD

Research has shown that chlamydia infection may be linked to ectopic pregnancy. One report showed 70% of the women they studied who had an ectopic pregnancy also had a chlamydia infection before they became pregnant. If you are trying to get pregnant, you may want to be screened for this STD, which is easily treated.

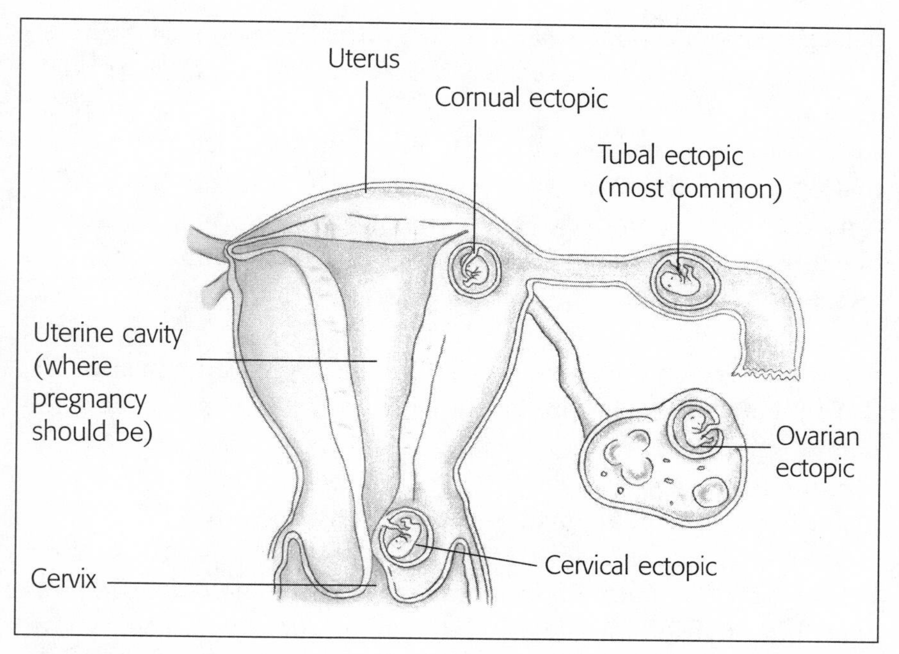

Sites of ectopic pregnancies.

How is an ectopic pregnancy diagnosed?

Diagnosis can be difficult and may require a couple of tests and some waiting. Tests include ultrasound, quantitative HCGs and laparoscopy (a visual examination inside the abdomen). Even with these tests, it may be a few days or weeks before your doctor can make a definite diagnosis.

Are there any symptoms with an ectopic pregnancy?

Yes; symptoms include abdominal pain and bleeding from the vagina. It may be confused with appendicitis, the flu or a bladder infection.

I've had some pain and bleeding, and my doctor is concerned about an ectopic pregnancy. Yesterday I had a quantitative HCG, and I'm supposed to have another one tomorrow. What is a quantitative HCG?

A quantitative HCG (human chorionic gonadotropin) is a special pregnancy test done with your blood. HCG is a hormone produced during pregnancy; it increases very rapidly early in pregnancy. A regular pregnancy test, using blood or urine, gives you a positive or negative ("yes" or "no") answer. A quantitative HCG assigns a number to tell how pregnant you are. The numbers aren't exact, but in a normal pregnancy they increase in a certain way. A quantitative HCG can help your doctor decide if your pregnancy is normal. This test is not used in normal pregnancies but can be very helpful when you are concerned about a miscarriage or ectopic pregnancy.

If I have an ectopic pregnancy, will a pregnancy test be positive?

Yes. The hormones produced with an ectopic pregnancy still make your pregnancy test positive.

If I have an ectopic pregnancy, what can my doctor do for me?

Many ectopic pregnancies result in reabsorption of the embryo before the tube ruptures. The woman may never know she was pregnant. If you are diagnosed with an ectopic pregnancy, you may be treated with methotrexate (medication), but often surgery is necessary to correct the problem, which results in loss of the pregnancy.

BLOOD CLOTS DURING PREGNANCY

I heard about a woman who had thrombophlebitis during pregnancy. Is that the same as a blood clot in the leg?

Yes, it is. The problem has several names, including *venous thrombosis, thromboembolic disease, thrombophlebitis* and *lower deep-vein thrombosis.*

Why do blood clots in the leg occur in pregnancy?

This condition is more likely to occur during pregnancy because of the changes in blood circulation. There is a slowing of blood flow in the legs because of pressure from the uterus on blood vessels and because of changes in the blood and its clotting mechanisms. Blood clots occur in less than 1% of all pregnancies.

What causes blood clots during pregnancy?

The most likely cause is decreased blood flow, called *stasis.*

I had a blood clot a few years ago. Is that relevant to my pregnancy?

Yes. Tell your doctor about it. This is important information!

I have a blood clot in my leg, but my doctor said it isn't serious because it's "superficial." What does that mean?

If a blood clot occurs in the veins near the surface of the leg, it is not serious. This type of thrombosis does not require hospitalization and is treated with mild pain relievers, elevation of the leg, heat and support of the leg with an Ace bandage or support stockings.

I have a deep-vein thrombosis, and my doctor said it is a serious problem. Why?

It is more serious because of the risk of the blood clot breaking loose and traveling to another part of the body, such as the lungs.

SIGNS AND SYMPTOMS OF DEEP-VEIN THROMBOSIS

Signs and symptoms can vary widely and include the following:

- paleness of the leg
- leg is cool to the touch
- a portion of the leg may be tender, hot and swollen
- skin of the leg may have red streaks over the veins
- squeezing the calf or walking may be very painful
- rapid, abrupt onset of the above symptoms

How is a deep-vein thrombosis diagnosed?

A pregnant woman will have an ultrasound of her legs. A non-pregnant woman will have either X-ray or ultrasound.

How is deep-vein thrombosis treated during pregnancy?

Treatment usually consists of hospitalization and administration of heparin to thin the blood and to allow the clot to dissolve. While receiving heparin, the woman is required to stay in bed with heat applied to her elevated leg.

I had a blood clot with my last pregnancy and just found out I'm pregnant. What should I do?

Call your doctor. If you have had a blood clot with a previous pregnancy, you will probably need heparin during this pregnancy. It should be started right away.

If heparin is used to prevent another blood clot, how is it given?

You give yourself injections 2 or 3 times a day, using a long-dwelling I.V. or a heparin pump.

Isn't there a blood thinner that can be taken as a pill?

Yes, it is called warfarin (Coumadin), but it is not usually given during pregnancy because it is not safe for the baby. Heparin is safe for use during pregnancy. After you deliver, you may have to take warfarin for a few weeks, depending on the severity of the blood clot.

How common is a pulmonary embolism in pregnancy?

It is a rare problem in pregnancy.

BREAST LUMPS IN PREGNANCY

I'm pregnant and just found a lump in my breast. What should I do?

Tell your doctor immediately! It's normal for your breasts to change and to grow larger during pregnancy, but you must have lumps checked out.

Are there any tests that can be done if I am pregnant and have a breast lump?

The first test is to examine yourself, then have your doctor check you if you find a lump. After your doctor's examination, you may have either a mammogram or an ultrasound. If you have a mammogram, tell them you are pregnant. They will cover your abdomen with a lead shield.

What can be done for a breast lump during pregnancy?

Often a lump in the breast can be drained or aspirated. If it cannot be drained, biopsy or removal of the lump may be necessary. Depending on how serious it is, surgery or other treatment may be needed.

Does a breast lump always mean cancer?

No, it doesn't, but it's important to get breast lumps checked.

Does pregnancy make breast cancer grow faster?

Not everyone agrees on the answer to this question. Most medical experts don't believe pregnancy accelerates the course or growth of breast cancer.

PRE-ECLAMPSIA IN PREGNANCY

I've heard about pre-eclampsia. What is it?

Pre-eclampsia is development of the following symptoms:

- hypertension (high blood pressure)
- protein in the urine
- swelling, usually in the legs, but also elsewhere in the body
- changes in muscle reflexes

Pre-eclampsia develops in about 5% of all pregnancies, usually in a woman's first pregnancy.

Why is pre-eclampsia serious during pregnancy?

Pre-eclampsia occurs *only* during pregnancy. It is serious because it can lead to eclampsia.

What is eclampsia?

Eclampsia refers to seizures or convulsions in a woman with pre-eclampsia.

What is a seizure?

A seizure is a loss of body control, similar to passing out. Seizures often include twitching, shaking or convulsions of the body. If you think you've had a seizure, call your doctor immediately!

How can I know if my pre-eclampsia is getting worse and I am beginning to develop eclampsia?

Watch for any of the following warning signs:

- pain under the ribs on the right side
- headache
- seeing spots or other changes in your vision

If my legs are swollen, does it mean I have pre-eclampsia?

No. Most pregnant women experience some swelling in various parts of the body. Development of pre-eclampsia includes evidence of the other symptoms in addition to swelling.

Does an elevation in my blood pressure mean I am getting pre-eclampsia?

Again, you may experience some of the symptoms without having pre-eclampsia.

What causes pre-eclampsia?

Researchers have not been able to isolate a definite cause for pre-eclampsia, but it occurs most often during a woman's first pregnancy.

How is pre-eclampsia treated?

The goal in treating pre-eclampsia is to avoid seizures, which can occur if the woman develops eclampsia. The first step in treatment is bed rest. The woman is also advised to drink lots of water, and to avoid salt and foods containing large amounts of sodium.

If pre-eclampsia doesn't get better with bed rest, drinking fluids and avoiding sodium, then what?

In some cases, medication is prescribed to prevent seizures. These medications include magnesium sulfate, antiseizure medicines, such as phenobarbital, and medications that reduce blood pressure.

Is there any way to prevent pre-eclampsia?

At this time, there is no reliable way to prevent pre-eclampsia. According to a recent study, if you consume between 1,500 and 2,000mg of calcium a day during pregnancy, you may lower your risk of developing the problem by at least 60%.

WHEN YOUR WATER BREAKS

I've heard about my water breaking. What does this mean?

When your water breaks, the amniotic sac that surrounds the baby and placenta actually ruptures. Some amniotic fluid inside the sac may initially gush out, then the rest leak out more slowly. This occurrence often signals the beginning of labor.

What is the bag of waters?

This is another name for the amniotic sac. These membranes must break when it is time for the baby to be born. If this does not happen naturally, the doctor will break them.

What does amniotic fluid look like?

It is usually clear, but it may have a bloody appearance, or it may be yellow or green.

What should I do when my water breaks?

Call your doctor. Don't have sexual intercourse; it can increase the possibility of an infection inside your uterus.

Are there any tests that can determine if my water has broken?

Yes, there are two. One is a *nitrazine test.* Fluid is placed on a piece of nitrazine paper; if membranes have ruptured, the paper changes color. The other test is a *ferning test.* When viewed under a microscope, dried amniotic fluid looks like a fern or the branches of a pine tree.

Every once in a while I feel a little wetness, as though I'm losing urine. Am I leaking amniotic fluid?

Probably not. As your pregnancy grows, your uterus grows larger and gets heavier. The uterus sits on top of the bladder—as it increases in size, it can put a great deal of pressure on your bladder and prevent your bladder from holding as much urine. Leakages can occur, especially when you lift something or bounce up and down. You may notice that your underwear or clothing is damp.

How do I know my water isn't broken when I find my clothing wet?

When your membranes rupture, you usually experience a gush of fluid or a continual leaking from inside the vagina. If you think your water has broken, call your doctor.

THE PLACENTA

I've heard of a woman having problems with the placenta. What is the placenta?

The *placenta* is a flat, spongy structure that grows inside the mother's uterus. It is attached to the fetus by the umbilical cord and carries nourishment and oxygen from the mother to the baby. It also carries waste products from the baby to the mother for excretion.

The placenta produces hormones called HCG (human chorionic gonadotropin), estrogen and progesterone.

Placenta Previa

I have a friend who had placenta previa. What is it?

With *placenta previa,* the placenta covers part or all of the cervix.

Why is this a problem?

When the cervix begins to open (dilate), the placenta is pulled away from the uterus, causing heavy bleeding. This can be dangerous for the mother-to-be and the baby.

What are the signs and symptoms of placenta previa?

The most characteristic symptom in placenta previa is painless bleeding.

If I experience this painless bleeding, what will my doctor do?

He or she will order an ultrasound exam to determine the location of the placenta. Your physician will not do a pelvic exam because it may cause heavier bleeding. If you see another doctor or when you go to the hospital, tell whomever examines you that you have placenta previa and should *not* have a pelvic exam.

Are there things I shouldn't do if I know I have placenta previa?

Most physicians recommend avoiding intercourse, traveling and pelvic exams.

If I have placenta previa, will I have to have a Cesarean section?

The baby is more likely to be in a breech position. For this reason, and also to avoid bleeding, you will most likely have a C-section.

How common is placenta previa?

It occurs in about 1 birth in 200.

Placental Abruption

In an article about pregnancy problems, I read placental abruption can be very serious. What is it?

Placental abruption is separation of the placenta from the wall of the uterus during pregnancy. Normally the placenta does not separate until after delivery of the baby.

Is placental abruption dangerous?

When the placenta separates before birth, it can be very serious for the baby.

How often does it occur?

The frequency of placental abruption is estimated to be about 1 in every 80 deliveries.

What causes placental abruption?

The cause of placental abruption is unknown; however, certain conditions make it more likely to occur:

- trauma to the mother, such as from a fall or a car accident
- an umbilical cord that is too short
- very sudden change in the size of the uterus, such as with the rupture of membranes
- hypertension
- dietary deficiency
- an abnormality of the uterus, such as a band of tissue in the uterus called a *uterine septum*

How will I know if I have placental abruption?

Watch for the following signs and symptoms:

- heavy bleeding from the vagina
- uterine tenderness
- uterine contractions
- premature labor
- lower-back pain

Placental abruption may occur without the presence of any or all of these symptoms.

Are there any tests available to help diagnose placental abruption?

Ultrasound may be helpful, but it does not always provide an exact diagnosis.

What are the risks to the woman with placental abruption?

Risks to the mother-to-be include shock, severe blood loss and the inability of the blood to clot.

How is it treated?

The most common treatment is delivery of the baby. However, the decision of when to deliver the baby depends on the severity of the problem.

If I have placental abruption, does it mean I have to have a C-section?

In some situations, if the baby needs to be delivered rapidly, you will need a Cesarean section. Each case must be handled on an individual basis.

Can a woman do anything to prevent placental abruption?

We now believe deficiency of folic acid may play a role in causing placental abruption. Extra folic acid may be prescribed during pregnancy. Maternal smoking and alcohol use may make it more likely for a woman to have placental abruption. If you smoke or drink alcohol, you will be advised to stop both activities.

Retained Placenta

I've heard about something called a retained placenta. What is this?

One complication following the birth of a baby is a placenta that does not deliver following the birth, called a *retained placenta.* Usually the placenta separates on its own from the uterus a few minutes after delivery. In some cases, it doesn't separate because it is attached to the wall of the uterus. This can be very serious and can cause extreme blood loss.

What causes a retained placenta?

Some reasons for a retained placenta include a placenta attaching over a previous C-section scar or other incision scar on the uterus in a place that has been curetted (scraped), such as with a D&C, or over an area of the uterus that was infected.

What problems can a retained placenta cause?

The most significant problem is heavy bleeding after delivery. If the placenta is not delivered, it must be removed some other way. One solution is to perform a D&C. However, if the placenta has grown into the wall of the uterus, it may be necessary to remove the uterus by performing a hysterectomy.

Is a retained placenta common?

No. It occurs in about 1% of all deliveries.

PART THREE

Childbirth

15

Labor and Delivery

The 9 months of your pregnancy are nearly over, and your baby will soon be with you. You may be happy that this time is near. You and your partner are probably looking forward to being a family with your new baby. You may also feel a little anxious about your labor and delivery.

It's normal to feel this way. You will be going through an experience you may have heard described in many ways from friends and family. Some labor-and-delivery experiences you've heard about might have been a little scary to you.

The best advice we can give you is to relax. No one knows what's going to happen during labor and delivery; even medical professionals are sometimes surprised by what occurs. But if you open yourself up to the experience, it can be wonderful.

The end result of your pregnancy, and labor and delivery, is the birth of your baby. You are also an important part of this equation—we want you to be healthy and happy, too. Work with your healthcare team to make this a positive experience. Learn what you need to know about being prepared, the medications you might be offered and any other concerns you may have. Before you know it, you'll be holding the baby you've been waiting so long to meet!

I've already felt some contractions, and I'm only 6 months' pregnant. Am I going into labor?

Probably not. You are probably experiencing Braxton-Hicks contractions, which are painless, nonrhythmical contractions. They can begin early in pregnancy and continue off and on until your baby is born. You feel them at irregular intervals and they may increase in number and strength when your uterus is massaged.

I heard a woman describe her baby as "dropping." Does this mean the baby was falling out?

No, it doesn't. The feeling of having your baby drop, also called *lightening,* means the baby's head has moved down deep into your pelvis. It is a natural part of the birthing process and can happen a few weeks to a few hours before labor begins.

How will I feel when my baby drops?

You may feel that you have more room to breathe when the baby descends into your pelvis, but you may also feel more pelvic pressure or discomfort.

I've heard stories about a woman's water breaking when she is out in public. Does this happen often?

Although it doesn't happen very often, it is possible, but don't waste energy worrying about it. If it happens to you, people will be understanding and helpful. At that stage of your pregnancy, your condition is quite obvious to them!

Does the water usually break before a woman goes into labor?

Sometimes the water breaks shortly before labor begins. However, in most cases, a doctor will rupture the membranes after the woman goes to the hospital and is in labor.

How will I know when my water breaks?

You may feel a gush of fluid, followed by slow leaking, or you may feel just a slow leaking, without the gush of fluid. A sanitary pad will help absorb the slow leaking.

What should I do when my water breaks?

Call your doctor immediately; you must take some precautions. If labor and delivery are imminent, you may be advised to go to the hospital. If you are not near term, you may be asked to come to the office for an examination. You may not be ready to deliver your baby, and your doctor wants to prevent any infection. Risk of infection increases when your water breaks.

My doctor said she might have to induce me. How is this done?

To induce labor, your doctor will break your bag of waters and give you oxytocin (Pitocin) intravenously. The medication is given in gradually increasing doses until contractions begin.

Why is labor induced?

Your doctor may decide to induce labor if you or your baby are at risk. There are many medical reasons why labor must be induced. Inducing labor is a decision your doctor will consider.

Can I ask my doctor to induce me?

You may be tempted to ask your doctor to induce your labor for convenience or because you are tired of being pregnant. Listen to your doctor's advice.

How long does labor last?

The length of your labor is extremely individual. It varies from pregnancy to pregnancy and depends on how many pregnancies you have already had.

SOME CAUSES OF PREMATURE LABOR

In most cases, the cause of premature labor is unknown. Causes we do understand include the following:

- a uterus with an abnormal shape
- a large uterus (such as with multiple fetuses)
- hydramnios (excessive amniotic fluid)
- an abnormal placenta
- premature rupture of the membranes
- incompetent cervix (a weak cervix that dilates very early)
- abnormalities of the fetus
- fetal death
- retained IUD
- maternal illness, such as high blood pressure, or some maternal infections
- incorrect estimate of gestational age, which means the baby is really not premature

PREMATURE LABOR AND BIRTH

What is preterm birth?

Preterm birth refers to a baby born more than 4 weeks early. It is also called *premature birth.*

How common is preterm birth?

About 10% of all babies are born more than 4 weeks early.

I've heard preterm birth can be dangerous for the baby. Why?

Preterm birth of a baby can be dangerous because the baby's lungs and other organ systems may not be ready to function on their own.

What will my doctor tell me to do if I go into labor too early?

It is important to try to halt the contractions. Most doctors start by recommending bed rest and increased fluids to stop labor. Bed rest means lying in bed on your side. Either side is OK, but the left side is best.

Why do I have to lie in bed?

It works. It may mean you have to modify or stop your activities, but we have found that bed rest helps end premature labor. Before we had medications, bed rest was the only treatment for premature labor. It is still often successful.

Is there any way for my doctor to know when I will go into labor?

No one knows when labor will begin.

I've heard there are medications to stop premature labor. Can't I take one of those medications instead of going to bed?

Even if you take medication, you will probably be advised to rest in bed. Bed rest is an essential part of the treatment plan for premature labor.

What kinds of medications are used to treat premature labor?

Medications that relax the uterus and decrease contractions include three types:

- magnesium sulfate, which is usually given through an I.V.; sometimes it is given orally
- beta-adrenergics, including ritodrine and terbutaline, which are given orally, through an I.V. or by injection
- sedatives or narcotics, which may be used in early attempts to stop premature labor

What are the benefits of stopping premature labor?

It is better for both mother and baby if premature labor is halted. Premature delivery increases the risks of fetal problems and maternal problems, such as the risk of C-section.

How long can I expect to be in labor with a first baby?

With a first pregnancy, the first and second stages of labor can last 14 to 15 hours, or more. A woman who has already had one or two children will probably have a shorter labor, but that's not always the case.

GOING TO THE HOSPITAL

I'm nervous about preparing to go to the hospital. What should I be concerned about?

Going to the hospital to have a baby can cause anyone a little nervousness, even an experienced mom. If you make some plans before you have to go, you'll have less to worry about.

- Tour the labor-and-delivery area of your hospital a few weeks before your due date. You may do this as part of your childbirth-education class.
- Ask about preregistering at the hospital.
- Plan the trip; know who will take you, and have a backup person available.
- Make a personal plan.
- Pack your bag.

I've never had a baby before. What do I need to take with me to the hospital?

There are a lot of things to consider, but the following list should cover most of what you might need:

- a cotton nightgown or T-shirt for labor
- extra pillows to use during labor
- lip balm, lollipops or fruit drops to use during labor
- light diversion, such as books or magazines, to use during labor
- 1 nightgown for after labor (bring a nursing gown if you are going to breastfeed)
- slippers with rubber soles
- 1 long robe for walking in the halls
- 2 bras (nursing bras and breast pads if you breastfeed)
- toiletries you use, including brush, comb, toothbrush, toothpaste, soap, shampoo and conditioner
- hairband or ponytail holder, if you have long hair
- eyeglasses (you can't wear contact lenses)
- underwear and loose-fitting clothes for going home
- sanitary pads, if the hospital doesn't supply them

PACK FOR YOUR PARTNER, TOO!

It's a good idea to include some things in your hospital kit to help your partner get through the experience. You might consider the following items:

- completed insurance or preregistration information
- baby powder or cornstarch for massaging you during labor
- a paint roller or tennis ball for giving you a low-back massage during labor
- tapes or CDs and a player, or a radio to play during labor
- labor handbook
- camera and film
- list of telephone numbers and a long-distance calling card
- change for telephones and vending machines

What should I bring for my new baby?

The hospital will probably supply most of what you will need for your baby; however, there are a few things you should have ready:

- clothes for the trip home, including an undershirt, sleeper, outer clothes (a hat if it's cold)
- a couple of receiving blankets
- diapers, if your hospital doesn't supply them

Be sure you have an approved infant car seat to take your baby home. It's important to put your baby in a car seat the very first time he or she rides in a car!

Do I need to preregister at the hospital?

It saves time if you register at the hospital a few weeks before your due date. It is wise to do this before you go to the hospital in labor because you may be in a hurry or concerned with other things.

How do I preregister at the hospital?

You will be able to preregister with forms that you receive from your doctor's office or from the hospital.

When I preregister, what do I need to know?

Take your insurance card or insurance information with you. It is important to know your doctor's name, your pediatrician's name and your due date. It is also helpful to know your blood type and Rh-factor.

If I am in labor, what can I expect once I get to the hospital?

After you are admitted, hospital staff will settle you in a labor room and check to see how much you have dilated. They will take a brief history of your pregnancy and note vital signs, including blood pressure, pulse and temperature. You may receive an enema, have your pubic area shaved or have an I.V. started. They will probably draw blood. You may have an epidural put in place, if you have requested it.

Will they be able to tell if my membranes have ruptured?

There are several ways to confirm if your membranes have ruptured.

- By your description of what happened, such as a large gush of fluid from your vagina.
- With nitrazine paper: Fluid is placed on the paper; if membranes have ruptured, the paper changes color.
- With a ferning test: Fluid is placed on a glass slide, allowed to dry and examined under a microscope. If it has a "fern" appearance, it is amniotic fluid.

Does a woman always need to have her pubic hair shaved before the birth of her baby?

No. Many are not shaved these days. However, some women who chose not to have their pubic hair shaved later said they experienced discomfort when their pubic hair became entangled in their underwear due to the normal vaginal discharge after the birth of their baby.

Is an I.V. always necessary?

Not always, but it is necessary with an epidural. If you have chosen not to have an epidural, it is not always required. Most physicians agree an I.V. is helpful if the woman needs medications or fluids during labor or delivery or after delivery.

Can I refuse to have an I.V.?

Discuss this with your doctor before the birth of your baby. In some situations, an I.V. can save your life.

A friend told me that when she got to the hospital, she found out her doctor was on vacation and someone she didn't know was going to deliver her baby! Is there anything I can do to prevent this from happening to me?

Talk to your doctor about this possibility. If your doctor believes he or she might be out of town when your baby is born, ask to meet doctors that "cover" when your doctor is unavailable. Although your physician would like to be there for the birth of your baby, sometimes it is not possible.

LABOR

What does labor feel like?

Your entire abdomen (the uterus) contracts (tightens) like a hard muscle, then relaxes. Tightening of the uterus can cause pain.

I've heard friends describe labor differently. One said her back hurt; another said it felt like the pain she had with diarrhea. Are these different types of labor?

No, these are not different types of labor. Labor is different for every woman; that's the reason we can't predict what your labor will be like before it begins. Your labor may also be different from one delivery to the next.

TRUE LABOR OR FALSE LABOR?

Considerations	True Labor	False Labor
Contractions	Regular	Irregular
Time between contractions	Comes closer together	Does not get closer together
Contraction intensity	Increases	Doesn't change
Location of contractions	Entire abdomen or back	Various locations
Effect of anesthetic or pain relievers	Will not stop labor	Sedation may alter frequency or stop contractions
Cervical change	Progressive cervical change (effacement and dilatation)	No cervical change

I've heard all sorts of stories about labor, but I don't really know what it is. Can you explain it for me?

Labor is defined as the dilatation (stretching and expanding) of your cervix. This occurs when your uterus, which is a muscle, tightens (contracts) to squeeze out its contents (your baby).

How will I know the difference between true labor and false labor?

There are differences between the two. Study the chart on the previous page so you'll be better able to distinguish the difference.

I've heard about different stages of labor. What are they?

Labor is divided into three stages—each stage is distinctly different and has a specific purpose. Review the chart on pages 294 to 296 to see what you might expect during the various stages of labor and delivery.

What is the 1st stage of labor?

Stage 1 of labor is the longest and consists of three phases—early, active and transition. The first stage of labor usually lasts 6 to 8 hours but can be longer for a first birth.

In the early phase, labor is just getting started and dilatation of the cervix has just begun. In the active phase, the cervix dilates at a fairly constant rate; transition includes complete dilatation. Contractions help the cervix dilate and thin out. They also help move the baby down the birth canal for delivery.

At the transition phase, the pace and intensity of labor increases, signaling that labor is moving into the second stage.

What is the 2nd stage of labor?

In stage 2 of labor, you are fully dilated and begin to push. Contractions change and become much harder, longer and more frequent. Along with your pushing, these contractions help deliver the baby. This stage can take 2 hours or longer. Anesthesia at this point, especially an epidural block, may prolong this stage of labor because your urge to push is decreased. At the end of the second stage, your baby is born.

STAGES OF LABOR

Stages 1—Early Phase

What's happening	• Cervix opens and thins out due to uterine contractions • Cervix dilates to about 2cm • This phase can last 1 to 10 hours
Mother is experiencing	• Membranes may rupture, accompanied by gush or trickle of amniotic fluid from vagina • Pinkish discharge may appear ("bloody show") • Mild contractions begin at 15- to 20-minute intervals; they last about 1 minute • Contractions become closer together and more regular
What mother or labor coach can do	• Mother should not eat or drink anything once labor begins • Mother may be able to stay at home, if she is at term • Begin using relaxation and breathing techniques learned in childbirth class • If water has broken, if labor is preterm, if there is intense pain, if pain is constant or there is bright red blood, contact doctor immediately!

Stage 1—Active Phase

What's happening	• Cervix dilates from about 2 to 10cm • Cervix continues to thin out • This phase can last 20 minutes to 2 hours
Mother is experiencing	• Contractions become more intense • Contractions come closer together • Contractions are about 3 minutes apart and last about 45 seconds to 1 minute
What mother and labor coach can do	• Keep practicing relaxation and breathing techniques • An epidural can be administered during this phase

Stage 1—Transition Phase

What's happening	• Stage 1 begins to change to stage 2 • Cervix is dilated to 10cm • Cervix continues to thin out • This phase can last a few minutes to 2 hours
Mother is experiencing	• Contractions are 2 to 3 minutes apart and last about 1 minute • Mother may feel strong urge to push; she shouldn't push until cervix is completely dilated • Mother may be moved to delivery room if she is not in a birthing room
What mother and labor coach can do	• Relaxation and breathing techniques help counteract mother's urge to push

Stage 2

What's happening	• Cervix is completely dilated • Baby continues to descend into the birth canal • As mother pushes, baby is delivered • Doctor or nurse suctions baby's nose and mouth, and clamps umbilical cord • This stage can last a few minutes to a few hours (pushing the baby can last a long time)
Mother is experiencing	• Contractions occur at 2- to 5-minute intervals and last from 60 to 90 seconds • With an epidural, mother may find it harder to push • An episiotomy may be done to prevent tearing vaginal tissues as baby is born
What mother and labor coach can do	• Mother will begin to push with each contraction after cervix dilates completely • Mother may be given analgesic or local anesthetic • Mother must listen to doctor or nurse when baby is being delivered; doctor or nurse will tell mother when to push • As mother pushes, she may be able to watch baby being born, if mirror is available

	Stage 3
What's happening	• Placenta is delivered • Doctor examines placenta to make sure all of it has been delivered • Doctor repairs episiotomy • This stage can last a few minutes to an hour
Mother is experiencing	• Contractions may occur closer together but be less painful
What mother and labor coach can do	• Meet and hold the baby • Mother may need to push to expel the placenta • Mother may be able to hold baby while the doctor repairs episiotomy • Nurse will rub or massage the uterus through the abdomen to help it contract and to control bleeding (during the next couple of days, the uterus will continue to contract, which is important to control bleeding)

What is the 3rd stage of labor?

Stage 3 of labor is usually short. During stage 3, the uterus contracts and expels the placenta (afterbirth). You will be given oxytocin to help contract the uterus.

Somewhere I read there's a 4th stage of labor. Is this true?

Some doctors describe a 4th stage of labor, referring to the time period after delivery of the placenta, while the uterus continues to contract. Uterine contraction is important in controlling bleeding after the birth of your baby.

When I am in labor, how is it determined that I will need a C-section?

Each situation, each labor must be considered individually. A reason for a C-section in the 1st stage of labor is if the cervix stops dilating; say, you get to be 5cm and then don't dilate any more. In the 2nd stage of labor, a reason for a C-section could be fetal distress or if you can't push the baby out.

My best friend told me she had a bloody show just before she went into labor. What is it?

You may bleed a small amount following a vaginal exam or at the beginning of labor. This bloody show occurs as the cervix stretches and dilates. If it causes you concern or appears to be a large amount of blood, call your doctor immediately.

I read that I may pass a mucus plug at the beginning of labor. Is this dangerous?

Along with a bloody show, you may pass some mucus, sometimes called a *mucus plug.* This is not dangerous. Passing this mucus doesn't always mean you'll have your baby soon or that you are beginning labor.

Timing contractions provides your doctor with information so he or she can decide whether you should go to the hospital.

I've heard how important it is to time contractions once labor begins. Why?

There are two reasons for timing contractions:

- to find out how long a contraction lasts
- to find out how often contractions occur

It's important for your doctor to have this information so he or she can decide if it's time for you to go to the hospital.

How do we time a contraction for how long it lasts?

Begin timing when the contraction starts, and end timing when the contraction lets up and goes away.

How do we time a contraction for how often it occurs?

Ask your doctor which method he or she prefers because there are two ways to time contractions.

- Start timing when the contraction starts, and time it until the next contraction starts. This is the most common method.
- Start timing when the contraction ends, and note how long it is until the next contraction starts.

What if I go into labor and my partner isn't with me?

Before your delivery date, sit down and talk with your partner about how you will stay in touch as your due date approaches. Some couples rent personal pagers for the last few weeks for the partner to carry. (Some hospitals or HMOs supply pagers for expectant couples the last few weeks.) With cellular phones readily available now, this may not be a problem. Line up a backup support person, in case your partner cannot be with you or if you need someone else to take you to the hospital.

I've heard I can't drink anything during labor. Why?

Women often get nauseated, which may cause vomiting. It is for your safety that you are not allowed to eat or drink anything during labor to keep your stomach empty.

THE PURPOSE OF A LABOR COACH

A labor coach can do a lot to help you through labor:

- time your contractions so you are aware of the progress of your labor
- encourage and reassure you during labor
- help you deal with your physical discomfort
- help create a mood in the labor room
- report symptoms or pain to the nurse or doctor
- protect your privacy
- control traffic into your room

If my labor is a long one, can I have anything to drink?

No, just sips of water or ice chips to suck on. If labor is long, you may be given fluids through an I.V.

What about food—if my labor is extremely long, can I eat anything?

No, you can't. It's for your safety that you will not be allowed anything to eat.

I'm nervous about whether my baby is too big for me to deliver. Can my doctor tell if I'll have problems before labor begins?

Even with an estimation of how much your baby weighs, your doctor cannot really know if the baby is too big for you until after labor begins. Usually labor must begin so your doctor can see how the baby fits into your pelvis and if there is enough room for the baby to pass through the birth canal.

I've heard many different stories from friends, but I need an answer. Will I have to have an enema when I go to the hospital to have my baby?

You may not be required to have an enema—it is usually a choice. Discuss this at one of your prenatal appointments. There are benefits to having an enema early in labor. It decreases the amount of contamination by bowel movement or feces during labor and at the time of delivery. It may also help you after delivery if you have an episiotomy, because having a bowel movement very soon after delivery can be painful.

What can I expect when I have my first bowel movement after delivery?

Your first bowel movement usually occurs a day or two after delivery. If you had an enema, it could take a few days longer. It could be painful, especially if you have had an episiotomy.

A friend said her doctor prescribed stool softeners for her, and they helped. Is this common?

Yes. Most doctors prescribe stool softeners after delivery to help with your bowel movements. They are safe to take, even if you are nursing.

What is back labor?

Back labor occurs when the baby comes out through the birth canal looking straight up. This type of presentation often causes lower back pain.

If my baby is looking up, will that make my labor longer?

This type of labor may take longer for delivery. It may require rotation of the baby's head so it comes out looking down at the ground rather than looking up at the sky.

My sister-in-law had all sorts of friends present during her labor and when she gave birth last year. I don't want anyone but my husband with me. Is this unusual?

Discuss this ahead of time with your partner. The birth experience is stressful. As long as it's acceptable to your doctor, you and your partner can make a lot of the decisions about labor and the birth. Too many people in the delivery room can be distracting. Delivery is a very personal experience for you both; it is not a spectator sport.

Tests during Labor

My doctor was mentioning fetal monitoring during labor and delivery. What is this?

In many hospitals, a baby's heartbeat is monitored throughout labor, making it possible to detect any problems early so they can be resolved.

What kind of monitoring do they do?

There are two types of fetal monitoring during labor—external fetal monitoring and internal fetal monitoring.

What is external fetal monitoring?

This type of monitoring can be done before your membranes rupture. A belt with a receiver is strapped to your abdomen, and it

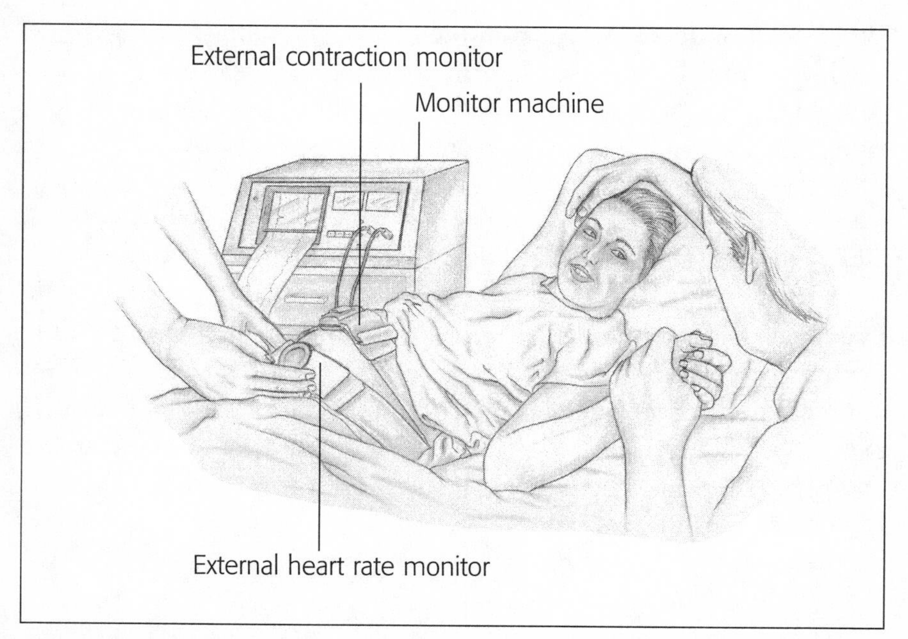

External monitoring during labor

records the baby's heartbeat. See the illustrations on the previous page and on page 86.

What is internal fetal monitoring?

Internal fetal monitoring is a more precise method of monitoring the baby. An electrode is placed on the fetal scalp to record the fetal heart rate; it gives a more exact reading. See the illustration on page 89.

I recently read about fetal blood sampling during labor. What is this test?

It is another way of evaluating how well a baby is tolerating the stress of labor.

How is fetal blood sampling done during labor?

Membranes must be ruptured, and the cervix must be dilated at least 2cm. Your doctor applies an instrument to the scalp of the baby to make a small nick in the skin. He or she collects the baby's blood in a small tube and checks its pH (acidity).

What can the doctor learn from fetal blood sampling?

The pH level can help determine whether the baby is having trouble during labor. Results help the physician decide whether labor can continue or if a Cesarean section is necessary.

DEALING WITH THE PAIN OF CHILDBIRTH

I've never had a baby before, and I'm scared of the pain of childbirth. Is it really bad?

Childbirth is accompanied by pain; expectation of this pain can evoke fear and anxiety in you. This is normal. If you're concerned about pain and how you'll handle it, the best way to deal with it is to become informed about it.

My friend told me I wouldn't feel like a real woman unless I have my baby without any pain relief. Is this true?

Some women believe they'll feel guilty after their baby is born if they ask for pain relief during labor. Sometimes they believe the baby will be harmed by the medication. Some believe they'll deprive themselves of the complete birth experience. The goal of every labor and delivery is a healthy baby and healthy mom. If a woman wants pain relief to help her, it doesn't mean she's failed in any way!

How can I find out more about the different pain-relief methods available during labor and delivery?

Discuss it with your doctor. Childbirth-education class is a good place to ask about these medications. You may also want to talk to friends to see what they did. Recent studies indicate more women are asking for pain relief during labor. One reason for this is that effective pain relief can be achieved with smaller doses of anesthetics, which helps reduce side effects and aftereffects. Today, about 66% of all women who deliver at large hospitals ask for pain relief during labor or delivery. In smaller hospitals, that number is around 42%.

Analgesia and Anesthesia

I've heard about analgesia and anesthesia for pain relief. What's the difference?

Analgesia is pain relief without total loss of sensation. *Anesthesia* is pain relief with total loss of sensation.

How does analgesia work?

An analgesic is injected into a muscle or vein to decrease the pain of labor, but it allows you to remain conscious. It provides pain relief but can make you drowsy, restless and nauseated. You may experience difficulty concentrating. It may slow the baby's reflexes and breathing, so it is usually given during the early and middle parts of labor.

How does anesthesia work?

With *general anesthesia,* you are completely unconscious; it is used only for some Cesarean deliveries and emergency vaginal deliveries. *Local anesthesia* affects a small area and is very useful for an episiotomy repair. *Regional anesthesia* affects a larger body area than local anesthesia.

Is general anesthesia dangerous?

There are some disadvantages to using general anesthesia—it is not used as much today as it was in the past. The advantage is that it can be administered very quickly in an emergency. Disadvantages include the mother being "asleep" or nausea that makes her vomit, with the risk of aspirating vomited food or stomach acid into her lungs. With general anesthesia, the baby may be asleep when delivered.

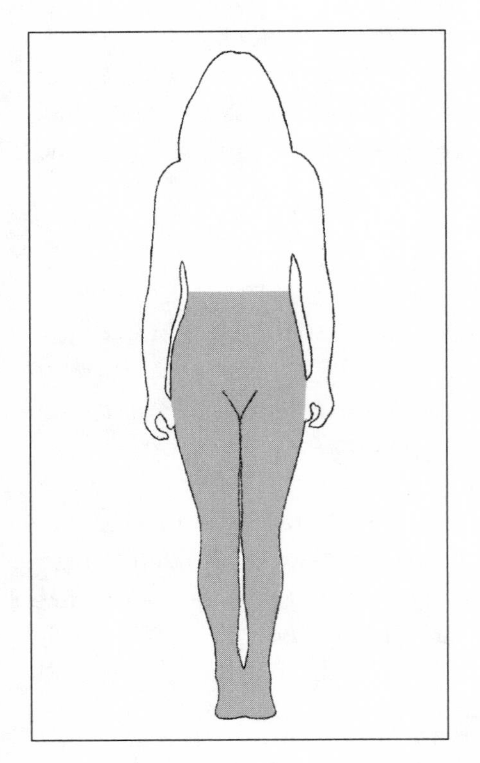

Regional anesthesia–area of anesthesia with spinal or epidural.

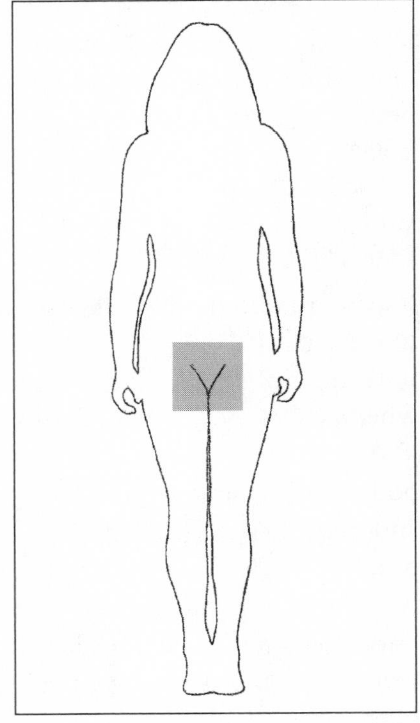

Local anesthesia–area of anesthesia with local anesthetic.

Do local or regional anesthesia affect the baby?

These anesthesias rarely affect the baby and usually have few lingering effects.

I've heard there are several types of regional anesthesia. What are they?

The three most common types of regional anesthesia are *pudendal block, spinal block* and *epidural block.*

What is a pudendal block?

A pudendal block is medication injected into the vaginal area to relieve pain in the vagina, the perineum and the rectum. Side effects are rare. It is considered one of the safest forms of pain relief; however it does not relieve the pain of contractions.

What is a spinal block?

With a spinal block, medication is injected into spinal fluid in the lower back, which numbs the lower part of the body. This type of block is administered only once during labor, so it is often used just before delivery. It works quickly and is an effective pain inhibitor. It is also used for a Cesarean delivery.

What is an epidural block?

With an epidural block, a tube is inserted into a space outside the mother's spinal column in the lower back. Medication is administered through the tube for pain relief. The tube remains in place until after delivery so additional medication can be administered when necessary, or it can be given continuously with a pump.

An epidural causes some loss of sensation in the lower part of the body. It helps relieve painful uterine contractions, pain in the vagina and rectum as the baby passes through the birth canal and the pain of an episiotomy. A woman can still feel pressure, so she can usually push adequately during vaginal delivery.

An epidural block is not effective in some women. Because an epidural may make it harder to push, vacuum extraction or forceps may be necessary during delivery.

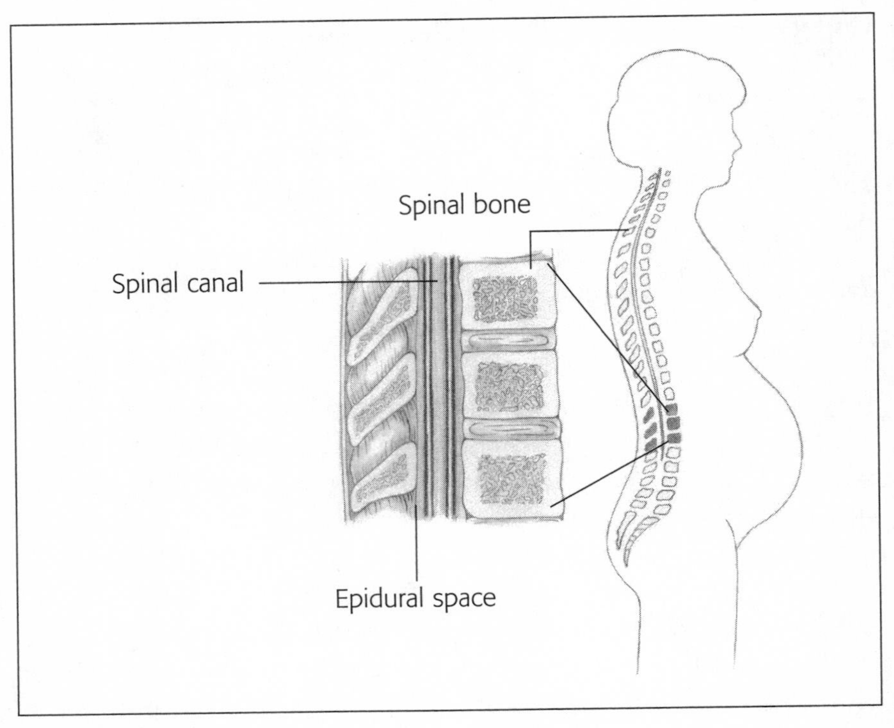

Epidural anesthesia.

What are the side effects of a spinal block or an epidural block?

Either block can cause a woman's blood pressure to drop suddenly, which in turn can cause a decrease in the baby's heart rate. These blocks are not used if the woman is bleeding heavily or if the baby has an abnormal heartbeat. A woman may experience a severe headache if the covering of the spinal cord is punctured during needle insertion with either type of anesthesia. This rarely happens.

Someone said if I have an epidural, I have a greater chance of having a Cesarean delivery. Was she right?

Experts don't agree on the answer to this question; each situation must be considered individually. Recent studies indicate that epidurals don't lengthen labor or increase the risk of C-section. If it affects your ability to push during the second stage of labor, your doctor can wait a little while and let the epidural wear off so you can push. Walking epidurals do not have as much of an effect on your ability to push.

What is a walking epidural or a walking spinal?

A walking spinal, also called *intrathecal anesthesia*, can be given to women who suffer extreme pain in the early stages of labor (dilated less than 5cm). A small amount of narcotic, such as Demerol, is injected through a thin needle into the spinal fluid, which eases the pain and causes few side effects.

Because the dose is small, neither the mother nor baby becomes overly drowsy. Sensory and motor functions remain intact, allowing the mother to walk around with help or sit in a chair.

What are the advantages of a walking epidural?

A walking epidural numbs you only in the pelvic area; it doesn't interfere with your ability to move your legs. Another advantage is that fewer women who have had a walking epidural have a "spinal headache" after the epidural wears off.

What are the disadvantages of a walking epidural?

As with a regular epidural, you must have an I.V. in place before you get the epidural. This is because the walking epidural, like a regular epidural, requires I.V. fluids to keep your blood pressure from falling.

CESAREAN DELIVERY

My doctor just told me I may need to have a Cesarean delivery, and I'm scared. What is it exactly?

When a woman has a Cesarean delivery (also called a *C-section*), her baby is delivered through an incision made in her abdominal wall and uterus.

I've read that more Cesareans are being done today. Is this true?

There has been a change in the rate of C-sections. In 1965, 4% of all deliveries were by Cesarean. In the 1980s and 1990s, the C-section rate rose to 20 to 25%. Today in the U.S., the rate has dropped, and only 15 to 20% of all deliveries are Cesarean deliveries.

POSSIBLE REASONS FOR A CESAREAN DELIVERY

There are many reasons for performing a C-section, but the main goal is to deliver a healthy baby. Specific reasons include the following:

- a previous Cesarean delivery
- to avoid rupture of the uterus
- baby is too big to fit through the birth canal
- fetal distress
- compression of the umbilical cord
- baby is in the breech position
- placental abruption
- placenta previa
- multiple fetuses (in some cases)

Why are there more Cesarean deliveries today than when my mom had me?

We believe the increase is related to better monitoring during labor and safer procedures for C-sections. Women are also having bigger babies. Another factor in this increase may be rising malpractice rates and the fear of litigation. However, the goal is the same—a safe delivery of the baby and the safety and health of the mother.

How is a C-section done?

The doctor makes an incision through the skin of the abdominal wall down to the uterus, then cuts the wall of the uterus. He or she cuts the amniotic sac containing the baby and placenta, and removes the baby through the incisions. After delivering the baby, your doctor removes the placenta and closes the uterus in layers with sutures that are absorbed (they don't have to be removed), then the abdomen is sewn together.

If I have to have a Cesarean, can I be awake?

With most C-sections, the anesthesiologist will give you an epidural or a spinal anesthetic. You are awake with these.

Can't my doctor tell if I'll need a C-section before I go into labor?

It would be nice to know this so you wouldn't have to go through labor, but it isn't that easy. We often have to wait for labor to see how your baby handles it and to see if the baby fits through the birth canal.

Research has indicated that a woman's weight may be an indicator of whether she will have a Cesarean delivery. A woman's body mass index (BMI)—a ratio of her height to her weight—may be used to predict whether a C-section may be necessary. A survey of over 2,500 women found that mothers with a higher BMI had more Cesarean deliveries. The reason it is important to determine whether risk of a Cesarean delivery is higher is to help medical personnel prepare for an emergency C-section. This can be done by

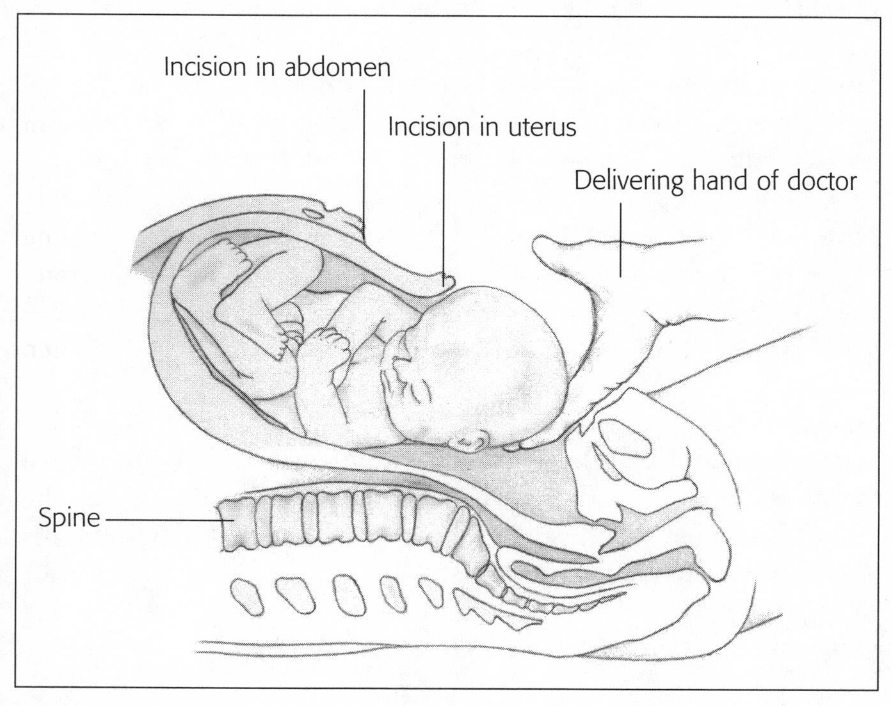

Cesarean delivery.

inserting an epidural catheter for regional anesthesia, which is considered safer than general anesthesia for obese women.

Are there any advantages to having a Cesarean delivery?

The most important advantage is delivery of a healthy baby. Babies usually do well after a C-section. Studies show babies who are delivered by Cesarean section do as well on the Apgar tests as babies that are born vaginally.

I'm sure there are disadvantages to having a C-section. What are they?

This is major surgery and carries with it the risks of major surgery. You will probably have to stay in the hospital 2 or 3 days.

Does walking during labor make labor easier and reduce the chance of a C-section?

A recent study found that walking did not provide any harm *or* benefit over resting in bed. Their conclusion was that a woman should be allowed to choose whichever option works best for her.

How long does it take to recover from a Cesarean?

Recovery at home takes longer with a Cesarean than it does with a vaginal delivery. The normal time for full recovery is 4 to 6 weeks.

How many Cesarean deliveries can a woman have?

There is no exact number. Many doctors recommend no more than two or three, but this is evaluated at the time of each delivery. We know of one woman who had *eight* C-sections! But this is unusual.

Some women at my childbirth-education class said if you have a Cesarean, you've failed as a woman. Is this true?

No! If you have a Cesarean, you have not failed in any way! The goal in pregnancy, labor and delivery is a healthy baby and a healthy mother. In many situations, the only way to achieve that is with a Cesarean delivery.

If a woman has repeat Cesarean sections, how does the doctor perform the surgery? Is a new, different incision made for every birth?

Usually your doctor will use the same incision site for each delivery. If you have a large scar, your doctor may cut out the old scar.

Vaginal Birth after Cesarean (VBAC)

I've heard that once you have a Cesarean, you must always have one. But don't some women deliver vaginally after having a Cesarean?

In the past it was believed that once a woman had a C-section, all later deliveries would have to be Cesarean also. Today it is becoming more common for women who have had a C-section to deliver vaginally with later pregnancies. This is called *vaginal birth after Cesarean (VBAC)*.

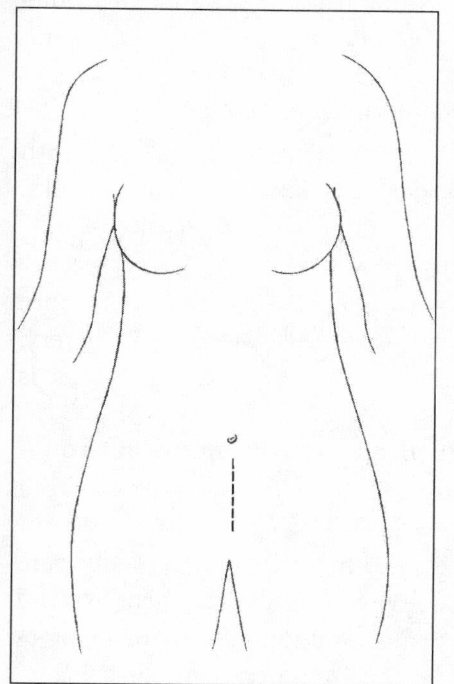

Midline Cesarean-section incision.

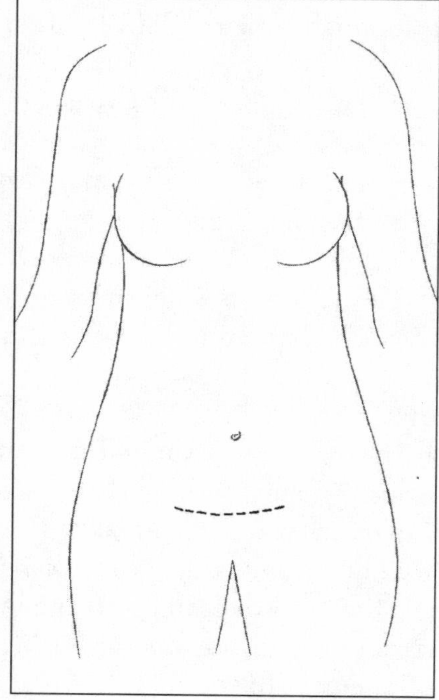

Bikini or pfanensteil Cesarean-section incision.

How does a woman know whether she can have a VBAC?

Your doctor must consider various factors in making this decision. The type of incision done with the Cesarean delivery is important. If the incision on the uterus (not the woman's abdomen) is high, labor is not permitted in subsequent pregnancies. If the woman is small and the baby is large, it may cause problems. Multiple fetuses and medical complications, such as diabetes or high blood pressure, may require a repeat C-section.

How many C-sections can I have and still be a candidate for VBAC?

The American College of Obstetricians and Gynecologists states two Cesarean deliveries are all right, other factors permitting. This is a very individual decision. Discuss it with your doctor.

What factors determine whether I can have a vaginal birth after having had a C-section?

The following situations give a woman the best chance of having a successful vaginal delivery after a C-section:

- The original cause for a Cesarean delivery is not repeated with this pregnancy.
- The woman has no major medical problems.
- The incision on the uterus from the previous C-section is low.
- The baby is a normal size.
- The baby is in the normal head-down position.

If I want to try a vaginal delivery after a C-section, what should I do?

The most important thing to do is to discuss it with your doctor well in advance of labor, so plans can be made. It may be helpful to get the records from your other delivery. Discuss the benefits and risks, and ask your doctor for his or her opinion as to your chances of a successful vaginal delivery. He or she knows your health and pregnancy history. Include your partner in this decision-making process.

EPISIOTOMY

What is an episiotomy?

An episiotomy is a surgical incision in the area behind the vagina, above the rectum; it is made during delivery to avoid tearing the vaginal opening or rectum.

Will I have to have an episiotomy?

This is something you need to discuss at your prenatal visits. Most women having their first or second baby will have an episiotomy. The more children a woman has had, the less likely she will need an episiotomy. It depends on the size of the baby. There are some situations that do not require an episiotomy, such as a small baby or a premature baby. Often the decision cannot be made until the time of delivery.

Why does a woman have an episiotomy?

An episiotomy is done to allow room for the baby to fit through the birth canal and to avoid tearing into other organs in the mother. If a woman has had a few pregnancies and deliveries, she may not need an episiotomy with her later children.

What factors determine whether I have to have one?

Some factors to consider include the following:

- the size of the mother's vaginal opening
- the size of the baby's head and shoulders
- the number of babies previously delivered
- whether it will be a forceps or vacuum delivery

I've heard some episiotomies are bigger than others. What does this mean?

Description of an episiotomy includes a description of the depth of the incision. There are 4 degrees that describe incision depth:

- 1st degree—cuts only the skin
- 2nd degree—cuts the skin and underlying tissue, called *fascia*

- 3rd degree—cuts the skin, underlying tissue and rectal sphincter, which is the muscle that goes around the anus
- 4th degree—goes through the three layers described above and the rectal mucosa, which is the lining of the rectum

How painful is an episiotomy?

After delivery of your baby, the most painful part of the birth process might be your episiotomy. Don't be afraid to ask for help with this pain. Many options are available for pain relief, including pain medication, ice, sitz baths and laxatives.

YOUR BABY'S BIRTH POSITION

I heard a woman at the doctor's office say her baby was in a breech position. What did she mean?

A *breech presentation* means the baby is not in a head-down position, and the legs or buttocks come into the birth canal first.

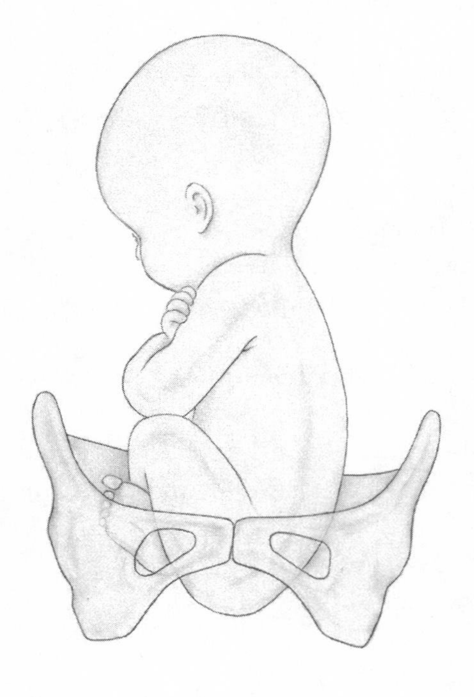

Complete breech presentation of baby.

If my baby is breech, is that bad?

Early in pregnancy, breech is common. By the last 4 to 6 weeks, your baby should be in a head-down position. If your baby is breech when it is time to deliver, your doctor may try to turn the baby or you may need a Cesarean delivery.

What causes a baby to be in a breech position?

One of the main causes is prematurity of the baby. Near the end of the 2nd trimester, it's more common for the baby to be in a breech position. As you progress through the 3rd trimester, the baby usually turns into the head-down position for birth.

How is a baby in the breech position delivered?

There is some controversy about this. For a long time, breech deliveries were performed vaginally, then it was believed the safest method was by C-section. Many doctors still believe a Cesarean

DIFFERENT BIRTH POSITIONS

There are different kinds of breech presentation as well as other positions, including the following:

- Frank breech—lower legs are flexed at the hips and extended at the knees. Feet are up by the face or head.
- Complete breech—one or both knees are flexed, not extended.
- Incomplete breech—a foot or knee enters the birth canal ahead of the rest of the baby.
- Face presentation—the baby's head is hyperextended so the face enters the birth canal first.
- Transverse lie presentation—the baby is lying almost as if in a cradle in the pelvis. The head is on one side of the mother's abdomen, and the bottom is on the other side.
- Shoulder presentation—shoulder enters the birth canal first.

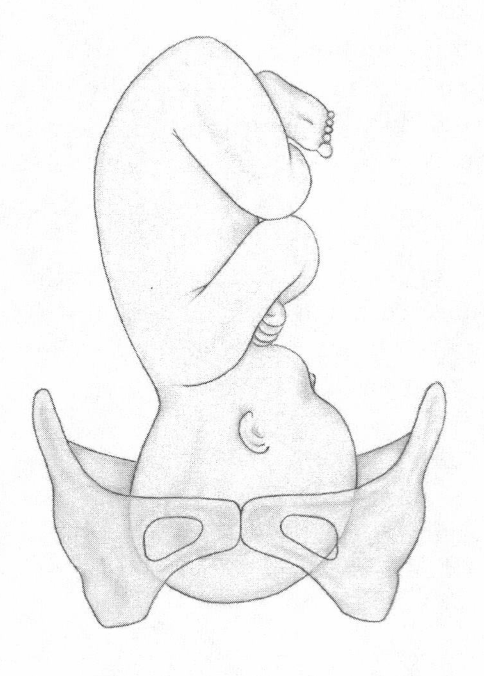

Preferable alignment for birth.

delivery is the safest way to deliver a baby in the breech position. However, some doctors believe a woman can deliver a breech baby without difficulty if the situation is right.

I've heard that sometimes the doctor will try to turn a baby in the breech position. Is that true?

Yes. Your physician may attempt to change its position by using external cephalic version (ECV).

How is the baby turned?

The doctor places his or her hands on your abdomen. Using gentle movements, he or she manually shifts the baby into the head-down position. An ultrasound is usually done first so the doctor can see the position of the baby. Then ultrasound is used during the procedure to guide the doctor in changing the baby's position.

When is external cephalic version usually done?

Most physicians who use this method do so before labor begins or in the early stages of labor.

How successful is ECV?

It is successful about 50% of the time.

DELIVERY OF YOUR BABY

How long does a vaginal delivery take?

The actual delivery of the baby and placenta (not including the laboring process) takes anywhere from a few minutes to an hour.

How long does a Cesarean delivery take?

It usually takes from 30 to 60 minutes. However, the part that takes the longest is not the birth of the baby—that is performed fairly quickly. Stitching closed the skin and muscle layers after the baby is born takes the greatest amount of time.

Will I deliver in the same room I labor in?

This is the setup in some hospitals and is called *LDRP,* which means *labor, delivery, recovery* and *postpartum*. With LDRP, you labor

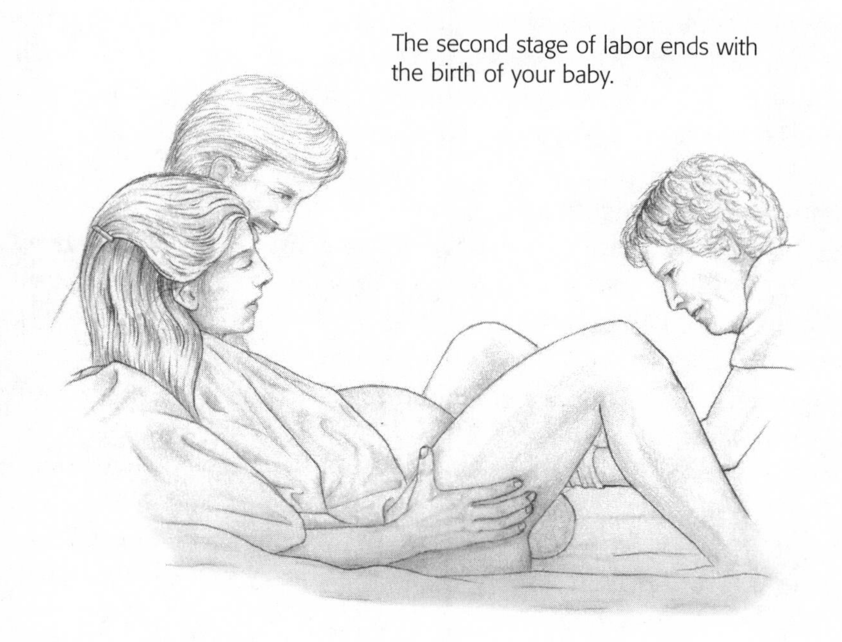

The second stage of labor ends with the birth of your baby.

and deliver in the same room, then remain there during your recovery and your stay at the hospital. Not all hospitals or birthing centers are equipped this way. In many places you will labor in one labor room, then move to a delivery room to deliver. Then you will recover in a wardlike setting, where you will remain until you go home.

I've read that other birth positions are possible besides lying on my back with my feet in stirrups. Is that true?

Yes. You may not have to use stirrups, or you may deliver lying on your side or squatting, if you make arrangements to do this.

Will my doctor have to use forceps during the delivery?

It depends on the situation at the time of delivery. The following factors are involved:

- the size of the baby
- the size of your pelvis
- how well you are able to push
- whether your baby needs to be delivered immediately.

What are forceps?

Forceps look like two metal hands and are used to protect the baby's head during delivery. However, they are not used as much today as they were in the past. Instead, physicians more often use a vacuum extractor or perform a Cesarean section.

What is a vacuum extractor?

A vacuum extractor is a plastic cup that fits on the baby's head by suction. When you push during labor, your doctor is able to pull and deliver the baby more easily.

My partner wants to take a video of the birth, but I don't want him to. Am I being unreasonable?

No, you're not. The birth process is very private for many women, and they don't want to be videotaped or photographed or forced to share it with others. If this is your wish, explain it to your partner. He should respect your wishes. If he won't listen, discuss the problem with your doctor. Ask him or her to explain your objections to your partner.

AFTER YOUR BABY IS BORN

What happens to my baby after it is born?

First, the baby's mouth and throat are suctioned to clear out any secretions. Then the doctor clamps and cuts the umbilical cord. The baby is wrapped in clean blankets and may be placed on your abdomen. At 1 minute and 5 minutes after birth, Apgar scores are recorded to show the baby's response to birth and to life outside the womb. An ID band is placed on the baby's wrist. Usually a brief physical or an assessment is done right after delivery. The baby receives eye drops to prevent infection and is given a vitamin-K shot to prevent bleeding.

You will be asked if you want your baby to receive the hepatitis vaccine. You may want to discuss this with your doctor or your baby's pediatrician. The vaccine is given to protect the baby against hepatitis in the future.

When the initial evaluation is complete, the baby is returned to you. See the chart on page 341 for a description of tests commonly performed on newborns.

My partner wants to cut the umbilical cord after the baby is delivered. Can he do this?

Talk to your doctor about your partner's participation in the delivery. What he is allowed to do varies from place to place and from doctor to doctor.

I've heard my uterus will contract after my baby is born. How much will it shrink?

Following the birth, the uterus shrinks from the size of a watermelon to the size of a volleyball. The uterus contracts and becomes smaller so it won't bleed.

How serious is bleeding after the birth of the baby?

You can expect to bleed after you deliver, but heavy bleeding is not very common. Bleeding is controlled by massaging the uterus (called *Credé*) and with medications; it lessens gradually over time, then stops.

Is it normal to bleed heavily after my baby is born?

It's not unusual to lose some blood during labor and delivery. However, heavy bleeding after the baby is born can be serious. A loss of more than 17 ounces (500ml) in the first 24 hours after your baby's birth is called *postpartum hemorrhage.*

What causes heavy bleeding?

Following are the most common causes of heavy bleeding:

- a uterus that won't contract
- tearing of the vagina or cervix during birth
- a large or bleeding episiotomy
- a tear, rupture or hole in the uterus
- failure of blood vessels inside the uterus to compress
- retained placental tissue
- clotting or coagulation problems

What if bleeding becomes heavy after a few days or weeks?

Contact your doctor. Sometimes the bleeding is normal, but it is best to talk to your doctor about it. He or she may want to see you to determine if the amount of bleeding is normal and, if necessary, to prescribe medication.

I've heard that we can have our baby's umbilical-cord blood saved and frozen for later use, if it is needed. Why would we want to do this?

Cord blood—blood saved from the umbilical cord—may be "banked" and saved for future use to treat cancer and genetic diseases that are now treated by bone-marrow transplants. Cord blood has been used successfully to treat childhood leukemia, some immune diseases and other blood diseases.

Blood is collected directly from the umbilical cord immediately after delivery. It is then transported to a bank facility where it is frozen and stored. There is no risk to the mother or baby.

Should we save and bank our baby's umbilical-cord blood?

That's a decision you and your partner will have to make. It is expensive and may not be for everyone. If you are interested, your doctor can give you more information.

POSTTERM BIRTH

What is a postterm birth?

Babies born 2 weeks or more past their due date are considered postterm or overdue births. Babies that are 41 weeks are *not* considered postterm.

How common is postterm birth?

About 10% of all babies are born more than 2 weeks past their due date.

Is a postterm birth dangerous for my baby?

Carrying a baby longer than 42 weeks can cause some problems for the fetus and the mother. Most pregnancies do well. Doctors conduct tests on these babies and induce labor, if necessary.

Why do they test a postterm baby?

A doctor can determine if a baby is moving around in the womb and if the amount of amniotic fluid is healthy and normal. If the baby is healthy and active, the mother-to-be is usually monitored until labor begins on its own. Tests are done as reassurance that an overdue baby is OK and can remain in the womb. These tests include a nonstress test, ultrasound, a contraction stress test and a biophysical profile. If problems are found, labor is often induced. (See the discussions of these tests in chapter 3.)

EMERGENCY CHILDBIRTH

What should I do if I go into labor and can't make it to the hospital?

Emergency childbirth can happen to anyone, so it's best to be prepared. Read and study the information on the following pages. Have the names and telephone numbers of your doctors and those of friends or family written down and near the phone. And if it happens to you, try to relax and follow the instructions provided.

EMERGENCY DELIVERY IF YOU ARE ALONE

1. Call 911 for help.
2. Call a neighbor, family member or friend (have phone numbers available).
3. Try not to push or to bear down.
4. Find a comfortable place, and spread out towels or blankets.
5. If the baby comes before help arrives, try to use your hands to ease the baby out while you gently push.
6. Wrap the baby in a clean blanket or clean towels; hold it close to your body to keep it warm.
7. Use a clean cloth or tissue to remove mucus from the baby's mouth.
8. Do not pull on the umbilical cord to deliver the placenta—it is not necessary.
9. If the placenta delivers on its own, save it.
10. Tie a string or shoelace around a section of the cord. You don't need to cut the cord.
11. Try to keep yourself and your baby warm until medical help arrives.

EMERGENCY DELIVERY AT HOME

1. Call 911 for help.
2. Call a neighbor, family member or friend (have phone numbers available).
3. Encourage the woman not to push or to bear down.
4. Use blankets and towels to make the woman as comfortable as possible.
5. If there is time, wash the woman's vaginal and rectal areas with soap and water.
6. When the baby's head delivers, encourage the woman not to push or bear down. Instead, have her pant or blow and concentrate on not pushing.
7. Try to ease the baby's head out with gentle pressure. Do not pull on the head.
8. After the head is delivered, gently push down on the head and push a little to deliver the shoulders.
9. As one shoulder delivers, lift the head up, delivering the other shoulder. The rest of the baby will quickly follow.
10. Wrap the baby in a clean blanket or clean towels.
11. Use a clean cloth or tissue to remove mucus from the baby's mouth.
12. Do not pull on the umbilical cord to deliver the placenta—it is not necessary.
13. If the placenta delivers on its own, wrap it in a towel or clean newspapers, and save it.
14. Tie a string or shoelace around a section of the cord. You don't need to cut the cord.
15. Keep the placenta at the level of the baby or above the baby.
16. Keep both mother and baby warm with towels or blankets until medical help arrives.

EMERGENCY DELIVERY ON THE WAY TO THE HOSPITAL

1. Stop the car.
2. Try to get help, if you have a cellular phone or a CB radio.
3. Put on your flashing warning lights.
4. Place the woman in the back seat, with a towel or blanket under her.
5. Encourage the woman not to push or to bear down.
6. When the baby's head delivers, encourage the woman not to push or bear down. Instead, have her pant or blow and concentrate on not pushing.
7. Try to ease the baby's head out with gentle pressure. Do not pull on the head.
8. After the head is delivered, gently push down on the head and push a little to deliver the shoulders.
9. As one shoulder delivers, lift the head up, delivering the other shoulder. The rest of the baby will quickly follow.
10. Wrap the baby in a clean blanket or clean towels. Use clean newspapers if nothing else is available.
11. Use a clean cloth or tissue to remove mucus from the baby's mouth.
12. Do not pull on the umbilical cord to deliver the placenta—it is not necessary.
13. If the placenta delivers on its own, wrap it in a towel or clean newspapers and save it.
14. Tie a string or shoelace around a section of the cord. You don't need to cut the cord.
15. Keep the placenta at the level of the baby or above the baby.
16. Keep both mother and baby warm until you can get them to the hospital or medical help arrives.

PART FOUR

After Your Baby Is Born

16

After Your Baby'

Pregnancy is over! Your baby has been born! You and your partner are parents to the new life you nurtured inside you for 9 months. You are finally a family.

As you begin your new life together, it's important to realize you and your partner need to take care of yourselves. You need to rest and to relax when possible. Support each other, and work together. By helping each other, you will discover the many joys of parenting your new baby.

Your doctor and the nurses at the hospital will have advice and suggestions to help you recover and to begin the task of taking care of your baby. Follow their advice. Ask questions about anything you are curious about. If you're a first-time parent and you decide to breastfeed, you probably won't have much of an idea of how to start. Ask for the help of the nurses; they've had lots of experience helping new moms get started.

If you have questions about the care of your newborn, ask them before you leave the hospital. Take advantage of all the people there who can help you.

When you get home, take it easy. You need time to recover and to get back on your feet. Your partner needs time and attention, too. It may take a little time to work out a schedule or divide up duties, but by working together, you'll be surprised how quickly things will fall into place.

VERY

ow long will I have to stay in the hospital?

Most women are discharged within a day or two, if labor and delivery are normal and the baby is doing well. If you have a Cesarean delivery, you will stay a few days longer.

What can I expect during my recovery from a vaginal delivery?

Hospital staff will check your blood pressure and bleeding closely for the first few hours after the birth. They will offer you medication for pain relief and encourage you to nurse your baby. The pressure that was exerted on your urethra during delivery may make it a bit more difficult to urinate after baby's birth. This will slowly clear up.

What can I expect during recovery if I have a Cesarean delivery?

You will be in a recovery area where a nurse will monitor you. You will be offered pain medication. After about an hour, you will be moved to your room.

I've heard the nurse will measure my urine output after delivery. Why?

This is done to make sure your kidneys and bladder are working.

What is the pain after childbirth like? What can I expect?

There are two main areas of pain—your abdomen and your episiotomy (if you have one). You can ask for pain medication for both.

How can I tell if my episiotomy is OK?

It will be hard for you to tell. The nurses will check it.

What should I do if I get an infection in the episiotomy incision?

This is unusual and doesn't usually show up for a few days. It requires antibiotics to treat it.

I've decided not to breastfeed. Will my doctor give me pills or a shot to dry up my milk?

We do not give medication to stop your milk from coming in. Bind or wrap your breasts to stop the milk flow.

What if I decide I want to breastfeed later. Can I?

No. If you stop your milk from coming in, you won't be able to start it later.

TUBAL LIGATION AFTER YOUR BABY'S BIRTH

If I don't want any more children, is it a good idea to have my tubes tied after I deliver my baby?

Some women opt to have a tubal ligation done while they are in the hospital after baby's birth. However this is not the time to make a decision about a tubal ligation if you haven't thought seriously about it before.

Are there advantages to having a tubal ligation after delivery?

Yes, there are. You are already in the hospital; if you have an epidural, you already have the anesthesia necessary for a tubal ligation.

What are the disadvantages to having a tubal ligation after delivering my baby?

Consider tubal ligation permanent and irreversible. If you have your tubes tied within a few hours or a day after having your baby, then change your mind, you will regret it.

If I didn't have an epidural, what kind of anesthesia is used for a tubal ligation?

If you didn't have an epidural for delivery, a tubal ligation usually requires general anesthesia.

GOING HOME WITH BABY

Are there any activities I should avoid after my baby is born?

Avoid lifting any objects heavier than the baby the first few weeks. If possible, avoid climbing stairs whenever you can.

Will I ever get my figure back?

It's natural to be concerned about your appearance after your baby's birth. Although you won't immediately regain your prepregnancy figure, there are a few things you can do to help you look and feel better.

- Buy and wear a well-fitting, supportive nursing bra.
- Oversized shirts (your partner's may do the trick) offer you variety. Stay away from your maternity clothes, which you probably want to burn anyway.
- Wear tops out—wait a little while for tummy muscles to tighten up before tucking tops in.
- Drawstring pants and stretch pants can be a good choice.
- A loose-fitting dress can be flattering because it doesn't hug your curves.

- Don't wear sloppy clothes, like sweat shirts and sweat pants all the time; sometimes when you wear sloppy clothes, you feel sloppy.

My friend said she was really tired after her baby was born. Is this normal?

Many women are surprised by how tired they are emotionally and physically the first few months after the birth of the baby. Your aerobic capacity can increase as much as 20% in the 6 weeks following baby's birth. This is good news if you feel overly fatigued. As your hormones return to a normal level, you'll probably have more energy. Take time for yourself—you'll have a period of adjustment.

I've heard I should get lots of sleep after the baby is born. Why?

Sleep and rest are essential after the baby is born to help you get back in shape. To get the rest you need, go to bed early when possible. Try taking a nap or resting when baby naps.

When you hold your baby, be sure to support the head with your hand.

It's exhausting dealing with my baby. How can I get my husband to help me?

Parenthood is easier and more enjoyable when both partners share the responsibilities and chores. Couples should form a parenthood partnership. It will take a cooperative effort from both of you, but it can be done.

How do we form this partnership?

Sit down together before the baby is born and discuss what changes you will face. You may be able to avoid problems before they occur. Sharing tasks, such as bathing and diaper changing, seems to work out the best.

My mother told me there are some warning signs of problems I may experience after birth. What are they?

You should not feel ill after birth. Call your doctor immediately if you experience any of the following:

- unusually heavy or sudden increase in vaginal bleeding (more than your normal menstrual flow or soaking more than two sanitary pads in 30 minutes)
- vaginal discharge with strong, unpleasant odor
- a temperature of 101F (38.3C) or more, except for the first 24 hours after birth
- painful or red breasts
- loss of appetite for an extended period of time
- pain, tenderness, redness or swelling in your legs
- pain in the lower abdomen or in the back

POSTPARTUM DISTRESS SYNDROME

I've heard about feeling blue after the baby is born. Is that normal?

After your baby is born, you may feel sad and cranky. It's called *postpartum distress syndrome (PPD)*, or the *baby blues;* up to 80% of all women experience this. It usually appears between 2 days and 2 weeks after the baby is born. The drop in estrogen and progesterone after delivery may contribute to the problem. The situation is temporary and tends to leave as quickly as it comes.

Is the problem treatable?

Postpartum reactions, whether mild or severe, are temporary and treatable. One of the most important ways you can help yourself is to set up support before the birth. Ask family members and friends to help. Ask your mother or mother-in-law to stay for a while. See if your husband can take some leave, or hire someone to come in and help each day. Do some form of moderate exercise every day. Eat nutritiously, and drink plenty of fluids. Go out every day.

SYMPTOMS OF POSTPARTUM DISTRESS

- anxiety
- crying for no reason
- exhaustion
- impatience
- irritability
- lack of confidence
- lack of feeling for the baby
- low self-esteem
- oversensitivity
- restlessness

Do some women have a higher chance of having postpartum distress syndrome?

Yes. If any of the following applies to you, you may be at higher risk of suffering from postpartum distress syndrome (PPD):

- your mother or sister suffered the problem—it seems to run in families
- you suffered from PPD with a previous pregnancy—chances are you'll have the problem again
- you had fertility treatments to achieve this pregnancy—hormone fluctuations may be more severe, which may cause PPD
- you suffered extreme PMS before the pregnancy—hormonal imbalances may be greater after the birth
- you have experienced any other major life changes recently—you may experience a hormonal drop as a result

I've heard that in severe cases, medication is necessary. Is that true?

With *postpartum depression,* a more severe problem than baby blues, medication may be necessary. Medications of choice include antidepressants and tranquilizers; often they are used together. In most cases, a course of antidepressants that lasts up to 1 year successfully treats the problem.

Can postpartum depression affect my partner?

Your partner can be affected if you suffer from the baby blues or postpartum depression. It's important to prepare him for this situation. Explain to him that if it happens to you, it is only temporary.

PHYSICAL CHANGES YOU MAY EXPERIENCE AFTER THE BIRTH

Will I ever regain the tightness of my abdominal skin now that my baby is here?

For some women, skin returns to normal naturally. For others, it never returns to its prepregnancy state. Abdominal skin is not like muscle, so it can't be strengthened by exercise. One of the main factors that affect your skin's ability to return to its prepregnancy tightness is connective tissue, which provides suppleness and elasticity. As you get older, your skin loses connective tissue and elasticity. Other factors include your state of fitness before pregnancy, heredity and how greatly your skin was stretched during pregnancy.

My breasts grew quite a bit during pregnancy. Will they return to their normal size?

Most women find their breasts return to their prepregnancy size or decrease a little in size. This is a result of the change in the connective tissue that forms the support system in a woman's breasts. Exercise will not make breasts firmer, but it can improve the chest area so breasts have better support.

I thought I'd feel thinner now that I'm no longer pregnant, but I still feel fat. What can I do about my weight?

It's normal to lose 10 to 15 pounds (4.5 to 6.75kg) immediately after your baby is born. Extra weight may be harder to lose. Your body stored about 7 to 10 pounds (3.15 to 4.5kg) of fat to provide energy for the first few months after birth. If you eat properly and get enough exercise, these pounds will slowly come off.

Shouldn't I go on a strict diet to lose the weight?

No! Don't go on a strict diet right away. Even if you bottlefeed your baby, your body requires a well-balanced, nutritious diet for you to stay healthy and to keep your energy levels up.

I've heard I shouldn't diet if I'm breastfeeding. Why?

All the nutrients your baby receives while breastfeeding depend on the quality of food you eat. Breastfeeding places more demands on your body than pregnancy does. Your body burns up to 1,000 calories a day just to produce milk. When breastfeeding, you need to eat an extra 500 calories a day. Be sure to keep fluid levels up.

You may not be getting enough zinc, vitamin D, vitamin E, calcium or folate. Lack of these vitamins and minerals may leave you feeling irritable and tired. Ask your doctor about continuing your prenatal vitamins while breastfeeding because they contain what you need.

I really want to get back to exercising now that my baby is here. How should I approach exercise?

Do something you enjoy, and do it on a regular basis. Walking and swimming are excellent exercises to help you get back in shape. However, before you start any postpartum exercise program, check with your doctor. He or she may have some particular advice for you.

I want to get back in shape as soon as possible. What can I do?

Be careful about beginning an exercise program too soon. Discuss it with your doctor first. Don't overtire yourself; get adequate rest.

What kind of activities can I start with?

Walking is a good exercise, but take it slowly. Ask your doctor when and how you can increase your exercise program.

YOUR POSTPARTUM CHECKUP

I'm scheduled for a postpartum checkup in 6 weeks. Do I really need to go?

Yes. Your postpartum checkup is the last part of your complete prenatal-care program. It is just as important as seeing your doctor during pregnancy. A postpartum checkup is scheduled between 2 and 6 weeks after delivery, depending on the circumstances of the birth.

What will my postpartum checkup cover?

You will have a physical exam, similar to the one at your first prenatal exam. Your doctor will also do an internal exam. If you had any birth tears or incisions, he or she will examine them to see how they are healing. This is a good time to discuss birth control, if you haven't already made plans.

Why do I have to have a pelvic exam now that my baby is born?

It's done to determine if your uterus is returning to its prepregnant size and position, which normally takes about 6 weeks. If there are any problems, they can be taken care of at this time.

BIRTH CONTROL AFTER PREGNANCY

When can I resume sexual relations with my partner?

Six weeks after delivery, if your recovery is normal. Wait until your postpartum checkup.

I've heard that breastfeeding is a good way to keep from getting pregnant. Is this true?

Breastfeeding decreases your chances of getting pregnant, but you *cannot* rely on breastfeeding or the lack of menstruation to protect

BIRTH CONTROL METHODS

Method	Effectiveness	Reasons to Use It
Oral contraceptives (estrogen and progestin)	99%	Bottlefeeding, not breastfeeding
Oral contraceptives (progestin only)	98%	Can use it while breastfeeding
Condoms	97%	Convenient and easy to use
Diaphragms	94%	Convenient to use; you can be fitted (or refitted) at your 6-week checkup
IUDs	98–99%	Don't have to think about birth control; it can be inserted at your 6-week checkup
Depo-provera	99%	Can use it while breastfeeding
Norplant	97%	Can use it while breastfeeding (may not be widely available)
Once-a-month birth-control Injection	99%	Can use it while breastfeeding

you against getting pregnant again. You need to use some type of protection when you resume intercourse.

What type of birth control can I use while breastfeeding?

There are many types of contraception you can use—condoms, "minipill" oral contraceptives, birth-control foam or jelly, diaphragms, IUDs, Norplant or Depo-provera injections. Discuss options with your doctor.

Should I talk to my doctor about contraception at my postpartum checkup?

This is the perfect time to discuss it. If you're not planning another pregnancy immediately, you need to discuss birth control with your doctor. Ask about contraceptive methods. You may decide on oral contraceptives, Norplant, Depo-provera or an IUD. You will need a prescription for an oral contraceptive. If you decide on Norplant, Depo-provera or an IUD, you will have to make arrangements for the procedure.

SAFETY FOR YOUR BABY

Safeguard your baby's environment by keeping the following in mind.

- Crib slats should be no farther apart than 2 3/8 inches (6cm).
- Be sure the mattress fits the crib securely.
- Keep the crib away from windows, wall decorations, heating units, climbable furniture, blind cords, drapery cords and other possible dangers.
- Reduce the risk of sudden infant death syndrome (SIDS) by keeping the crib free of extras—no bumper pads, quilts, blankets, pillows or toys. Keep baby warm with a blanket-sleeper.
- Keep the dropside up and locked when baby is in the crib.
- Keep mobiles and other crib toys out of baby's reach. You may have to remove them as baby grows older.
- Never hang a pacifier or anything else around baby's neck.
- Never leave baby unattended on a sofa, chair, changing table or any other surface above the floor.
- Never put an infant seat on the counter or a table.
- Use safety straps with all baby equipment.
- Never leave a baby unattended in *any* water. A baby can drown in 1 inch of water.
- Never hold baby while cooking or drinking a hot beverage.
- If you warm formula or baby food in the microwave, it can heat unevenly, causing hot spots. Shake the bottle or stir the food well, then test its temperature before serving.
- Don't hang anything on stroller handles, such as a purse or bag. The extra weight could cause the stroller to tip over.
- Always put your baby in a car seat, even for a short ride. Be sure the car seat is safety approved and installed correctly.

17

Your New Baby

One of the first things you probably did after your baby was born was check him or her out from head to toe. It's normal—we did it with our babies, too! Getting to know your baby is fun and exciting. You may be surprised by how strong your feelings are for your baby. And you may feel a little overwhelmed when you realize you and your partner are mommy and daddy to your little one.

You may be a little nervous as you begin the task of parenting. It can help to understand that babies are very resilient—you don't have to handle yours as if he or she is made of china. You must be careful to support the baby's head, keep baby comfortably dressed (not too hot, not too cold), and feed and change him or her, but as you get the hang of things, these tasks become much easier.

The most important thing you can give your baby is your love. This won't be a difficult task. Babies are lovable; it's hard not to give all of your time to them! Our best advice to you is to enjoy this wonderful, magical time with your child. To help you understand your baby and appreciate all that is occurring with him or her, you might want to read our book *Your Baby's First Year Week by Week*. It contains a great deal of practical advice on raising a child during his or her first year of life.

TESTS ON THE NEWBORN

Test	How Test Is Performed	What Test Indicates
Apgar test	At 1 and 5 minutes after birth, baby is assessed for color, heart rate, muscle tone, reflex response, breathing. Each category receives a score from 0 to 2 points, for a maximum of 10 points.	Gives an indication of baby's general condition at birth. Helps hospital staff. decide if newborn needs extra care. Does not indicate what future may hold.
Blood screen	Blood is taken from baby's heel.	Detects phenylketonuria, anemia and hypothyroidism.
Coombs test	Blood is taken from umbilical cord if mother's blood is Rh-negative, type O or has not been tested for antibodies.	Detects whether Rh-antibodies have been formed.
Reflex assessment	Tests several specific reflexes, including the rooting and grasping reflexes.	If a particular reflex is not present, further evaluation is necessary.
Assessment of neonatal maturity	Many characteristics of baby are assessed to evaluate neuromuscular and physical maturity.	Each characteristic is assigned a score; sum indicates infant's maturity.
Brazelton neonatal behavioral assessment	Tests broad range of behaviors in babies where a problem is suspected. Some hospitals test all babies.	Provides information to doctors and parents about how a newborn responds to the environment.

Other blood tests	Blood is taken from heel to test for sickle-cell anemia, abnormal blood-glucose levels or other problems.	Results indicate whether baby needs further evaluation.

TESTS FOR BABY

I've heard that my baby will have to have a lot of tests after he's born. What are they?

The tests performed depend on your medical history, findings obtained during examination of the newborn and other factors. Tests performed on the baby include the following:

- Apgar test at 1 minute and 5 minutes after birth
- Brazelton neonatal behavioral assessment scale
- Coombs test
- assessment of neonatal maturity
- reflex assessment
- screening for hyperphenylketonuria, anemia and hypothyroidism
- additional blood tests

See the preceding chart for an explanation of these tests.

YOUR BABY'S APPEARANCE

What does the baby look like at birth?

The baby is wet and usually has some blood on her. Vernix, a white or yellow waxy substance, may cover part or much of the body.

I always thought all newborns were beautiful, but my new baby isn't very pretty. His head looks too big. What's wrong with him?

A baby's head is large in proportion to the rest of his body. At birth, it measures 1/4 of his entire length. As he grows, this will change until his head is 1/8 of his adult height.

My little girl looks like she's been in a fight—her nose is flat and lumpy. Will she need plastic surgery?

The shape of your little girl's nose at birth has little to do with what it will look like when she's an adult. A newborn's nose may look too flat to breathe through, but babies manage to breathe through them.

My little boy's head is misshapen. Will it always be like this?

If your baby made his appearance into this world through the birth canal, he may have an elongated head. The shape is only temporary and will become more "normal" in the next few days.

My husband and I each have lots of hair, but our daughter is completely bald. Our son had lots of hair when he was born. Why the difference?

Your baby may be born with lots of hair or none at all. Don't worry about it. If she has lots of hair, this first hair may fall out during the first 6 months and will be replaced by hair that may be entirely different in color and texture. If she doesn't have any hair, it's not a permanent condition either. She will eventually grow hair.

My baby's eyes seem to be swollen. What causes this?

A newborn's eyes are often swollen or puffy immediately after birth. The pressure he or she experienced while passing through the birth canal causes this; it subsides in a few days.

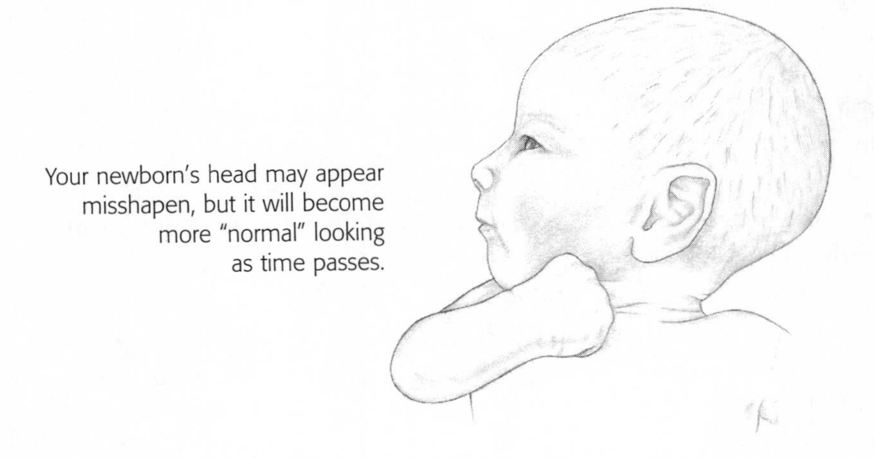

Your newborn's head may appear misshapen, but it will become more "normal" looking as time passes.

When they brought my baby to me in my room, his eyes looked greasy and were kind of red. What did they do to him?

Your baby's eyes may have been slightly irritated and reddened by the drops or ointment applied to his eyes shortly after birth. Drops or ointment prevent eye infections. Redness usually disappears within 48 hours after birth.

My little girl has one eye that seems to wander when she looks at me. Is this an indication of some major problem?

One of your baby's eyes may wander when she looks at you, or she may look cross-eyed. Don't worry. Her eye muscles aren't strong enough yet to control eye movements. A wandering eye usually corrects itself by the time the baby is 6 months old. If she still has a problem after that, discuss it with your pediatrician.

My little boy looks as if he's squinting at me. Are his eyes all right?

The skin folds at the inner corners of his eyes make it look as if he's squinting. As time passes, these folds become less prominent, and he won't look as if he's squinting any more.

My baby's skin seems dry and flaky. I always heard a baby's skin is soft and beautiful. Should I be concerned?

Within hours after birth, a baby's skin begins to dry out and may become flaky and scaly. This can last for a few weeks after birth. You

RASHES

Different kinds of rashes are common in newborns and usually nothing to worry about. Following are a few your baby may have.

- Diaper rash is the most common. Keep the area dry and clean, and apply a protective ointment that contains zinc oxide.
- A red, blistery rash may be prickly heat. Apply cornstarch to the affected area, and don't overdress the baby.
- Tiny yellow bumps on the face, called *milia,* affect about half of all newborns.
- Large yellow pimples on splotchy skin is called *newborn rash.* It affects about 70% of all newborns.
- Swollen pink pimples are called *newborn acne.*

Treatment for milia, newborn rash and newborn acne is time—you don't need to do anything. They will disappear on their own in a little while.

really don't need to treat it, but you may want to rub a little lotion on your baby's delicate skin.

A friend told me my baby will probably get a lot of different rashes. Is this normal?

Yes, but don't be alarmed about them. Contact your pediatrician if any rash lasts longer than a few days or if your baby seems to be extremely uncomfortable.

I know a baby's skin is sensitive. Is it OK to take my baby out in the sun?

Avoid exposing your baby to sunlight. A newborn's skin has little or no ability to protect itself from damage by the sun. Sunscreens are not recommended for babies under 6 months, so keep your little one in the shade for the best protection. Dress baby in a hat and protective clothing for even a brief outing in the sun, especially in very hot, sunny areas like the Southwest.

YOUR BABY'S HEALTH

I've never had a baby before. I'm concerned that I won't know when he's ill or when I should call the doctor. Do you have any recommendations?

If your baby exhibits any of the following symptoms, call your doctor:

- fever higher than 101F (38.3C)
- inconsolable crying for long periods of time
- problems with urination
- projectile vomiting, in which stomach contents come out with great force
- baby appears lethargic or floppy when held
- severe diarrhea
- unusual behavior
- poor appetite

Any of these could be an indication your baby is ill.

My brother's baby suffers from ear infections. How will I be able to tell if my baby has an ear infection?

It may be difficult for you to determine that your baby has an ear infection. The following symptoms may indicate an ear infection in babies under 6 months of age:

- irritability that lasts all day
- sleeplessness
- lethargy
- feeding difficulties

These symptoms may be hard to discern and may not be accompanied by fever. For babies between 6 and 12 months of age, symptoms are similar, except that fever is more common. The onset of ear pain may be sudden, acute and more noticeable.

I understand that dehydration is extremely dangerous in a baby. How will I know if my baby is dehydrated?

If dehydration occurs, call your baby's doctor immediately. Below are some warning signs to watch for.

- Baby wets fewer than six diapers a day.
- Baby's urine is dark yellow or orange; it should be pale yellow.
- Baby has fewer than two loose stools a day.
- Baby seems to be having trouble sucking.
- The soft spot on baby's head is sunken in.
- Baby is listless or otherwise appears unhealthy.

I've heard it's dangerous for a baby to have diarrhea. How will I know if my baby has diarrhea?

If you're concerned, call your pediatrician. A change in the number of diapers soiled or a change in the consistency of the bowel movement are the first clues.

What should I do if my baby has diarrhea?

Call the doctor. If your baby has diarrhea, he or she will need extra water and minerals to prevent dehydration. The doctor may recommend an oral electrolyte solution to help replenish baby's lost fluids and minerals.

Jaundice

I've heard about newborns with jaundice. What is jaundice?

Jaundice is the yellow staining of the skin, sclera (eyes) and deeper tissues of the body. It is caused by the newborn's inability to handle bilirubin, a chemical produced in the liver.

Is jaundice dangerous for a newborn?

Yes. Jaundice can be dangerous for the baby if it is left untreated, but with treatment, it is usually not a serious problem.

How is jaundice diagnosed?

The pediatrician and the nurses in the baby nursery observe the baby's color. The baby looks yellow because of the excess amounts of bilirubin in the blood. Bilirubin is measured by a blood test.

The *Colormate LTC Bilitest* doesn't involve taking baby's blood—no needles! It measures the yellow tinge of baby's skin with a handheld device. It is 95% accurate, and results are available in a few minutes.

How is it treated?

Phototherapy is the treatment of choice. The baby is placed under special lights; light penetrates the baby's skin and destroys the bilirubin. In some parts of the country, such as the Southwest, special lights may not be necessary. The baby is merely placed in the sunshine for short periods of time, and the sunlight destroys the excess bilirubin. In more severe cases, blood-exchange transfusions may be necessary.

Colic

Both of my sister's babies had colic. What is it exactly?

Colic is a condition marked by episodes of loud, sudden crying and fussiness, which can often last for hours, in a baby that is otherwise healthy. About 20% of all babies experience the pain and crying caused by colic. In full-blown colic, the abdomen becomes distended and the infant passes gas often.

What should I do if I think my baby has colic?

The only way to know if your baby has colic is to see your pediatrician or family physician. He or she can determine if it is colic or if your baby is having some other problem.

When does colic appear?

It usually appears gradually in the infant about 2 weeks after birth. As days pass, the condition worsens, then often disappears around the age of 3 months but occasionally lasts until 4 months. Colic attacks usually occur at night beginning in the late afternoon and early evening and last 3 to 4 hours. Attacks cease as quickly as they begin.

DEALING WITH COLIC

Most doctors recommend using a variety of methods to try to ease the baby's discomfort.

- Offer the baby the breast or a bottle of formula.
- Try noncow's milk formula, if you bottlefeed.
- Carry your baby in a sling during an episode. Motion and closeness often help somewhat.
- Try a pacifier to soothe the baby.
- Put the baby on her stomach across your knees and rub her back.
- Wrap the baby snugly in a blanket.
- Massage or stroke the baby's tummy.

What causes colic?

Researchers have been studying colic and its causes for a long time, but we still have little understanding of why it occurs. Theories about its causes include the following:

- immaturity of the digestive system
- intolerance to breast milk or cow's-milk protein in formula
- fatigue in the infant

YOUR BABY'S SLEEPING HABITS

I've heard stories about how difficult it is to get a baby to go to sleep at night. What can I do about this?

The wisest thing is to establish a routine to help your baby develop healthy sleeping habits.

- Wait until your baby is tired to put him or her to bed.

- Develop a regular, predictable routine for bed.
- Use a pacifier to help soothe and comfort baby.

My brother's new baby wants to sleep all day and stay up all night. Is there any way to get a baby to sleep at night and be up during the day?

There are some things a parent can do to try to change the day/night situation with the baby.

- Limit daytime naps to a few hours each.
- Don't overstimulate baby when you get up for nighttime feedings.
- By day, let baby nap in a light area, with some noise. At night, put baby in a very quiet, dark room to sleep.
- Keep baby up during the day by talking and singing or providing other stimulation.

I heard that it's better to put a baby down to sleep on his side or back, rather than on his stomach. Is this true?

Yes. We have discovered the back or side positions greatly reduce the incidence of SIDS (sudden infant death syndrome) by about 50%!

Someone told me that there's a difference in the sleep habits between bottlefed and breastfed babies. Is this true?

Yes, it may be. Bottlefed babies often sleep longer at night as they mature. Breastfed infants may not shift to longer sleep patterns until around the time they are weaned. See the chart below for a comparison of bottlefed and breastfed babies' sleep patterns.

NIGHTTIME SLEEP PATTERNS

Age Babies	Bottlefed Babies	Breastfed
Newborn	5 hours	4 to 7 hours
4 months	8 to 10 hours	4 to 7 hours
6 months	9 to 10 hours	4 to 7 hours
Total Sleep in 24 hours	13 to 15 hours	11 to 14 hours

TAKING CARE OF BABY

I'm nervous about dealing with the baby's umbilical cord. What should I do?

It isn't difficult to deal with the stump of the umbilical cord. It will fall off 7 to 10 days after birth. Until it does, clean your baby with sponge baths instead of tub baths. Follow your pediatrician's advice.

My baby's eyes are all gooey. How can I safely clean them?

To remove sleepers from baby's eyes, use a moistened cotton ball. Place the cotton ball at the inner corner of the eye, and wipe vertically down the nose. Or wipe from the inner corner of the eye to the outer corner.

How can I clean my baby's nose?

Never put anything inside your baby's nose. If you need to remove dried nasal secretions, gently wipe around the nose. Your baby will often sneeze out dried nasal secretions.

Is there an easy way to clean my baby's ears?

Never probe in your baby's ears with any object! Ear wax is there for a purpose. It's OK to clean around the outside of the ears with a soft washcloth, but don't put anything inside your baby's ears.

I've been trying to decide between cloth and disposable diapers for my new baby. Is one better than the other?

You must take into consideration your lifestyle, your budget and your baby. Disposable diapers are convenient. You don't need pins or plastic pants, and you never have to wash them. Cloth diapers can be used many times. Some styles don't need pins or plastic pants. You need adequate washing and drying facilities, or you may choose a diaper service. Many families use a combination of disposable and cloth diapers.

My little girl was pretty big when she was born, and I don't want her to be fat. Should I be concerned about how fat she is now?

No, that's not a concern at this early age. Focus on whether your baby is growing and developing appropriately, not how fat she is. Do *not* put your baby on a diet to keep her slim!

Will my doctor tell me if my baby is too fat?

Your doctor will be more concerned about where your child fits on the growth charts in relation to other children. Usually a child's weight (and height) are given using a percentile. For example, if you are told your son is in the 80th percentile for weight, it means 80 out of 100 children weigh less than he does and 20 children weigh more. (Percentile is also used for height.)

Is there any way I can keep my baby from being obese?

There are some tips to help you give your baby the best nutritional start possible.

- Breastfeed your baby.
- Do not introduce solid foods until between 4 and 6 months of age.
- Feed your baby in response to hunger not to meet other needs or just because it's "time to eat."
- Encourage physical activity and sound eating habits for everyone in your family.

CAR SEATS—FOR THE SAFETY OF YOUR BABY

Does my baby need to ride in a car safety-restraint seat all the time?

Yes. In an accident, an unrestrained child becomes a missilelike object in a car. The force of a crash can literally pull a child out of an adult's arms!

Where is the safest spot in the car to put the baby's car seat?

The safest spot is in the middle of the back seat. In this position, your baby is more protected in the event of a side collision. Manufacturers recommend not putting the car seat in the front seat, especially if you have a passenger-side air bag. If the bag inflates, it can knock the car seat around or even injure the baby.

What about short trips; what can happen to my baby?

It's incredible, but one study showed more than 30 deaths a year occur to unrestrained infants going home from the hospital after birth! In nearly all these cases, if the baby had been in an approved

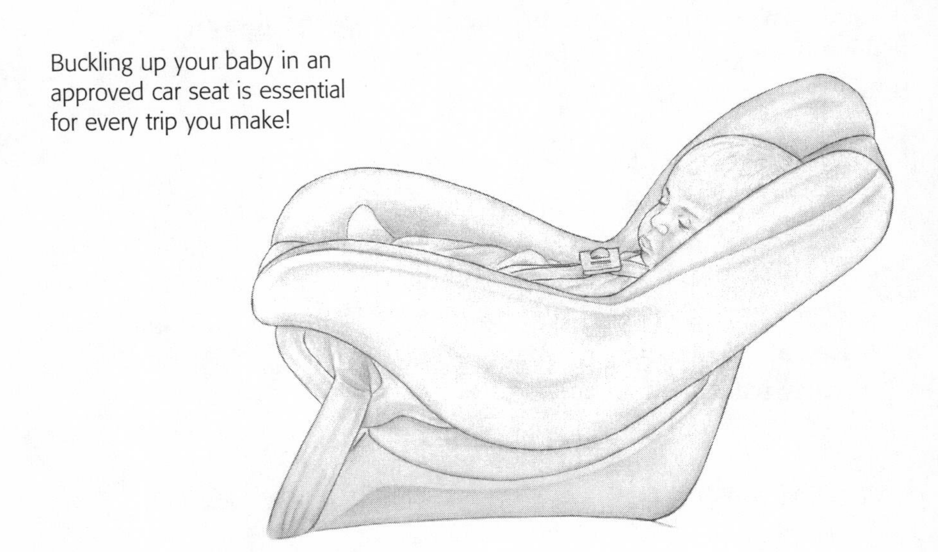
Buckling up your baby in an approved car seat is essential for every trip you make!

infant-restraint system, he or she would have survived the accident. Don't take chances—keep your baby safely restrained.

My mother said that it's against the law to let babies ride in a car without a safety-restraint system. Is this true?

All states have laws that govern safety-restraint systems. Call your local hospital or police department, and ask for information. Some hospitals won't let you take the baby home if he or she is not going to ride in an approved safety-restraint seat. Many hospitals have loaners you can borrow until you get your own.

18

Feeding Your Baby

As a parent, you do many things for your baby. You give your baby love. You give comfort when he or she's fussy. You change your baby when he or she needs it. You take care of your baby's many needs. Feeding your baby is one of the most important tasks you will perform. The nutrition you give your baby now will have an effect on the rest of his or her life.

You may decide to breastfeed your baby. This is probably the best nutrition you can provide. The baby receives more than just breast milk from you. He or she also receives important nutrients, antibodies to help prevent infections and other substances important for growth and development. However, you may choose not to breastfeed—if you bottlefeed, you are in the majority. You can still provide good nutrition for your baby. You just have to be aware of the various nutrients that different formulas provide.

The purpose of this chapter is to help you give your baby the best start nutritionally. If you have questions about a particular area, discuss them with your OB-GYN or your baby's pediatrician. Work together as a team in this important undertaking.

FEEDING BASICS

How often does a baby need to feed?

Early in life, most babies eat every 3 to 4 hours, although some babies feed as often as every 2 hours. It may help your baby get on a schedule if you feed at regular intervals. Or you can let your baby

How will I know when my baby is hungry?

Your baby will exhibit definite signs of hunger:

- *fussing*
- *putting his hands in his mouth*
- *turning his head and opening his mouth when his cheek is touched*

set a schedule—some babies need to feed more often than others. Sometimes your baby will need to feed more often than he or she usually does. See how often your baby wants to feed and whether he or she is growing properly. These are the best feeding guides. Usually as baby grows older, he or she waits longer between feedings and feeds longer at each feeding.

How much should I feed my baby at each feeding?

A baby is usually the best judge of how much to take at each feeding. Usually a baby will turn away from the nipple (mother or bottle) when he or she is full.

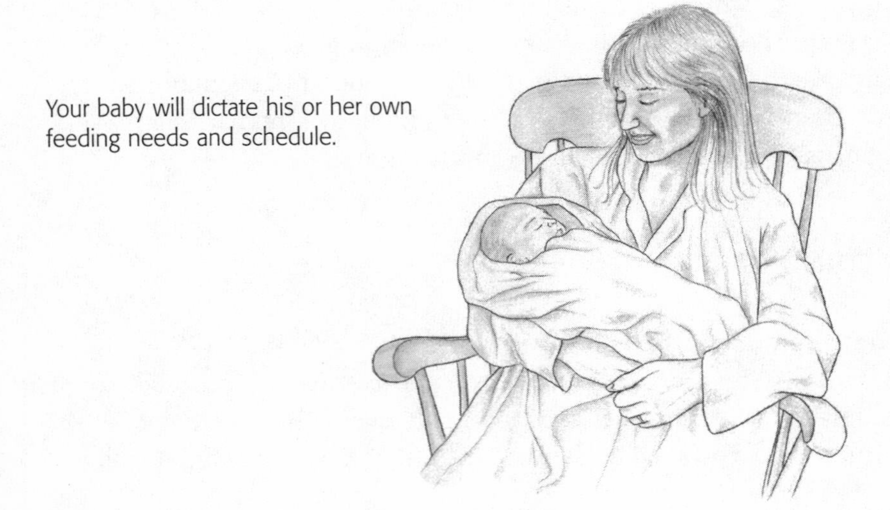

Your baby will dictate his or her own feeding needs and schedule.

I've heard that babies don't need to be fed breast milk or formula every time they're thirsty, that water is OK sometimes. How do I know when I should give water?

Discuss this with your pediatrician. Much depends on your baby's weight, how well he or she is doing and whether he or she is hungry or thirsty.

Do all babies need to be burped?

It's a good idea to burp your baby after each feeding. Some babies need to be burped during a feeding as well. Hold your baby over your shoulder or sit your baby in your lap, and gently rub or pat his or her back. You will probably want to place a towel over your shoulder or at least have one handy in case he or she spits up. If your baby doesn't burp, don't force it.

Is spitting up common in babies?

It is common during the early months of life because the muscle at the top of the stomach is not yet fully developed. When a baby spits up enough to propel the stomach contents several inches, it is called *vomiting.* If your baby vomits after a feeding, do not feed him or her again immediately—his or her stomach may be upset. Wait until the next feeding.

Is it true breastfeeding is the best choice for my baby?

If you can breastfeed, it is best for the baby. Breast milk contains all the nutrients a baby needs, and it's easy to digest. Breastfed babies have lower rates of infections, and breastfeeding provides the baby a sense of security and the mother a sense of self-esteem. However, if there are reasons you cannot or choose not to breastfeed, be assured that your baby will do well on formula.

My sister had problems and couldn't breastfeed. What if something like that happens to me and I can't breastfeed—will it harm my baby?

No, it will not harm your baby. We don't want any mother to feel guilty because she doesn't breastfeed her baby. Sometimes you cannot breastfeed because of a physical condition or other problem. Sometimes you choose not to breastfeed because of other demands on your time, such as a job or other children to care for. Your baby can still get all the love and attention and nutrition he or she needs if breastfeeding is not possible for you.

I've heard some babies can't breastfeed. Why not?

Some infants may have problems breastfeeding, or they will be unable to, if they have a cleft palate or cleft lip. Lactose intolerance can also cause breastfeeding problems.

BOTTLEFEEDING

I may be in the minority, but I want to bottlefeed, not breastfeed. Will I be a terrible mother because I feel this way?

No, you will not be a terrible mother because you choose not to breastfeed. In fact, statistics show that more women choose to bot-

I've heard all the great things about breastfeeding. Aren't there any good things to be said about bottlefeeding?

There are advantages to bottlefeeding that are often overlooked. Some women enjoy the freedom bottlefeeding provides. Someone else can help care for the baby. Fathers can be more involved in the care of the baby. Bottlefed babies are often able to last longer between feedings because formula is usually digested more slowly than breast milk. And you can determine exactly how much formula your baby is taking in at each feeding.

tlefeed than breastfeed their babies. We know that through the use of iron-fortified formula, your baby can receive good nutrition if you bottlefeed. Don't berate yourself or feel guilty if you bottlefeed—it's a personal decision that you must make.

BOTTLEFEEDING TIPS

- Snuggle baby close to you during feeding.
- Heat the formula to body temperature by running it under warm water.
- Hold the baby in a semi-upright position, with the head higher than his or her body.
- Place the bottle's nipple right side up, ready to feed.
- Don't touch the tip of the nipple.
- Brush the nipple lightly over the baby's lips, and guide it into the baby's mouth. Don't force it.
- Tilt the bottle so the neck is always filled, keeping the baby from sucking in too much air.
- Remove the bottle during feeding to let the baby rest. It usually takes 10 to 15 minutes to finish feeding.
- Don't leave the baby alone with the bottle. Never prop up a bottle and leave the baby alone to suck on it.
- Never put a baby down to bed with a bottle.

Do I have to warm up the formula before I feed it to my baby?

There's no evidence that feeding refrigerated formula without warming it will harm your baby. If you usually warm it, your baby will probably prefer it that way. If your baby is usually breastfed, he or she will probably prefer a warmed bottle. Be careful that formula is not too hot.

Are there different types of formula?

Yes, there are. Most babies do very well on milk-based formula, but some babies need specialized formulas.

What types of formulas are there besides regular milk-based formula?

Several types are available on the market today:

- milk-based, lactose-free formula for babies with feeding problems, such as fussiness, gas and diarrhea, caused by lactose intolerance
- soy-based formula—milk-free and lactose-free for babies with cow's milk allergies or sensitivity to cow's milk
- hypoallergenic protein formula—easier to digest and lactose free for babies with colic or other symptoms of milk-protein allergy

I recently read that bottlefeeding with a bottle that is slanted is better for the baby. Why?

Research has shown this design keeps the nipple full of milk, which means baby takes in less air. A slanted bottle also helps ensure baby is sitting up to drink. When a baby drinks lying down, milk can pool in the Eustachian tube, where it can cause ear infections.

How long should a baby receive formula?

The American Academy of Pediatrics recommends that a baby be fed iron-fortified formula for the first year of life. Feeding for this length of time helps maintain adequate iron intake.

BREASTFEEDING

When can I begin breastfeeding?

You can usually begin breastfeeding your baby within an hour after birth. This provides your baby with colostrum, the first milk your breasts produce. Colostrum contains important factors that help boost the baby's resistance to infection. Breastfeeding also

Bottlefeeding is a choice for many women. It allows them more freedom and the opportunity for other members of the family to participate in feeding the baby.

causes your pituitary gland to release oxytocin, which causes the uterus to contract and to decrease bleeding.

I'm nervous about breastfeeding. How do I start?

Don't be discouraged if it doesn't feel natural at first. It takes some time to find out what will work best for you and your baby. Hold your baby so he can reach the breast easily while nursing. Hold him across your chest, or lie in bed. Your baby should take your nipple fully into his mouth, so his gums cover the areola. He can't suck effectively if your nipple is only slightly drawn into his mouth.

I've heard that breastfeeding is the best way to bond with my baby. Is this true?

Breastfeeding is an excellent way to bond with your baby because of the closeness between mother and child established during the feeding process. However, there are other ways you can bond with your baby. Studies have shown that carrying your baby close to your body in a slinglike carrier helps the bonding process, which is great because dads can bond with baby, too.

Breastfeeding provides baby the best start in life.

I read that breastfeeding can prevent milk allergies. How?

It's nearly impossible for a baby to become allergic to his or her mother's breast milk. This is important if there is a history of allergies in your family or your partner's family. The longer a baby breastfeeds, the less likely he or she is to be exposed to substances that could cause allergic problems.

If my baby is sick or premature, can I still breastfeed?

Yes. If your baby is sick or premature, and you want to breastfeed, pump your breasts and store the milk until you can feed your baby. This helps establish your milk production, and you'll have a good supply of breast milk on hand when baby starts to feed. If you have enough breast milk stored, you may want to consider donating your extra breast milk to a breast-milk bank. Call your local La Leche League for information.

Everyone always mentions the advantages of breastfeeding. What are some of the disadvantages?

The greatest disadvantage for many mothers is the fact they are tied down to the baby so completely. They must be available when their baby is hungry. Breastfeeding can also make other family members feel left out. Mothers who breastfeed must pay careful attention to their diet, both for the nourishment they take in and the avoidance of substances that pass into their breast milk and could cause problems for the baby. Caffeine, alcohol and some medications can pass into breast milk.

I've heard stories about friends having to be up half the night to breastfeed. How long does it usually take for a baby to nurse?

Usually most babies will breastfeed every 2 to 3 hours for 5 to 15 minutes per breast.

Breastfeeding Precautions

Someone told me I had to drink lots of fluids (water mostly) while I'm breastfeeding. Is this true?

It's a good idea to keep your fluid intake up if you breastfeed.

Can I diet if I'm breastfeeding?

It's best *not* to diet while breastfeeding. All the nutrients your baby receives from breastfeeding depend on the quality of the food you eat. Breastfeeding places more demands on your body than pregnancy. Your body burns up to 1,000 calories a day just to produce milk. When breastfeeding, you need to eat an extra 500 calories a day.

I've heard that breastfeeding is a good way to keep from getting pregnant. Is this true?

Hormone changes that go along with breastfeeding make it less likely that you'll get pregnant, but *don't* rely on breastfeeding to protect you against getting pregnant again. You need to use some type of protection when you resume intercourse.

My friend said I shouldn't use birth-control pills while I'm breastfeeding. Why?

The hormones in regular oral contraceptives get into your milk and are passed along to your baby, possibly causing problems with the baby's development. However, the minipill is a good choice, or choose some other form of birth control until you are finished breastfeeding.

My sister told me not to eat spicy food while I'm breastfeeding. Can this cause some problem?

Many substances you eat or drink (or take orally, as medication) can pass to your baby in your breast milk. Spicy foods, chocolate, cabbage, broccoli and caffeine are some things your baby can react to when you ingest them. Be careful about what you eat and drink while breastfeeding.

How is caffeine a problem during breastfeeding?

Caffeine in breast milk can cause irritability and sleeplessness in a breastfed baby.

I read that a breastfeeding woman shouldn't eat peanuts or peanut products. Why?

Recent studies indicate exposure to peanuts and peanut products in a child under age 3 may cause a peanut allergy. Substances in peanuts can pass into breast milk, which could cause a breastfeeding child to become sensitized, leading to various allergic reactions.

I read an article the other day that mentioned a condition called "insufficient milk syndrome." What is it?

Insufficient milk syndrome is rare. The baby becomes dehydrated because of breastfeeding problems, such as the mother's low milk supply or the baby's failure to drink enough milk.

How does this syndrome occur?

It can happen when a mother has the idea that breastfeeding is the only "right" method of feeding and takes it to extremes. This woman views using a bottle as a personal failure, even when breastfeeding complications occur. It can also happen when a mother is unable to produce enough breast milk, due to genetic defect, injury or breast surgery. However, this problem is rare.

Your Milk Production

How will I know I'm producing enough breast milk?

If you are not producing enough milk, you may notice some of the following signs:

- your breasts show little or no change during pregnancy
- no engorgement after baby's birth
- no breast milk by the 5th postpartum day
- you can't hear baby gulping while he or she breastfeeds
- your baby loses more than 10% of his or her birthweight
- baby wets fewer than six diapers and has fewer than three stools a day
- baby never seems satisfied

My mother said she couldn't nurse me because she didn't have enough milk. Is this a common problem?

This is not a common problem. With some practice and lots of patience, nearly every woman can breastfeed her baby.

What problems keep a woman from breastfeeding?

A woman may be unable to breastfeed if she is extremely underweight or has some medical conditions, such as a prolactin deficiency, heart disease, kidney disease, tuberculosis or HIV.

I have a cousin whose breast milk never came in after her triplets were born. Is this common with multiple births?

No, it isn't.

I recently read that I can express my breast milk so my baby can drink it when I'm away from home. How do I do that?

By using a breast pump that is hand, battery or electrically operated to empty your breasts. You can store expressed milk.

How long does it take to express my breast milk?

You'll need 10 to 30 minutes to do this, depending on the type of pump you have. You'll probably need to do it 1 to 4 times a day (around the time you would normally nurse). You also need a refrigerated place to store the milk and a comfortable, private place where you can relax enough for milk letdown to occur.

I've heard I can freeze breast milk. How do I do that?

For longer storage, keep it in a refrigerator freezer for 6 months or in a deep freezer (–20F; –29C) for up to 12 months. Fill a contain-

STORING BREAST MILK

There are several steps you must take to store breast milk safely.

- Pump or express milk into a clean container.
- Label the container with the date and amount of milk collected.
- Freshly pumped breast milk can be kept at room temperature for up to 2 hours, but it's best to refrigerate milk as soon as possible.
- You may store breast milk safely in the refrigerator for up to 72 hours.

er only 3/4 full to allow for expansion during freezing. Freeze milk in small portions, such as 2 to 4 ounces (57 to 114ml), because these amounts thaw more quickly.

Is it possible to combine fresh breast milk with frozen breast milk?

Yes, this is possible. First, cool breast milk before combining it with previously frozen milk. The amount of thawed breast milk must be more than the amount of fresh breast milk. Never refreeze breast milk!

What's the best way to thaw frozen breast milk?

- Put the container of frozen milk in a bowl of warm water for 30 minutes, or hold container under warm running water.
- Never microwave breast milk; it can alter its composition.
- Swirl the container to blend any fat that might have separated during thawing.
- Feed thawed milk immediately, or store in the refrigerator for up to 24 hours.

The lady at La Leche League told me that if I bottlefeed formula part of the time, my milk supply will be reduced. Is this true?

Yes, it is. Your milk supply is driven by the baby's demand. If you bottlefeed with formula part of the time, your baby will not be demanding the breast milk from you, and your body will slow down its production.

Some Common Problems during Breastfeeding

Will it be painful when my milk comes in?

Breast milk becomes more plentiful between 2 and 6 days after birth, when it changes from colostrum to more nourishing mature milk. Your breasts may become engorged and could cause you some pain for 24 to 36 hours. Continue breastfeeding during this time. Wear a support bra, and apply cold compresses to your breasts for short periods. Take acetaminophen (Tylenol) for pain, or ask your doctor for something stronger.

My friend says she feels a tingling in her breasts when her baby nurses. What causes this?

Soon after a baby begins to nurse, the mother experiences tingling or cramping in her breasts called *milk letdown,* which means milk is flowing into the breast ducts. It occurs several times during feeding. Occasionally a baby will choke a bit when the rush of milk comes too quickly.

I've read that many new mothers have problems with sore nipples. Why?

If your baby doesn't take your nipple into his or her mouth fully during breastfeeding, his or her jaws can compress the nipple and make it sore. But take heart—sore nipples rarely last longer than a couple of days. Continue breastfeeding while your breasts are sore.

Is there any other way to prevent sore nipples?

Nipple shields, worn inside your bra between the nipple and fabric, provide some relief. (It keeps tender skin from rubbing on the bra fabric.) You can also apply a mild cream to sore nipples to provide some soothing relief. Ask your pharmacist or doctor for the names of products that are OK to use during nursing.

My best friend had a very bad breast infection with her last baby. How will I know if I have one?

Large red streaks that extend up the breast toward the armpit usually indicate a breast infection. If you experience this, call your doctor. An infection can cause a fever to develop within 4 to 8 hours after the appearance of the red streaks.

How is a breast infection treated?

If you have a plugged duct, apply a warm compress to the affected area or soak the breast in warm water. Then express milk or breastfeed while massaging the tender area. If you develop flulike symptoms with a sore breast, call your doctor. Antibiotic treatment will be started. You may also need to rest in bed, and empty the infected breast by pumping or breastfeeding every hour or two.

What happens if a breast infection isn't treated?

It can turn into an abscess. This is very painful and may need to be opened and drained.

PREVENT BREAST INFECTION

There are several things you can do to help prevent an infection.

- Eat right, drink lots of fluid and get enough rest. This helps reduce stress and keeps your immune system in top fighting form.
- Don't wear tight-fitting bras—especially underwire bras—because they can block milk flow. This can cause an infection.
- Empty your breasts on a regular schedule to avoid engorgement.
- After each feeding or pumping, let nipples air dry for a few minutes.

Should I stop nursing if I get a breast infection?

No. It's important to continue breastfeeding. If you stop, the infection may get worse.

I recently read that milk ducts in the breast can get plugged up. What does this mean?

A plugged milk duct in the breast prevents milk from flowing freely. It results in tender or firm areas of the breast that become more painful after breastfeeding. A plugged duct may not be red, and you may not have a fever.

How is a plugged duct treated?

It usually takes care of itself if you continue to nurse frequently. Apply warm compresses to the sore area to help with the pain and to open the duct. You may also take acetaminophen.

If I'm sick, can I still breastfeed?

If you have a cold or other virus, it is all right to breastfeed. It's OK to breastfeed if you're taking an antibiotic, as long as you know the drug is OK to use during nursing. Ask your pharmacist or doctor if any medication prescribed for you should not be taken while breastfeeding. Be sure to ask *before* you begin taking it.

You Should Also Know

My breasts are very small. How do I know I'll have enough breast milk?

The size of your breasts doesn't influence the amount of milk you have, so this usually isn't a problem.

I'm embarrassed when I think about breastfeeding my baby in public. Is it really acceptable?

In many countries, breastfeeding is a natural part of life. In North America, people are now more accepting of breastfeeding than in the past. Gauge each situation separately. If you're comfortable nursing at a friend's house, go ahead. If you feel uncomfortable nursing in a public place, go into the ladies' room or a lounge. Look at each instance separately—you'll soon learn how comfortable you feel feeding your baby away from home.

My sister-in-law said she didn't keep breastfeeding her son because he wouldn't settle into a pattern. Is this common?

You may be unprepared for how often your baby will want (and need) to nurse in the first few weeks after birth. You may wonder if it's worth it to continue. Relax and be patient. It takes time for baby to establish a nursing pattern, but he or she will establish one and begin to sleep longer between feedings.

Is it OK to substitute bottles for some breastfeeding sessions?

It's best to avoid bottles, if possible, for the first 4 to 6 weeks of breastfeeding for two reasons. First, your baby may come to prefer feeding from a bottle (it's not as hard to suck). Second, your breasts may not produce enough milk.

I don't know how long I'll be able to breastfeed my baby because I have to go back to work. Is there a time that is the most important for me to nurse my baby?

Nursing the first 4 weeks of your baby's life provides the most protection for your baby and the most beneficial hormone release to help you recover after the birth. Nursing for the first 6 months is very beneficial for your baby—it provides excellent nutrition and protection against illness. After 6 months, the nutrition and protection aspects are not as critical. If you can nurse only a short period of time, the first 4 weeks of your baby's life are the most important time to do so.

I want to continue breastfeeding my baby after I go back to work. Is this possible?

Yes. If you breastfeed exclusively, you'll have to pump your breasts or arrange to see your baby during the day. Or you can nurse your baby at home and provide formula for when you're away.

A friend told me that support at work for her breastfeeding seemed to disappear after 4 or 5 months. What can I do about this?

You may have to talk to your employer and co-workers about the situation and attempt to work out a solution that is equitable for everyone.

If I have to be out of town on business for a few days, will my breast milk dry up?

You probably will need to pump your breast milk while you are gone. You may be very uncomfortable if you don't because your milk will continue to come in. Take a breast pump with you and discard the breast milk after you pump it.

I've heard there are special bras to wear while breastfeeding. What are they?

Nursing bras are worn for breastfeeding. They have cups that open so you can breastfeed without having to get undressed.

How soon can I buy a nursing bra?

Wait until at least the 36th week of your pregnancy. If you buy it sooner, it will be difficult to buy one that fits.

How can I be sure a nursing bra will fit correctly?

Your breasts will become larger when your milk comes in, so buy a bra with at least a finger's width of space between any part of the cup and your breast. Be sure to make allowances for the room taken up by nursing pads. When trying on the bra, fasten the hooks at their loosest setting. That will make it possible for you to tighten it as your ribcage shrinks after your baby is born.

Are there any other special clothes I should consider for breastfeeding?

Nighties, shift dresses and full-cut blouses have been designed with discreet openings so you don't have to get undressed to breastfeed. You can reach up inside your outer clothing, unhook your nursing bra and place your baby at your breast without anyone noticing. Draping a light towel or blanket over your shoulder, over the baby's head, adds further coverage.

A few years ago, I had my very small breasts enlarged. Can I breastfeed my baby after it is born?

Ask your doctor. Many women who have had breast-enlargement surgery are able to breastfeed successfully. Some doctors have advised women not to breastfeed if they have had silicone implants.

Because of back problems caused by extremely large breasts, I had my breasts reduced. Will this affect my ability to breastfeed?

You should still be able to breastfeed. The surgery may result in decreased milk production, but usually there is enough.

Someone told me that if I breastfeed, my nipples will drip milk when my baby cries. This isn't true, is it?

It is true. This may occur when your baby, or any other baby you are around, cries. This is the milk letdown response and is normal. To protect your clothing, wear breast shields or pads.

I'm sure my partner will feel left out if he can't feed the baby. Is there any way he can participate in feeding?

Your partner can help out by getting up at night and bringing the baby to you or by changing the baby. Your partner can also feed your baby expressed breast milk.

I know my stepdaughter will want to help me feed the baby, but I'll be nursing. How can I include her?

You can include your stepdaughter by letting her hold or burp the baby after a feeding. If you express your milk, she could feed the baby a bottle of it at some feedings.

Should I switch breasts during breastfeeding?

Yes, but wait until your baby finishes with one breast before switching to the other one. The consistency of breast milk changes from thinner to richer as the baby nurses. At the next feeding, start your baby on the breast you nursed last. This will help you keep both breasts stimulated. If your baby only wants to nurse from one breast during a feeding, switch to the other breast the next feeding.

If I have any problems breastfeeding, what can I do?

Many hospitals have breastfeeding specialists you can call for help. Also call your doctor's office—they may be able to refer you to someone knowledgeable. You can look in the telephone book for the La Leche League, which is an organization that promotes breastfeeding. Someone from the local group can give you advice and encouragement.

How do I discontinue nursing when my baby is old enough to stop?

You can either taper off gradually or stop cold turkey. Each way has its advantages. If you want to taper off gradually, start offering a bottle every other feeding or offer bottles during the day and nurse at night. If you stop cold turkey, you may have some sleepless nights with a screaming baby, and you may be quite uncomfortable physically with engorged breasts. However, this method takes less time.

At what age (of the baby) do most women stop breastfeeding?

That varies from woman to woman. Some women like to nurse until they return to work. Others nurse through the first year. It depends on your situation and your desire, and when your baby gets teeth!

RESOURCES

GENERAL INFORMATION FOR PARENTS

All Print USA (unique birth announcements)
877–685–6397
www.info@allprintusa.com

American Academy of Pediatrics
141 Northwest Point Boulevard
Elk Grove Village, IL 60007–1098
847–434–4000
www.aap.org

American College of Obstetricians and Gynecologists
Resource Center
409 12th Street, SW
P.O. Box 96920
Washington, DC 20090–6920
www.acog.org

Baby Center
www.babycenter.com

Baby Talk and Shop
800–628–5113
www.babytalkandshop.com

Child Magazine
www.childmagazine.com

Children's Defense Fund
25 E Street NW
Washington, DC 20001
202–628–8787
www.childrensdefense.org

Family and Medical Leave Act
800–522–0925

Maternity Center Association
www.maternity.org

Miserly Moms
www.miserlymoms.com

Moms Online
www.momsonline.com

National Maternal and Child Health Clearinghouse
2070 Chain Bridge Road, Suite 450
Vienna, VA 22182–2536
888–434–4624
www.nmchc.org

Social Security Administration
800–772–1213
www.ssa.gov

The Women's Bureau Publications
(for summary of state laws on family leave)
U.S. Department of Labor
Women's Bureau Clearing House
Box EX
200 Constitution Avenue, NW
Washington, DC 20210
800–827–5335

AT-HOME MOMS

International MOMS Club (Mothers Offering Mothers Support)
25371 Rye Canyon Road
Valencia, CA 91355
www.momsclub.org
momsclub@aol.com
To find a MOMS club near you, e-mail or mail your address and names of other cities in your area.

Mothers at Home
9493-C Silver King Court
Fairfax, VA 22031
800–783–4666
www.mah.org

BREASTFEEDING

Avent
475 Supreme Drive
Bensenville, IL 60106
800–542–8368
www.aventamerica.com

Best Start
4809 E. Busch Boulevard, Suite 104
Tampa, FL 33617
800–277–4975

International Lactation Consultant Association
1500 Sunday Drive, Suite 102
Raleigh, NC 27607
919–787–5181
www.ilca.org

La Leche League
1400 North Meacham Road
Schaumburg, IL 60173–4048
847–519–7730
www.lalecheleague.org

Medela, Inc.
P.O. Box 660
McHenry, IL 60051–0660
800–435–8316
www.medela.com

Wellstart
4062 First Avenue
San Diego, CA 92103–2045
619–295–5192
www.aiha.com

CHILDBIRTH

American Academy of Husband-Coached Childbirth
(Bradley Method)
P.O. Box 5224
Sherman Oaks, CA 91413–5224
800–422–4784
www.bradleybirth.com

American College of Nurse-Midwives (ACNM)
818 Connecticut Avenue NW, Suite 900
Washington, DC 20006
202–728–9860
www.midwife.org

American Society for Pyschoprophylaxis in Obstetrics (ASPO/Lamaze)
2025 M Street, Suite 800
Washington, DC 20036–3309
800–368–4404
www.lamaze-childbirth.com

Association of Labor Assistants and Childbirth Educators
P.O. Box 382724
Cambridge, MA 02238–2724
617–441–2500
www.alacehq.hypermart.net

Doulas of North America
13513 North Grove Drive
Alpine, UT 84004
801–756–7331
www.dona.com

Informed Home Birth
2110 Londonderry Road
Ann Arbor, MI 48104
734–662–6857

International Cesarean Awareness Network (ICAN)
1304 Kingsdale Avenue
Redondo Beach, CA 90278
310–542–6400
www.ican-online.org

International Childbirth Education Association
P.O. Box 20048
Minneapolis, MN 55420–0048
952–854–8660
www.icea.org

Midwives Alliance of North America (MANA)
5462 Madison Street
Hilliard, OH 43026
888–923–6262

National Association of Childbearing Centers (NACC)
3123 Gottschall Road
Perkiomenville, PA 18074
215–234–8068
www.birthcenters.org

Public Citizen Health Research Group
(for information on C-sections and VBAC)
1600 20th Street NW
Washington, DC 20009
202–588–1000
www.citizen.org

CHILD CARE

Au Pair in America
River Plaza
9 West Broad Street
Stamford, CT 06902–3788
800–727–2437
www.aupairinamerica.com

Child Care Aware
800–424–2246
www.childcareaware.org

Department of Health and Human Services National Child Care Information Center
243 Church Street, NW
2nd Floor
Vienna, VA 22180
800–616–2242

International Nanny Association
900 Haddon Avenue, Suite 438
Collingswood, NJ 08108
856–858–0808
www.nanny.org

Internal Revenue Service
(for information on child-care expenses)
800–829–1040

National Resource Center for Health and Safety in Child Care
UCHSC at Fitzsimons
Campus Mail Stop F541
P.O. Box 6508
Aurora, CO 80045–0508
800–598–5437
nrc.uchsc.edu

National Association for the Education of Young Children
1509 16th Street, NW
Washington, DC 20036–1426
800–424–2460
www.naeyc.org

Working Mother magazine
www.workingmother.com

DADS

A Man's Life
http://www.manslife.com

A Daddy's Home
www.daddyshome.com

At-Home Dad newsletter
61 Brightwood Avenue
North Andover, MA 01845
www.athomedad.com

Baby Center Dad Zone
www.babycenter.com/dads

Boot Camp for New Dads
www.newdads.com

Father's World, Inc.
P.O. Box 433
Massapequa, NY 11758–0433
516–795–3096
www.fathersworld.com

Full-Time Dads
193 Shelley Avenue
Elizabeth, NJ 07208
908–355–9722 FAX
908–355–9723
http://www.fathersworld.com/fulltimedad

DOWN SYNDROME

The Arc of the United States
1010 Wayne Avenue, Suite 650
Silver Spring, MD 20910
301–565–3842
www.thearc.org

Association for Children with Down Syndrome (ACDS)
4 Fern Place
Plainview NY, 11803
516–933–4700
www.acds.org

National Down Syndrome Society (NDSS)
666 Broadway
New York, NY 10012–2317
800–221–4602

MATERNITY CLOTHES

Baby Becoming Plus Size Maternity Fashions
888–666–6910
www.babybecoming.com

Belly Basics
www.nystyle.com/bellyb

E-Styles Maternity Clothes
877–378–9537
www.maternityclothes.com

Liz Lange Maternity
888.616.5777
www.lizlange.com

MOTHER'S HEALTH

American Cancer Society
800-ACS–2345
www.cancer.org

Group-B Strep Association
P.O. Box 16515
Chapel Hill, NC 27516
919–932–5344
www.groupbstrep.org

Sidelines
(for women experiencing complicated pregnancies)
P.O. Box 1808
Laguna Beach, CA 92652
Candace Hurley, executive director: 714–497–2265
www.sidelines.org

MULTIPLES

Center for Loss in Multiple Birth (CLIMB, Inc.)
c/o Jean Kollantai
P.O. Box 91377
Anchorage, AK 99509
907–222–5321
www.climb-support.org

Center for Study of Multiple Births
333 E. Superior Street, Suite 464
Chicago, IL 60611
312–908–7532
www.multiplebirth.com

Mothers of Supertwins (M.O.S.T.)
(triplets or more)
P.O. Box 951
Brentwood, NY 11717
631–859–1110
www.mostonline.org

National Online Fathers of Twins Club (NOFOTC)
c/o Jeff Maxwell
2804 NW 163rd
Edmond, OK 73013
www.nofotc.org

National Organization of Mothers of Twins Clubs, Inc. (NOMOTC)
Executive Office
P.O. Box 438
Thompson Station, TN 37179–0438
877–540–2200
www.nomotc.org

Triplet Connection
P.O. Box 99571
Stockton, CA 95209
209–474–0885
www.tripletconnection.org/

Twin to Twin Transfusion Syndrome (TTTS) Foundation
411 Longbeach Parkway
Bay Village, OH 44140
440–899–8887
www.tttsfoundation.org

Twin Services
P.O. Box 10066
Berkeley, CA 94709
510–524–0863

The Twins Foundation
P.O. Box 6043
Providence, RI 02940–6043
401–729–1000
www.twinsfoundation.com

Twins Magazine
5350 S. Roslyn Street, Suite 400
Englewood, CO 80111
888–558–9467
www.twinsmagazine.com

NUTRITION

Beechnut Nutrition Hotline
800–523–6633

Center for Food Safety and Applied Nutrition; Special Document Request Line
800–332–4010

USDA Center for Nutrition Policy and Promotion
Food Guide Pyramid
1120 20th Street, NW
Suite 200, North Lobby
Washington, DC 20036–3475
www.nal.usda.gov/fnic/Fpyr/pyramid.html

POSTPARTUM DEPRESSION

Postpartum Support International
927 N. Kellogg Avenue
Santa Barbara, CA 93111
805–967–7636
www.chss.iup.edu/postpartum

PREMATURE INFANTS

ECMO (Extracorporeal Membrane Oxygenation) Moms and Dads
c/o Gayle Wilson
Route 1, Box 176AA
Idalou, TX 79329
806–892–3348
E-mail: bgw@odsy.net

SAFETY FOR YOUR BABY

The Danny Foundation
(information on crib dangers)
800–83-DANNY
www.dannyfoundation.org

National Child Abuse Hotline
800–4A-CHILD (800–422–4453)

SafetyBeltSafe USA
P.O. Box 553
Altadena, CA 91003
www.carseat.org

U.S. Consumer Products Safety Commission
800–638–2772
www.cpsc.gov

SINGLE MOTHERS

National Organization of Single Mothers
P.O. Box 68
Midland, NC 28107–0068
704–888-KIDS (704–888–5437)
www.singlemothers.org

GLOSSARY

abortion. Termination or end of pregnancy; giving birth to an embryo or fetus before it can live outside the womb, usually defined as before 20 weeks of gestation. Abortion may be spontaneous, often called a *miscarriage,* or induced, as in a medical or therapeutic abortion performed to terminate a pregnancy.

acquired immune deficiency syndrome (AIDS). Debilitating and frequently fatal illness that affects the body's ability to respond to infection. Caused by the human immune deficiency virus (HIV).

aerobic exercise. Exercise that increases your heart rate and oxygen intake.

afterbirth. Placenta and membranes expelled after the baby is delivered. See *placenta.*

alpha-fetoprotein (AFP). Substance produced by the unborn baby as it grows inside the uterus. Large amounts of AFP are found in amniotic fluid. Larger-than-normal amounts may be found in the maternal bloodstream if neural-tube defects are present in the fetus.

amino acids. Substances that act as building blocks in the developing embryo and fetus.

amniocentesis. Removal of amniotic fluid from the amniotic sac; fluid is tested for some genetic defects or fetal lung maturity.

amniotic fluid. Fluid surrounding the baby inside the amniotic sac.

amniotic sac. Membrane that surrounds baby inside the uterus. It contains the baby, placenta and amniotic fluid.

anemia. Any condition in which the number of red blood cells is less than normal. Term usually applies to the concentration of the oxygen-transporting material in the blood.

anencephaly. Defective brain development combined with the absence of the bones normally surrounding the brain.

angioma. Tumor, usually benign, or swelling composed of lymph and blood vessels.

antigen. Substance formed in the body or introduced into the body that causes formation of antibodies, which interact specifically with the substance.

anti-inflammatory medications. Drugs to relieve pain and inflammation.

Apgar score. Measurement of a baby's response to birth and life on its own. Taken 1 and 5 minutes after birth.

areola. Pigmented or colored ring surrounding the nipple of the breast.

arrhythmia. Irregular or missed heartbeat.

aspiration. Swallowing or sucking a foreign body or fluid, such as vomit, into an airway.

asthma. Disease marked by recurrent attacks of shortness of breath and difficulty breathing. Often caused by an allergic reaction.

atonic uterus. Uterus that is flaccid or relaxed; lacks tone.

baby blues. Mild depression in woman after delivery.

back labor. Pain of labor felt in lower back.

bilirubin. Breakdown product of pigment formed in the liver from hemoglobin during the destruction of red blood cells.

biophysical profile. Method of evaluating a fetus before birth.

biopsy. Removal of a small piece of tissue for microscopic study.

birthing center. Facility in which a woman labors, delivers and recovers in the same room. It may be part of a hospital or a freestanding unit. Sometimes called *LDRP*, for *labor, delivery, recovery* and *postpartum*.

blood pressure. Push of the blood against the walls of the arteries, which carry blood away from the heart.

bloody show. Small amount of vaginal bleeding late in pregnancy; often precedes labor.

board certification. Doctor has had additional training and testing in a particular specialty. In the area of obstetrics, the American College of Obstetricians and Gynecologists offers this training. Certification requires expertise in care of women.

Braxton-Hicks contractions. Irregular, painless tightening of uterus during pregnancy.

breech presentation. Abnormal position of the fetus. Buttocks or legs come into the birth canal before baby's head.

carcinogen. Any cancer-producing substance.

cervix. Opening of the uterus.

Cesarean section (delivery). Delivery of a baby through an abdominal incision rather than through the vagina.

Chadwick's sign. Dark blue or purple discoloration of the mucosa of the vagina and cervix during pregnancy.

chemotherapy. Treatment of disease by chemical substances or drugs.

chlamydia. Sexually transmitted venereal infection.

chloasma. Extensive brown patches of irregular shape and size on the face or other parts of the body.

chorionic villus sampling (CVS). Diagnostic test done early in pregnancy. A biopsy of tissue is taken from inside the uterus through the abdomen or the cervical opening to determine abnormalities of pregnancy.

chromosomal abnormality. Abnormal number or abnormal makeup of chromosomes.

chromosomes. Thread in a cell's nucleus that contains DNA, which transmits genetic information.

clomiphene-challenge test. Way of testing for ovulation using a drug that stimulates the ovaries.

colostrum. Thin, yellow fluid that is the first milk to come from the breast. Most often seen toward the end of pregnancy. It is different in content from milk produced later during nursing.

condyloma acuminatum. Skin tags or warts that are sexually transmitted, caused by human papilloma virus (HPV). Also called *venereal warts.*

congenital problem. Problem present at birth.

consanguinity. Being related by blood to the person you are married to.

constipation. Infrequent or incomplete bowel movements.

contraction stress test. Test of response of fetus to uterine contractions to evaluate fetal well-being.

contractions. Squeezing or tightening of uterus, which pushes the baby out of the uterus during birth.

corpus-luteum cyst. Normal cyst on ovary after ovulation.

cystitis. Inflammation of the bladder.

cytomegalovirus (CMV) infection. Group of viruses from the herpes-virus family.

D&C (dilatation and curettage). Surgical procedure in which the cervix is dilated and the lining of the uterus is scraped.

developmental delay. Slower than normal development of the baby or child.

diastasis recti. Separation of abdominal muscles.

differentiating. Changing, especially because of growth.

dilatation. Opening or stretching of the cervix during a baby's birth.

dizygotic twins. Twins derived from two different eggs. Often called *fraternal twins.*

due date. Date your baby is expected to be born. Most babies are born near this date, but only 1 of 20 are born on the actual date.

dysplasia. Abnormal, precancerous changes in the cells of the cervix.

dysuria. Difficult or painful urination.

eclampsia. Convulsions and coma in a woman with pre-eclampsia. Not related to epilepsy.

ectopic pregnancy. Pregnancy that occurs outside the uterine cavity.

EDC (estimated date of confinement). Baby's anticipated due date. Calculated from the first day of the last menstrual period, counting forward 280 days.

Edwards' syndrome. See *trisomy 18.*

effacement. Thinning of cervix.

electronic fetal monitoring. Use of electronic instruments to record the fetal heartbeat.

embryo. Organism in the early stages of development.

embryonic period. First 10 weeks of gestation.

endometrium. Mucous membrane that lines the inside of the uterine wall.

enema. Fluid injected into the rectum to clear the bowel.

engorgement. Congestion, as filled with fluid.

epidural block. Type of anesthesia injected around the spinal cord during labor or some types of surgery.

episiotomy. Surgical incision of the perineum (area behind the vagina, above the rectum). Done during delivery to avoid tearing of the vaginal opening and rectum.

estimated date of confinement. See *EDC.*

expressing breast milk. Manually removing milk from the breast.

external cephalic version (ECV). Procedure done late in pregnancy, in which doctor manually attempts to move a baby in the breech position into the normal head-down position.

face presentation. Baby comes into the birth canal face first.

Fallopian tube. Tube that leads from the cavity of the uterus to the area of the ovary. Also called *uterine tube.*

false labor. Tightening of uterus without dilatation of the cervix.

false-negative test result. Result indicates negative outcome, but it is actually positive.

false-positive test result. Result indicates positive outcome, but it is actually negative.

fasting blood-sugar test. Blood test to evaluate the amount of sugar in the blood following a period of fasting.

fertilization. Joining of the sperm and egg.

fertilization age. Dating a pregnancy from the time of fertilization; 2 weeks earlier than the gestational age. Also called *ovulatory age.*

fetal anomaly. Fetal malformation or abnormal development.

fetal arrhythmia. See *arrhythmia.*

fetal distress. Problems with the baby that occur before birth or during labor, requiring immediate delivery.

fetal-growth restriction. See *intrauterine-growth restriction.*

fetal monitor. Device used before or during labor to listen to and record the fetal heartbeat. Monitoring of the baby inside the uterus can be external (through maternal abdomen) or internal (through maternal vagina).

fetal period. Time period following the embryonic period (first 10 weeks of gestation) until birth.

fetus. Refers to the unborn baby after 10 weeks of gestation until birth.

forceps. Special instrument placed around the baby's head, inside the birth canal, to help guide the baby out of the birth canal during delivery.

fragile-X syndrome. Abnormal X chromosome.

frank breech. Baby presenting buttocks first. Legs are flexed and knees extended.

fraternal twins. See *dizygotic twins.*

full-term infant. Baby born between 38 and 42 weeks of pregnancy.

gene regulator. Gene that regulates the operation of another gene.

genetic counseling. Consultation between a couple and specialists about genetic defects and the possibility of presence or recurrence of genetic problems in a pregnancy.

genital herpes simplex. Herpes simplex infection involving the genital area. It can be significant during pregnancy because of the danger to a newborn infected with herpes simplex.

gestational age. Dating a pregnancy from the first day of the last menstrual period; 2 weeks longer than fertilization age. Also called *menstrual age.*

gestational diabetes. Occurrence or worsening of diabetes during pregnancy (gestation).

globulin. Family of proteins from plasma or serum of the blood.

glucose-tolerance test. Blood test done to evaluate the body's response to sugar. Blood is drawn at intervals following ingestion of a sugary substance.

glucosuria. Sugar in the urine.

gonorrhea. Contagious venereal infection, transmitted primarily by intercourse. Caused by the bacteria *Neisseria gonorrhea.*

group-B streptococcal infection. Serious infection occurring in the mother's vagina and throat.

habitual miscarriage. Occurrence of three or more spontaneous miscarriages.

heartburn. Discomfort or pain that occurs in the chest, often after eating.

hematocrit. Determines proportion of blood cells to plasma. Important in diagnosing anemia.

hemoglobin. Pigment in red blood cell that carries oxygen to body tissues.

hemolytic disease. Destruction of red blood cells. See *anemia.*

hemorrhoids. Dilated blood vessels in the rectum or rectal canal.

heparin. Medication used to prevent excessive clotting of the blood.

high-risk pregnancy. Pregnancy with complications that requires special medical attention, often from a specialist. See *perinatologist.*

human chorionic gonadotropin. Hormone produced in early pregnancy. Measured in a pregnancy test.

hydramnios. Increased amniotic fluid.

hydrocephalus. Excessive accumulation of fluid around the baby's brain. Sometimes called *water on the brain.*

hyperbilirubinemia. Extremely high level of bilirubin in the blood.

hyperemesis gravidarum. Severe nausea, dehydration and vomiting during pregnancy, most frequently during the first trimester.

hyperglycemia. High blood-sugar levels.

hyperkeratosis. Increase in the size of the horny layer of the skin.

hypertension, pregnancy-induced. High blood pressure that occurs during pregnancy. Defined by an increase in the diastolic or systolic blood pressure.

hyperthyroidism. Elevation of the thyroid hormone in the blood.

hypoglycemia. Low blood-sugar levels.

hypoplasia. Defective or incomplete development or formation of tissue.

hypotension. Low blood pressure.

hypothyroidism. Low or inadequate levels of thyroid hormone in the blood.

identical twins. See *monozygotic twins.*

immune globulin preparation. Substance used to protect against infection from certain diseases, such as hepatitis or measles.

in utero. Within the uterus.

in vitro. Outside the body.

incompetent cervix. Cervix that dilates painlessly, without contractions.

incomplete miscarriage. Miscarriage in which part, but not all, of the uterine contents are expelled.

induced labor. Labor started by the doctor, using a medication.

inevitable miscarriage. Pregnancy complicated by bleeding and cramping. Usually results in miscarriage.

insulin. Peptide hormone made by the pancreas; promotes body's use of glucose.

intrauterine-growth restriction (IUGR). Inadequate growth of the fetus during pregnancy.

iron-deficiency anemia. Anemia produced by lack of iron in the diet; often seen in pregnancy. See *anemia.*

isoimmunization. Development of specific antibody directed at the red blood cells of another individual, such as a baby in utero. Occurs when Rh-negative woman carries Rh-positive baby or when she is given Rh-positive blood.

jaundice. Yellow staining of the skin, sclera (eyes) and deeper tissues of the body. Caused by excessive amounts of bilirubin.

ketones. Breakdown product of metabolism found in the blood, particularly in starvation or uncontrolled diabetes.

kidney stones. Small mass or lesion found in the kidney or urinary tract that can block the flow of urine.

Klinefelter's syndrome. Abnormal number of sex chromosomes (XXY).

labor. Process of expelling a fetus from the uterus.

laparoscopy. Surgical procedure performed for tubal ligation, diagnosis of pelvic pain, diagnosis of ectopic pregnancy or for other diagnoses.

leukorrhea. Vaginal discharge characterized by white or yellowish color. Primarily composed of mucus.

lightening. Often described as the baby "dropping"; a sensation of pressure in the pelvis near term.

linea nigra. Line of increased pigmentation running down the abdomen from the bellybutton to the pubic area during pregnancy.

lochia. Vaginal discharge that occurs after delivery of baby and placenta.

mammogram. X-ray study of the breasts to identify normal and abnormal breast tissue.

mask of pregnancy. Increased pigmentation over the area of the face under each eye. Commonly has the appearance of a butterfly.

meconium. First intestinal discharge of the newborn; green or yellow in color. It consists of epithelial or surface cells, mucus and bile. Discharge occurs before or during labor or soon after birth.

melanoma. Pigmented mole or tumor that may be cancerous.

meningomyelocele. Congenital defect of the central nervous system of the baby. Membranes and spinal cord protrude through an opening or defect in the vertebral column.

menstrual age. See *gestational age.*

menstruation. Regular or periodic discharge of a bloody fluid from the uterus.

microcephaly. Abnormally small development of the head in the developing fetus.

miscarriage. See abortion.

missed miscarriage. Failed pregnancy, without bleeding or cramping. Often diagnosed by ultrasound weeks or months after a pregnancy fails.

monilial vulvovaginitis. Infection caused by yeast or monilia. Usually affects the vagina and vulva.

monozygotic twins. Twins conceived from one egg. Often called *identical twins.*

morning sickness. Nausea and vomiting found primarily during the first trimester of pregnancy. Also see *hyperemesis gravidarum.*

mucus plug. Secretions in cervix; often released just before labor.

natural childbirth. Labor and delivery in which no medication is used, and the mother remains awake to help deliver the baby. The woman may or may not have taken classes to prepare her for labor and delivery.

neural-tube defects. Abnormalities in the development of the spinal cord and brain in a fetus. See also *anencephaly; hydrocephalus; spina bifida*.

nonstress test. Test in which movements of the baby felt by the mother or observed by a doctor are recorded, along with changes in the fetal heart rate.

nurse-midwife. Nurse who has received extra training in the care of pregnant patients and the delivery of babies.

obstetrician. Physician who specializes in the care of pregnant women and the delivery of babies.

oligohydramnios. Lack or deficiency of amniotic fluid.

omphalocele. Congenital hernia at the bellybutton.

osteopathic physician. Physician who has trained in osteopathic medicine, a system of treating medical ailments based on the belief that ailments generally result from the pressure of displaced bones on nerves and are curable with manipulation. Osteopaths rely on physical, medicinal and surgical methods, much as their medical-doctor counterparts.

ovarian cycle. Regular production of hormones from the ovary in response to hormonal messages from the brain. The ovarian cycle governs the endometrial cycle.

ovulation. Cyclic production of an egg from the ovary.

ovulatory age. See *fertilization age.*

oxytocin. Medication that causes uterine contractions; used to induce labor. Also the hormone produced by pituitary glands.

palmar erythema. Redness of palms of the hands.

Pap smear. Routine screening test that evaluates presence of premalignant or cancerous conditions of the cervix.

paracervical block. Local anesthetic for pain from cervical dilatation.

Patau's syndrome. See *trisomy 13*.

pediatrician. Physician who specializes in the care of babies and children.

percutaneous umbilical blood sampling. Removal of blood from the umbilical cord while a baby is still inside the uterus.

perinatal death. Death of a baby around the time of delivery.

perinatologist. Physician who specializes in the care of high-risk pregnancies.

perineum. Area between the rectum and the vagina.

phenylketonuria (PKU). Hereditary disease that prevents oxidation of phenylananine (an amino acid) into tyrosine. Left untreated, brain damage may occur.

phospholipids. Fat-containing phosphorous. The most important are lecithins and sphingomyelin, which are important in the maturation of fetal lungs before birth.

physiologic anemia of pregnancy. Anemia during pregnancy caused by an increase in the amount of plasma (fluid) in the blood compared to the number of cells in the blood. See *anemia.*

PKU. See *phenylketonuria.*

placenta. Organ inside the uterus that is attached to the baby by the umbilical cord. Essential during pregnancy for growth and development of the embryo and fetus.

placenta previa. Low attachment of the placenta, very close to or covering the cervix.

placental abruption. Premature separation of the placenta from the uterus.

pneumonitis. Inflammation of the lungs.

polyhydramnios. See *hydramnios.*

postmature baby. Pregnancy of 42 or more weeks' gestation.

postpartum blues. See *baby blues.*

postpartum depression. Depression after delivery.

postpartum hemorrhage. Bleeding more than 15 ounces (450ml) at delivery.

postterm baby. Baby born 2 weeks or more past its due date.

pre-eclampsia. Combination of symptoms significant to pregnancy, including high blood pressure, edema, loss of protein in the urine and changes in reflexes.

pregnancy diabetes. See *gestational diabetes.*

premature delivery. Delivery before 38 weeks' gestation.

prenatal care. Program of care for a pregnant woman before the birth of her baby.

prepared childbirth. Woman takes classes to know what to expect during labor and delivery. She may request pain medication if she feels she needs it.

presentation. Describes which part of the baby comes into the birth canal first.

preterm birth. Baby born before 38 weeks of pregnancy.

products of conception. Tissue passed with a miscarriage.

proteinuria. Protein in urine.

pruritis gravidarum. Itching during pregnancy.

pubic symphysis. Bony prominence in the pelvic bone found in the midline. Landmark from which the doctor often measures during pregnancy to follow growth of the uterus.

pudendal block. Local anesthesia during labor.

pulmonary embolism. Blood clot from another part of the body that travels to the lungs. Can cause closed passages in the lungs and decreased oxygen exchange.

pyelonephritis. Serious kidney infection.

quickening. Feeling the baby move inside the uterus.

RDA. Recommended dietary allowance; an amount of a substance as established by the Food and Drug Administration.

Rh-negative. Absence of rhesus antibody in the blood.

RhoGAM. Medication given during pregnancy and following delivery to prevent isoimmunization. Also see *isoimmunization.*

Rh-sensitivity. See *isoimmunization.*

round-ligament pain. Pain caused by stretching ligament on the sides of the uterus during pregnancy.

rupture of membranes. Loss of fluid from the amniotic sac. Also called *breaking of waters.*

seizure. Sudden onset of a convulsion.

sexually transmitted disease (STD). Infection transmitted through sexual intercourse or other sexual activity.

sickle cell anemia. Anemia caused by abnormal red blood cells shaped like sickles or cylinders.

sickle cell trait. Presence of the trait for sickle cell anemia. Not sickle cell disease itself.

sickle crisis. Painful episode caused by sickle cell disease.

skin tag. Flap or extra buildup of skin.

sodium. Element found in many foods, particularly salt. Ingestion of too much sodium may cause fluid retention.

spina bifida. Congenital abnormality characterized by a defect in the vertebral column. The spinal cord and membranes of the spinal cord protrude outside the protective bony canal of the spine.

spinal anesthesia. Anesthesia given in the spinal canal.

spontaneous miscarriage. Loss of pregnancy during the first 20 weeks of gestation.

stasis. Decreased flow.

station. Estimation of the baby's descent in the uterus in preparation for birth.

steroids. Group of hormone-based medications often used to treat diseases. Includes estrogen, testosterone, progesterone, prednisone.

stillborn. Baby is not alive when it is born.

stress test. Test in which mild contractions of the mother's uterus are induced; fetal heart rate in response to the contractions is noted.

stretch marks. Areas of the skin that are stretched. Often found on the abdomen, breasts, buttocks and legs.

surfactant. Phospholipid present in the lungs that controls surface tension of lungs. Premature babies often lack sufficient amounts of surfactant to breathe without assistance.

syphilis. Sexually transmitted venereal infection caused by *Treponema pallidum*.

systemic lupus erythematosus (SLE). Connective-tissue disorder common in women in the reproductive ages. Antibodies made by the person act against person's own tissues.

Tay-Sachs disease. Inherited disease characterized by mental and physical retardation, convulsions, enlargement of the head and eventually death. Trait is usually carried by Ashkenazi Jews.

telangiectasias. Dilatation or swelling of a small blood vessel; sometimes called an *angioma*. During pregnancy, another common name is *spider angioma*.

teratogenic. Causes abnormal development.

teratology. Branch of science that deals with teratogens.

term. Baby is considered "term" when it is born after 40 weeks. Also called *full term*.

thalassemia. Group of inherited disorders of hemoglobin metabolism, which results in a decrease in the amount of hemoglobin formed. Most commonly found in people of Mediterranean descent.

threatened miscarriage. Bleeding during the first trimester of pregnancy without cramping or contractions.

thrombosis. Formation of a blood clot (thrombus).

thrush. Monilial or yeast infection occurring in the mouth or mucous membranes of a newborn infant.

thyroid disease. Abnormality of the thyroid gland and its production of thyroid hormone. See *hyperthyroidism; hypothyroidism*.

tocolytic agents. Medications to stop labor.

toxic shock syndrome. Overwhelming reaction to poisons made by bacteria.

toxic strep A. Bacterial infection that can cause severe damage to person; usually starts in a cut on the skin, not as a sore throat, and spreads very quickly. It can involve the entire body very quickly.

toxemia. See *pre-eclampsia.*

toxoplasmosis. Infection caused by *Toxoplasma gondii.*

transverse lie. Fetus is turned sideways in uterus.

trichomonal vaginitis. Venereal infection caused by trichomonas.

trimester. A 13-week period of pregnancy.

triple screen. Measurement of three blood tests to determine fetal well-being.

trisomy. Extra chromosome.

trisomy 13. Extra chromosome 13.

trisomy 18. Extra chromosome 18.

Turner's syndrome. Missing chromosome 45X.

umbilical cord. Cord that connects the placenta to the developing baby. It removes waste products and carbon dioxide from the baby and brings oxygenated blood and nutrients from the mother to the baby.

ureters. Tubes from the kidneys to the bladder that drain urine.

urinalysis. Test of the urine. Doctor tests urine during pregnancy to check for signs of disease or infection.

uterus. Organ an embryo/fetus grows in. Also called a *womb.*

vaccine. Mild infection given to cause production of antibodies to protect against subsequent infections of the same type.

vacuum extractor. Device used to provide traction on fetal head during delivery; used to help deliver a baby.

vagina. Birth canal.

varicose veins. Blood vessels (veins) that are dilated or enlarged.

vascular spiders. See *telangiectasias.*

vena cava. Major vein in the body that empties into the right atrium of the heart. It returns unoxygenated blood to the heart for transport to the lungs.

venereal warts. See *condyloma acuminatum.*

womb. See *uterus.*

yeast infection. See *monilial vulvovaginitis; thrush.*

INDEX

X–Z